Athlete Transitions into Retirement

Transitions in sport can be either normative (relatively predictable) or non-normative (less predictable) and are critical times in the development of athlete's careers. Whilst retirement from sport is inevitable, the timing of retirement can be less predictable. If an athlete copes well with the transition, they may be better able to adjust to life after sport. However, not coping with the transition can lead to a crisis and negative consequences for the athlete.

Transition periods from sport, and in particular retirement from sport, have been identified as high-risk periods for athletes in terms of psychological distress. However, circumstances surrounding the athlete's retirement are a critical factor in the transition into life after sport. Voluntarily retiring from sport, for example, leads to a smoother transition than being forced into retirement through injury or deselection. Research indicates that retirement from sport should be seen as a process rather than a single moment, with many athletes taking up to 2 years to successfully transition out of sport.

Currently, there are few bodies of work that are solely devoted to retirement transition. *Athlete Transitions Into Retirement: Experiences in Elite Sport and Options for Effective Support* provides contemporary viewpoints on athlete transitions from elite sport in a global context. This volume is a collaboration of research from leading authors around the world, offering global perspectives to athlete transitions into retirement and is key reading for both researchers and practitioners in the fields of Sport Psychology and Coaching as well as the Athletes themselves.

Deborah Agnew, PhD, is a senior lecturer in the Bachelor of Sport, Health and Physical Activity in the College of Education, Psychology and Social Work at Flinders University, Australia.

Routledge Psychology of Sport, Exercise and Physical Activity
Series Editor: Andrew M. Lane, *University of Wolverhampton, UK*

This series offers a forum for original and cutting-edge research exploring the latest ideas and issues in the psychology of sport, exercise and physical activity. Books within the series showcase the work of well-established and emerging scholars from around the world, offering an international perspective on topical and emerging areas of interest in the field. This series aims to drive forward academic debate and bridge the gap between theory and practice, encouraging critical thinking and reflection amongst students, academics and practitioners. The series is aimed at upper-level undergraduates, research students and academics and contains both authored and edited collections.

Available in this series:

Feelings in Sport
Theory, Research, and Practical Implications for Performance and Well-being
Edited by Montse C. Ruiz and Claudio Robazza

Sport Injury Psychology
Cultural, Relational, Methodological, and Applied Considerations
Edited by Ross Wadey

Stress, Well-Being, and Performance in Sport
Edited by Rachel Arnold and David Fletcher

Athlete Transitions into Retirement
Experiences in Elite Sport and Options for Effective Support
Edited by Deborah Agnew

Analytical Psychology of Football
Professional Jungian Football Coaching
Edited by John O'Brien and Nada O'Brien

For more information about this series, please visit: www.routledge.com/sport/series/RRSP

Athlete Transitions into Retirement

Experiences in Elite Sport and Options for Effective Support

Edited by Deborah Agnew

NEW YORK AND LONDON

First published 2022
by Routledge
605 Third Avenue, New York, NY 10158

and by Routledge
2 Park Square, Milton Park, Abingdon, Oxon, OX14 4RN

Routledge is an imprint of the Taylor & Francis Group, an informa business

© 2022 Taylor & Francis

The right of Deborah Agnew to be identified as the author of the
editorial material, and of the authors for their individual chapters,
has been asserted in accordance with sections 77 and 78 of the
Copyright, Designs and Patents Act 1988.

All rights reserved. No part of this book may be reprinted or
reproduced or utilised in any form or by any electronic, mechanical,
or other means, now known or hereafter invented, including
photocopying and recording, or in any information storage or
retrieval system, without permission in writing from the publishers.

Trademark notice: Product or corporate names may be trademarks
or registered trademarks, and are used only for identification and
explanation without intent to infringe.

Library of Congress Cataloging-in-Publication Data
A catalog record for this book has been requested

ISBN: 978-0-367-43286-7 (hbk)
ISBN: 978-1-032-04776-8 (pbk)
ISBN: 978-1-003-02018-9 (ebk)

Typeset in Baskerville
by Apex CoVantage, LLC

This book is dedicated to the memory of my father, David, who taught me to love sport. Without such a passionate role model, I may never have taken the career path towards helping those who are trying to cope with life after sport.

Contents

List of Figures	x
List of Tables	xi
About the Contributors	xii
Foreword	xvii

Introduction: Athlete Transitions in Sport 1
DEBORAH AGNEW

PART I
Socio-Cultural and Psychological Aspects of Athlete Retirement Transition 7

1 **The Influence of the Cultural Context on the Transition Out of Elite Sport in Europe** 9
ANDREAS KÜTTEL

2 **Psychosocial Aspects of Sport Retirement Amongst Collegiate Student-Athletes in the United States** 21
ASHLEY BRAUER

3 **The Professionalisation of Paralympic Sport and Implications for the Retirement Experiences of Paralympians** 32
ANDREA BUNDON

4 **Considering the Connections Between Doping and Transitions Out of Sport: Desperate Times and Desperate Measures?** 46
LAURIE PATTERSON

viii *Contents*

5 **Exploring Transitions in UK Professional Football**   58
ALAN TONGE

6 **Athlete Identity and Career Transition: Implications
for Retirement Outcomes**   71
SUZANNE M. COSH

7 **Retirement Through Injury: A Case Study Approach
Exploring Mental Health Issues and the Retirement
Experiences of Two Ex-English Premier
League Footballers**   84
THOMAS A. BUCK

PART II
Supporting Athletes Transitioning Into Retirement   99

8 **Delisted Footballers: Supporting Well-Being Through
Continued Participation in State-Based Levels**   101
DEBORAH AGNEW AND ELIZABETH ABERY

9 **Understanding Parents' Experiences With
Athlete Retirement**   113
PATRICIA LALLY AND RICHARD LALLY

PART III
Contextual Insights From Global Sports   127

10 **The Next Logical Step? An Examination of Elite Athletes'
Transitions Into Post-Athletic High-Performance
Coaching Roles**   129
ALEXANDER D. BLACKETT, ADAM B. EVANS, AND DAVID PIGGOTT

11 **Time's Up! Indigenous Australian Sportsmen
and Athlete Transitions**   145
MEGAN STRONACH

12 **Transitions in Disability Sport**   158
JEFFREY J. MARTIN AND EVA PROKESOVA

Contents ix

13 A Holistic Perspective to Elite Athletes' Career Development and Post-Sport Career Transition in an African Context 170

TSHEPANG TSHUBE, LEAPETSWE MALETE AND DEBORAH L. FELTZ

14 Autobiographical Insights Into Athlete Transitions From Sport 188

KITRINA DOUGLAS

Conclusion 206

DEBORAH AGNEW

Index 212

Figures

1.1	Ecological framework for studying the transition out of elite sport (Kuettel, 2017)	11
7.1	Illustration of themes. All themes were found to link to Adverse Mental Health within participants and shared links with other related themes within the analysis	89
10.1	Distinction between 'active' and 'passive' coach pathways (Blackett et al., 2018)	137
10.2	Categories for destination of first formalised coaching role	138

Tables

1.1	Overview of macro, meso, and cultural aspects of Switzerland, Denmark, and Poland	13
2.1	Example structure of sport retirement workshop	28
10.1	Competitive-athletic career characteristics and coaching roles of participants at each interview	134
13.1	Athletes' entourage profiles by stage	175

About the Contributors

Elizabeth Abery has held academic and research roles at Flinders University, Adelaide, Australia, for over 10 years. In her academic roles, she is involved in teaching topics directed at health science and education of students that encompass health, health contexts and practice, and well-being at organisational, social and individual levels. Her academic research explores student and staff well-being and the complexities of supporting transition and preparation processes from the educational environment to the future workplace. She also has an interest in emotional labour and its impact on academic roles and well-being, particularly in areas where student support is imperative. In recent years, her research roles and interests have expanded to investigating the role and implementation of coach education in junior community and elite sports and the "lived experience" of elite footballers who are transitioning out of their sport into planned or unplanned retirement through identifying the barriers and facilitators of the transition process.

Deborah Agnew is a senior lecturer in Sport, Health and Physical Activity at Flinders University in South Australia. As part of this role, she oversees the Sport Work Integrated Learning practical placement and liaises with industry organisations locally, nationally and internationally. Her research interests include Australian football, masculinity, sports retirement and men's health. She is passionate about athlete welfare and supporting athletes as they transition out of sport.

Alexander D. Blackett is course leader of the undergraduate BA (Hons) Sport Coaching degree and the fully online, part-time MSc Sport Coaching degree at Staffordshire University, UK. Alex's research interests centre on coach learning and education. Alex is primarily a football coach, having coached all over the world. Whilst retaining an interest in football, Alex has become more involved in delivering multi-skills and fundamental movement skills coaching along with delivering inclusive physical activity sessions to vulnerable groups.

About the Contributors xiii

Ashley Brauer is a clinical and sport psychologist who specialises in treating athletes with mental health disorders. Dr. Brauer holds a position with The Victory Program at McCallum Place, an eating disorder treatment programme for athletes. In addition, she helps athletes navigate mental health and sport concerns through an outpatient practice in New York City. Dr. Brauer's clinical and research interests focus on the intersection of clinical health and performance psychology, including evidence-based interventions to address health behaviours, injury, eating disorders and sleep.

Thomas A. Buck is a lecturer at UCFB Etihad Campus and a PhD student at Liverpool John Moores University, UK. He teaches sport and exercise psychology, research methods, and supervises a range of undergraduate dissertation projects across psychology, and coaching subjects. His primary research interest is the investigation of mental health issues in elite-level sport, exploring a range of associated factors, including transitions, identity, long-term injuries and adaptive/maladaptive coping strategies. Other research areas include decision-making, elite player development and existential psychology.

Andrea Bundon is Assistant Professor in the School of Kinesiology at the University of British Columbia, Canada. Her research spans the sociology of sport and critical disability studies. Working with qualitative methodologies and participatory research frameworks, she explores the intersections of sport, physical activity, disability and social inclusion.

Suzanne M. Cosh is a senior lecturer in Clinical Psychology in the School of Psychology, University of New England, USA. Her primary research interests relate to athlete mental health and wellbeing, especially post-retirement. Other research interests also include disordered eating behaviours of athlete and non-athlete populations, as well as athlete and exercise identity.

Kitrina Douglas is a video/ethnographer/researcher/storyteller, musician and narrative scholar whose research spans the arts, humanities and social sciences. Along with David Carless, she has carried out research for a variety of organisation, including Department of Health, Addiction Recovery Agency, Royal British Legion, Women's Sports Foundation, UK Sport, local authority and NHS Primary Mental Health Care Trusts, with a common theme of mental health. These research projects have provoked us to find ways to communicate our research outside traditional academic reporting channels; therefore, we publish our research as films, documentaries and musical theatre, as well as through peer-reviewed publications, magazine articles, online publications and books. She is a professor of narrative and performance at the University of West London and a visiting professor at the University of Coimbra in Portugal and a fractional contract at Leeds Beckett University. She is xiv *About the Contributors*

also director of the Boomerang-Project.org.uk, an arts-based network for public engagement and performance of social science research and produces the online qualitative research series "Qualitative Conversations."

Adam B. Evans is Associate Professor at the University of Copenhagen, Scandinavia, after joining them in the Department of Nutrition, Exercise and Sport (NEXS) in July 2015. Adam is a co-founder of the HART research group and current editor-in-chief of the *European Journal for Sport and Society*.

Deborah L. Feltz is University Distinguished Professor and Chairperson Emerita in Kinesiology at Michigan State University, USA. She earned her PhD in kinesiology from The Pennsylvania State University. Her research interests, over her 37-year career, have focused primarily on relationships amongst self-efficacy beliefs, motivation and performance for athletes, teams and coaches. She synthesised this research in her book, *Self-Efficacy and Sport*. She is a Fellow in the American Psychological Association and National Academy of Kinesiology.

Andreas Küttel is Assistant Professor at the Department of Sport Sciences and Clinical Biomechanics, University of Southern Denmark, Denmark, where he teaches courses in talent development, sports psychology and project governance. Before starting his academic career, he was a Swiss national team ski jumper for 15 years, participated at three Olympics and took a gold medal at the World Championships in 2009. Besides conducting research related to athletes' careers and transitions and their mental health, Andreas also works applied as a sport psychology consultant and career adviser with both individual athletes and teams.

Patricia Lally is Professor of Sport and Performance Psychology in the College of Business, Information Systems and Human Services at Lock Haven University, USA, where she teaches graduate courses in Sport and Exercise Psychology. Her research interests include athletic identity, athletic retirement and athlete mental health, as well as the experiences of international student-athletes and social media literacy amongst athletes.

Richard Lally is Professor in the College of Business, Information Systems and Human Services at Lock Haven University, USA. He teaches both undergraduate and graduate courses in Sport Studies. His research interests include the Psychology of Athletic Retirement and Transition and Sport Ethics.

Leapetswe Malete is Associate Professor in Kinesiology at Michigan State University, USA. Based in the Institute for the Study of Youth Sports, his teaching and research interests are on international dimensions of youth psychosocial development through sport and physical activity. He has served as a project leader and co-investigator in a number of

About the Contributors xv

international multidisciplinary research projects on youth development, physical activity and health, with most of these involving African youth. He has also served as sport psychology consultant to national teams and Olympic athletes in Botswana.

Jeffrey J. Martin is Professor at Wayne State University in Detroit, MI, USA. He has published over 250 research articles and book chapters in sport and exercise psychology. His major research agenda has been on the psychosocial aspects of disability sport and physical activity, investigating topics ranging from performance enhancement for Paralympians to the role of physical activity in promoting quality of life for military veterans. He is the current editor of the *Adapted Physical Activity Quarterly*, a premier international journal for adapted physical activity and sport for individuals with disabilities.

Laurie Patterson is Senior Lecturer in Sport and Exercise Psychology within the School of Sport at Leeds Beckett University, UK. She teaches sport and exercise psychology in the Bachelor of Science (Hons) Sport and Exercise Science and Sport and Exercise Nutrition degree courses and supervisors both undergraduate and postgraduate research students. Her principal research interest is investigating (anti-)doping behaviour amongst athletes and athlete support personnel, to inform effective anti-doping practice, programmes and policy. Beyond this, Laurie has conducted research related to the efficacy of nutritional supplements, coach development and education, and athlete development in youth sport settings.

David Piggott is Senior Lecturer in Sports Coaching at Leeds Beckett University, UK, where he leads the MSc programme. David has 20 years' experience as a coach and coach developer and has previously coached professional basketball in the United Kingdom. He has also delivered a number of research and consultancy projects for some of the world's biggest governing bodies, such as the Premier League, The FA, the ECB, UK Sport and UEFA. Between 2018 and 2020, David was also the Research Lead for the Performance Insights team at the English FA.

Eva Prokesova is an academic at the Department of Adapted Physical Education and Sport Medicine at the Charles University, Faculty of Physical Education and sport, Czech Republic. She is also a contact person for students with special needs at the same faculty. Her primary interest as a practitioner in a field of Adapted physical activity is in the area of adapted indoor skydiving for people after spinal cord injury.

Megan Stronach is Research Fellow at the University of Technology Sydney, Australia, and teaches at the University of Tasmania. Megan has

xvi *About the Contributors*

published widely in areas of sport management, cultural and women's issues in sport and has a keen interest in sport history. Most recently, her attraction to history has culminated in publications focusing on issues of topical relevance in Tasmania, including cultural challenges resulting from the interface between tourism and extractive industry development in Southern Tasmania. Her current research interests centre on the histories of Indigenous people in Van Diemen's Land (Tasmania), particularly the culturally important activities of women.

Alan Tonge is Lecturer in Football and Research at UCFB, Etihad Campus, UK. He currently supervises undergraduate and postgraduate student dissertation projects based on topics such as transitions and mental health and well-being. Alan's research interests include examining critical moments and how they impact upon professional football player identity.

Gearoid Towey is an Olympian and Founder of Crossing the Line Sport. Born in County Cork. Gearoid was a member of the Irish Olympic Team Sydney 2000, Athens 2004 and Beijing 2008. He is a former World Champion and three-time world bronze medallist.

In 2015, Gearoid founded Crossing the Line Sport, a charity where athletes can share their stories and receive expert advice and information on mental health, wellbeing and transitioning to the next stage of their career. He is also the co-founder of The Athlete Advantage, a programme that empowers athletes to become more self-aware, resilient and well-balanced and to transition successfully to life after sport.

Tshepang Tshube is Senior Lecturer in the Department of Sport Science at the University of Botswana. Tshube holds a PhD in Sport and Exercise Psychology from Michigan State University. He is an active researcher in Southern Africa published in areas of dual-career, life skills, coach-athlete relations and elite athlete retirement transition. In addition to his academic work, Tshube is a member of the Botswana National Olympic Committee High-Performance Commission. He has consulted with Team Botswana at major international games, including the 2016 Olympic Games, 2018 Commonwealth Games and several Africa Championships.

Foreword

Being an athlete means that you occupy a different world with a different set of rules. It is an intense and exciting world to be part of. Singular focus is applauded and encouraged as athletes continue to push the boundaries of human performance, year after year. Most athletes will tell you they would give anything to reach the top of their sport. Admirable dedication that can come with a high price.

Every athlete in the world has the same thing in common: one day, they will be an ex-athlete. How they finish their sport is a crucial element in how well they transition out. Many athletes have their dreams stolen from them through injury or burn-out, their vision of standing on the podium forever contained in a cruel figment of their imagination. On the other hand, some get to retire on their own terms: mission accomplished. Regardless of how perfect or imperfect their career was, the question they must all face is, "Who am I now?"

It is a simple question and one they could likely answer proudly and confidently since they were children. When sport is no longer their focus, many do not have an answer and not having an answer can be mentally crippling and ego destroying. The challenges of athlete transition are complex with many factors at play. An identity crisis is one of the most profound challenges, sending many a great athlete into a downward spiral that they never came back from. It is difficult to explain to an athlete what an identity crisis feels like, since their identity is so clear and strong. Therefore, we must be there to help them through it, if or when it happens.

This is why this book is so important to our sporting community. In 2009, a year after my retirement from Olympic rowing, I was crying out for a book like this. I needed information and advice that directly related to what I was experiencing and that was difficult to find at that time. I wanted to hear from those who had walked the path I was on and how they dealt with what I was feeling.

xviii *Foreword*

I know this book is going to help countless athletes and their families to navigate the tricky waters of career transition. On behalf of those who read these pages, thank you Deb for dedicating yourself to providing this valuable resource to those who need it now and those who do not know they need it, yet.

Gearoid Towey

Introduction
Athlete Transitions in Sport

Deborah Agnew

Transitions in sport are either normative (relatively predictable) or non-normative (less predictable) and are critical times in the development of athlete's careers (Alfermann & Stambulova, 2007; Stambulova, 2010). While retirement from sport is inevitable, the timing of retirement can be less predictable. If an athlete copes well with the transition, they are better able to adjust to life after sport. However, not coping with the transition can lead to a crisis and negative consequences for the athlete (Stambulova, 2010). Factors that can affect the transition into retirement can be athletic or non-athletic and include the voluntariness of retirement, the athlete's perception of their career achievements, the athlete's education levels and the prevalence of athletic identity (Cecić Erpič, Wylleman, & Zupančič, 2004). The level of acceptance of not playing their chosen sport again as well as the prospect of finding an alternative career can also impact on the retirement transition experiences of athletes (Price, 2007).

In addition to everyday stressors, elite athletes face additional sport-related stressors and physical demands (Lebrun & Collins, 2017). Transition periods, and in particular retirement from sport, have been identified as a high-risk period for athletes in terms of psychological distress (Reardon & Factor, 2010; Hughes & Leavey, 2012). However, the circumstances surrounding the athlete's retirement are a critical factor in the transition into life after sport. Voluntarily retiring from sport leads to a smoother transition than being forced into retirement through injury or deselection (Gordon & Lavallee, 2012; Cosh, Crabb, & LeCouteur, 2013). Further, voluntary retirement has been linked to higher life satisfaction in life after sport (Martin, Fogarty, & Albion, 2014).

Research indicates that retirement from sport should be seen as a process rather than a single moment and includes the continual decision to remain retired (Kelly & Hickey, 2008; Agnew, 2011; Cosh, McNeil, & Tully, 2020), with many athletes taking up to two years to successfully transition out of sport. However, although many athletes experience feelings of loss during the transition period out of sport, most are able to work through the changes and rebuild their lives. Some athletes even relish the opportunity for self-exploration during this time (Lally, 2007). Around 20% of retiring

2 Deborah Agnew

athletes experience a crisis transition requiring professional help (Alfermann & Stambulova, 2007; Stambulova & Wylleman, 2014). However, crisis transitions do not necessarily mean that the athlete unsuccessfully transitions out of sport. The crisis has the potential to be a pivotal moment in the transition process through instigating seeking assistance, which can then lead to a delayed, but successful transition (Stambulova, 2017).

Growing concern for the well-being of athletes transitioning out of elite sport has led to an increase in the number of support organisations and services across the globe. Particularly in the online community organisations such as Crossing the Line (Australia), Switch the Play (the United Kingdom), LAPS: Life After Professional Sport (the United Kingdom), The Final Whistle and Career After Sport (the United Kingdom), there is recognition for the need to provide ongoing and readily available access to resources for retiring athletes. Lebrun and Collins (2017, p. 234) state that "normal rules do not apply to non-normal people and elite athletes are, by definition, not 'normal' in the sense of average." Therefore, it is arguable that applying strategies designed to assist the general population improve positive health and well-being is not appropriate for elite athletes.

This book brings together leading and emerging researchers in the field of athlete transitions. This book is divided into three sections, which focus on 1) the socio-cultural and psychological aspects of athlete retirement transitions, 2) supporting athletes transitioning into retirement and 3) contextual insights from global sports.

Part I Socio-Cultural and Psychological Aspects of Athlete Retirement Transition

This section includes an overview of the socio-cultural and psychological factors influencing the athlete retirement transition experience. In chapter 1, Andreas Küttel compares three European perspectives to explore how different factors can facilitate or hinder transitions out of elite sport. The cultural context of sport is highlighted as an important factor in retirement transition, contributing to a better understanding of how macro and meso contexts influence career trajectories. The psychosocial factors influencing sports retirement at the US collegiate level are explored in chapter 2 by Ashley Brauer. Both psychosocial risk factors and positive sport retirement experiences are outlined as well as an overview of an educational workshop that can be utilised by practitioners in the field. Chapter 3 uses empirical qualitative data to discuss the pathways for Paralympians and how the Olympification of Paralympic sport can lead to inequitable outcomes for Paralympics. With a focus on the impact on retirement, Andrea Bundon examines the implications of professionalisation of Paralympic sport and provides insight into how Paralympians may be supported in the transition out of sport. There is growing evidence that athletes may be vulnerable to doping in preparing to leave elite sport. In chapter 4, Laurie Patterson explores

Introduction 3

the factors contributing to an increased risk of athlete doping during the transition out of sport and provides recommendations for reducing these risks for athletes. Chapter 5 uses narratives to outline the experiences of UK professional footballers as they transition out of sport. Specifically using a story-analyst approach, Alan Tonge gives voice to athlete concerns over the support received by footballers as they negotiate the critical moments both within the game and as they leave professional sport. In chapter 6, Suzanne M. Cosh provides insight into athlete identity and synthesises current developments in the field to inform support strategies and services for retiring athletes in relation to identity. In particular, the relationship between identity and career transition outcome is explored. Part I concludes with a case study of two footballers' mental health experiences as they leave professional sport. In chapter 7, Thomas A. Buck explores themes associated with adverse mental health, including transitions, identity, injuries and coping strategies to offer new insight into the experiences of athletes leaving Premier League Football.

Part II Supporting Athletes Transitioning Into Retirement

The focus of this section is on providing support to athletes who are transitioning out of elite sport. Chapter 8 explores the unique experiences of athletes who are deselected from an elite team and are thus forced into retirement, however, choose to keep playing at a lower level of their sport. Deborah Agnew and Elizabeth Abery highlight the need for continued support during the transition 'down a grade' and who is responsible for providing this care. Part II concludes with insight into an under-researched area, the experiences of parents as they support their children transitioning out of elite sport. Patricia Lally and Richard Lally examine the impact of sports retirement on parents as central figures in the athlete retirement process.

Part III Contextual Insights From Global Sports

This section provides insight into transition out of elite sport from around the world. In chapter 10, Alexander D. Blackett, Adam B. Evans and David Piggott consider the transition from elite athlete to high-performance coach in the United Kingdom and why some athletes making the transition to coach flourish while others experience more challenges. They conclude with how governing bodies can support the transition to coach process through strategies to minimise the challenges faced. Retirement from sport for Indigenous Australians is complex due to athletic identity, assumptions made about their natural ability as athletes, racialised stereotypes, and broader family and community commitments. In chapter 11, Megan Stronach suggests strategies to support Indigenous athletes in their retirement out of sport, while analysing the roles and responsibilities of sport organisations in providing a duty of care during this time. Chapter 12

4   *Deborah Agnew*

considers the unique experiences of athletes with a disability and the coping strategies adopted by Paralympians. Jeffrey J. Martin and Eva Prokesova highlight social activism as a potential path forward for athletes as well as the support services provided by Paralympic sports organisations. African perspectives are presented in chapter 13 by Tshepang Tsube, Leapetswe Malete and Deborah L. Feltz, who make a case for cross-cultural and holistic approaches to athlete development. Specifically using a lifespan approach, the retirement experiences of African athletes emphasise challenges throughout careers, including talent identification, development and dual careers. Part III concludes with an autobiographical account of the process from entry into sport, life as an athlete and leaving professional sport. Kitrina Douglas explores her journey from professional golfer to a career in academia in chapter 14, using narratives and news reports from her career to give personal insight into meaning of life in sport and career transitions out of sport.

Using This Book

This book is a comprehensive discussion of the various aspects of athlete retirement. With different experiences from a variety of sports, it highlights the similarities and differences across the breadth of athletes from different places and the nuances of place and culture presented side by side for a textured picture of the experience of athlete retirement. This book is unique in that it is solely dedicated to retirement transitions in sport.

One of the benefits of this book is that the insights are grounded in empirical research and provides recommendations for how to support athletes during a time where they are most vulnerable. Covering various levels of competition including college, elite and second-tier competitions, this book offers a proactive approach to caring for athletes during the transition out of sport. This book is intended to engage academics, undergraduate and postgraduate students and practitioners who are working with athletes in the transition out of sport process. Each chapter contains a specific section on the practical implications of the research to help guide practitioners in supporting athletes who are transitioning out of elite sport.

References

Agnew, D. (2011). *Life after football: The construction of masculinity following a career in elite Australian Rules football* (Thesis PhD). Flinders University, Adelaide, Australia.

Alfermann, D., & Stambulova, N. (2007). Career transitions and career termination. In G. Tenenbaum & R. C. Eklund (Eds.), *Handbook of sport psychology* (pp. 712–733). New York: John Wiley & Sons, Inc.

Cercić Erpič, S., Wylleman, P., & Zupančič, M. (2004). The effect of athletic and non-athletic factors on the sports career termination process. *Psychology of Sport and Exercise, 5*(1), 45–59.

Cosh, S. M., Crabb, S., & LeCouteur, A. (2013). Elite athletes and retirement: Identity, choice, and agency. *Australian Journal of Psychology, 65*(2), 89–97.

Cosh, S. M., McNeil, D. G., & Tully, P. J. (2020). Poor mental health outcomes in crisis transitions: An examination of retired athletes accounting of crisis transition experiences in a cultural context. *Qualitative Research in Sport, Exercise and Health,* 1–20.

Gordon, S., & Lavallee, D. (2012). Career transitions. In T. Morris & P. Terry (Eds.), *The new sport and exercise psychology companion* (pp. 567–582). Morgantown, WV: Fitness Information Technology.

Hughes, L., & Leavey, G. (2012). Setting the bar: Athletes and vulnerability to mental illness. *The British Journal of Psychiatry, 200*(2), 95–96.

Kelly, P., & Hickey, C. (2008). *The struggle for the body, mind and soul of AFL footballers.* North Melbourne: Australian Scholarly.

Lally, P. (2007). Identity and athletic retirement: A prospective study. *Psychology of Sport and Exercise, 8*(1), 85–99.

Lebrun, F., & Collins, D. (2017). Is elite sport (really) bad for you? Can we answer the question? *Frontiers in Psychology, 8,* 324.

Martin, L. A., Fogarty, G. J., & Albion, M. J. (2014). Changes in athletic identity and life satisfaction of elite athletes as a function of retirement status. *Journal of Applied Sport Psychology, 26*(1), 96–110.

Price, N. (2007). *Game of two halves: Preparing young elite rugby players for a future beyond the game* (PhD thesis). Faculty of Education, University of Wollongong. Retrieved from http://ro.uow.edu.au/theses/46

Reardon, C. L., & Factor, R. M. (2010). Sport psychiatry: A systematic review of diagnosis and medical treatment of mental illness in athletes. *Sports Medicine, 40*(11), 961–980.

Stambulova, N. B. (2010). Counseling athletes in career transitions: The five-step career planning strategy. *Journal of Sport Psychology in Action, 1*(2), 95–105.

Stambulova, N. B. (2017). Crisis-transitions in athletes: Current emphases on cognitive and contextual factors. *Current Opinion in Psychology, 16,* 62–66.

Stambulova, N. B., & Wylleman, P. (2014). Athletes' career development and transitions. In A. G. Papaioannou & D. Hackfort (Eds.), *International perspectives on key issues in sport and exercise psychology. Routledge companion to sport and exercise psychology: Global perspectives and fundamental concepts* (pp. 605–620). East Sussex: Routledge and Taylor & Francis Group.

Part I

Socio-Cultural and Psychological Aspects of Athlete Retirement Transition

1 The Influence of the Cultural Context on the Transition Out of Elite Sport in Europe

Andreas Küttel

Introduction

> Career termination is the clearest example of a normative and even inevitable transition, which mixes sport-related and unrelated contexts in the athletes' retirement planning, reasons for termination, and adaptation to the post-career experiences including studies, work, identity change, and renewing social networks.
>
> (Stambulova, Alfermann, Statler, & Côté, 2009, p. 398)

Athletic retirement has attracted sports science researchers since international sport became more professionalised in the 1960s. There has been a substantial increase in research related to career-end studies both in their quantity and quality since the end of the 1980s. In the beginning, the end of an elite sports career was associated with a rather negative perception using terms such as "crisis" or "social death" (Lavallee, 2000). In the early 1990s, sport researchers adapted a more positive view using Schlossberg's (1981) model of human adaptation to transition and emphasised that athletic retirement should be understood as a coping process—for which athletes and their entourage can prepare—rather than a single point in time (Stambulova et al., 2009). In 2013, Park, Lavallee, and Tod conducted a systematic review about athletic retirement and concluded that pre-retirement planning, social support, a multifaceted identity, and appropriate coping strategies are the main factors that facilitate the transition out of sport. However, as noted by Stambulova and Ryba (2013), all these factors may work differently in different countries and contexts. This chapter aims to provide a better understanding of the relationship between the national/cultural context and athletic transitions by comparing the athletic retirement of former Swiss, Danish, and Polish athletes.

A transition has been defined by Schlossberg (1981) as "an event or non-event which results in a change in assumptions about oneself and the world and thus requires a corresponding change in one's behaviour and relationships" (p. 5). According to Schlossberg's model of human adaptation to

10 *Andreas Küttel*

transition, three major sets of factors interact during a transition, namely (a) the characteristics of the individual experiencing the transition, (b) the perception of the particular transition, and (c) the characteristics of the pre-transition and post-transition environments. Regarding the perception of a particular transition, Schlossberg suggested that role change, affect, source, onset, duration, and the degree of stress are all important factors to consider. These aspects of Schlossberg's model emphasise the phenomenological nature of transitions, in that it is not just the transition itself that is of primary importance, but especially the individual perception of the event and its circumstances. For retiring athletes, Sinclair and Orlick (1993, p. 138) have acknowledged this position by suggesting that "every career transition has the potential to be a crisis, relief, or combination of both, depending on the athlete's perception of the situation." Overall, it can be estimated that around 15%–20% of the athletes experience serious adjustment difficulties when ending their elite sports career (Park et al., 2013).

Nowadays, athletic career development and transition research do not only look at the transition out of sport but have a focus on within-career transitions (e.g. the junior-to-senior transition) that is typically integrated in the so-called "whole-career" approach. Several descriptive models of an athletic career (e.g. Côté, 1999; Weissensteiner, 2017; Wylleman, Reints, & De Knop, 2013) highlight the different phases and the corresponding normative transitions that can be expected when athletes start in the initiation stage, progress in the development stage, achieve the perfection/mastery stage, and finally reach the discontinuation stage of competitive sport involvement. Since previous transition experiences affect how new transitions challenges are handled, the transition out of elite sports cannot be understood without taking into account athletes' previous career development. The holistic athletic career model (Wylleman et al., 2013) further highlights a "whole-person" lifespan perspective, viewing athletic career transitions in their relation to developmental challenges and transitions in other spheres of an athlete's life (i.e. on the psychological, psychosocial, the academic/vocational, and the financial levels).

In recent years, the focus has shifted away from understanding how significant persons within the micro-context (i.e. coaches, family, peers) influence athletes' transition to consider macro-context factors (i.e. sports system and cultural dimensions) as other important factors. Athletes' careers are heavily coloured by the way talent development programmes are organised (Storm, 2015), how elite sport is promoted and recognised (De Bosscher, Shibli, Westerbeek, & van Bottenburg, 2015; Ronglan, 2015; Stambulova & Ryba, 2013), and how elite athletes are supported in their efforts to combine sport with school or work in different countries (Kuettel, Christensen, Zysko, & Hansen, 2020).

The *ecological framework for studying the transition out of elite sport* (Kuettel, 2017) displayed in Figure 1.1 incorporates the perspective that the

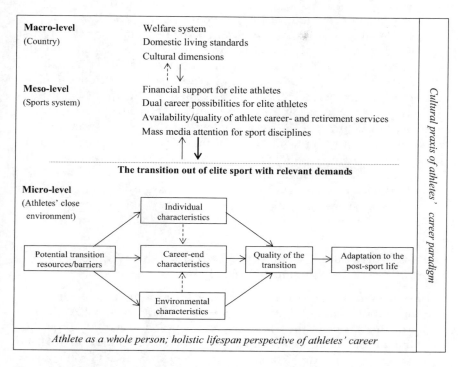

Figure 1.1 Ecological framework for studying the transition out of elite sport (Kuettel, 2017)

macro-context influences the sport and educational system on the meso level, which further influences the transition out of elite sport with its relevant demands. The *macro level* represents the welfare system of the country (e.g. liberal, conservative, social-democratic; Esping-Andersen, 1990), the cultural dimensions (e.g. power distance, individualism, masculinity; Hofstede, Hofstede, & Minkov, 2010), as well as general macro-level dimension such as the living standard, the geographical location and size, and the size of population of a country. The *meso level* represents various characteristics of the elite sports systems and is described by the financial support for elite athletes (De Bosscher et al., 2015), job/dual-career possibilities (Aquilina & Henry, 2010), athlete career and retirement services (Andersen & Morris, 2000; Stambulova & Wylleman, 2014), mass media attention for sport, as well as the embedded values within the institutions and organisations responsible for the elite sports' development. The *micro level* represents the athletes' close environment (i.e. coaches, family, sporting peers, and friends) and includes the transition out of elite sport along

12 Andreas Küttel

with the respective demands such as dealing with bodily changes, adapting to a new social environment, and adjustment to a new lifestyle and job situation. Potential transitional resources and barriers (Stambulova, 2003) that influence the quality of the transition and the following adaptation to the post-sport life are divided into individual (e.g. age, gender, athletic identity, skills), career end (e.g. voluntariness, reasons for career end, timing), and environmental characteristics (e.g. support from private and sporting environment) according to Schlossberg's (1981) model. The *cultural praxis of athletes' career paradigm* (Stambulova & Ryba, 2013) emphasises the contextual sensitivity of the model. Applying this cultural praxis paradigm, researchers and practitioners are urged to apply a holistic perspective in viewing athletes, to investigate the idiosyncratic career patterns and pathways of athletes in their specific contexts, and to position their projects (and themselves) in relevant socio-cultural contexts with contextual awareness and reflexivity.

Cross-Cultural Comparison of the Transition Out of Elite Sport of Swiss, Danish, and Polish Athletes

The overall aim of the study was to compare the transition out of elite sport of Swiss, Danish, and Polish athletes in terms of (a) transitional characteristics, (b) the quality of the transition, and (c) the adaptation to the post-sport life. In this chapter, the countries Switzerland, Denmark, and Poland were chosen on the basis of their contrasting characteristics on the macro and meso levels (displayed in Table 1.1) that potentially affect athletes' transition process out of elite sport.

Switzerland supports elite athletes through athlete career programmes including financial support, career counselling/planning, and help to find internships. Nevertheless, solutions to combine higher education and elite sport are limited and based on individual solutions. In *Denmark*, a strong emphasis is traditionally placed on the dual career of athletes, providing grants for student-athletes on all levels. Athlete career programmes are offered to both active and retired athletes during and is part of the socially responsible approach to elite sport (by law) in Denmark. In *Poland*, as a relic from the former communist era where elite sport was used to promote nationalistic interests, a more centralised approach to elite sport is still dominant. Elite athletes are granted financial support and get flexible educational solutions in the sport studies. Olympic medal winners receive a life-long pension, but no athlete career programme is available when athletes retire from elite sports. The short description and overview of the three countries under study (Table 1.1) highlights the diversity of the socio-cultural contexts in terms of their macro, meso, and cultural dimensions. According to the ecological framework that guided this study, these dimensions are hypothesised to influence athletes' sports careers, their transitions, and their post-elite sport life situation.

Table 1.1 Overview of macro, meso, and cultural aspects of Switzerland, Denmark, and Poland

Aspect	Switzerland (CH)	Denmark (DK)	Poland (PL)
Population size (2014)	8.2 million	5.6 million	38.5 million
GDP/capita (2014)	$59,536	$46,000	$24,952
Unemployment rate (2014)	4.5%	6.6%	9.0%
Welfare system	Liberal	Social-democratic	Conservative
Power distance	Low-medium (34)	Very low (18)	High (68)
Individualism	High (68)	High (74)	Medium-high (60)
Masculinity	Medium-high (70)	Very low (16)	Medium-high (64)
Uncertainty avoidance	Medium (58)	Low (23)	Very high (93)
Long-term orientation	High (74)	Low (34)	Low (38)
Indulgence	High (66)	High (70)	Low (29)
Organisation of sport system	Bottom-up	Mixed-complementary	Top-down
Dual-career typology in higher education	Laissez-faire: no formal structure	State/National Sport organisation as facilitators	State-centred approach
Athlete career programme	Both during and after career	Both during and after career	Only during career

Note: GDP/capita and unemployment rates were derived from the Organisation for Economic Co-operation and Development (OECD) database. The welfare state classification relates to the terminology of Esping-Andersen (1990). The cultural dimensions (power distance—indulgence) measured on a scale ranging from 0 to 100 relate to the work of Hofstede et al. (2010). Dual-career typologies were described by Aquilina and Henry (2010).

Methodology

After receiving approval from the regional ethics committee, former elite athletes who had finished their career between 2008 and 2013 were included in the study and provided information about their sporting career (e.g. success, training and working hours, educational level, skills, income), their transition period (e.g. reasons for career end, duration, adaptation difficulties), and their current situation in the life after elite sport (e.g. job situation, life satisfaction). With a response rate of 62%, a total of 401 former elite athletes (231 from Switzerland, 86 from Denmark, and 84 from Poland) from a wide range of team and individual sports (summer and winter) completed the online survey in 2014 in a German-, Danish-, or Polish-language version (Kuettel, Boyle, Christensen, & Schmid, 2018). In all countries, athletes had competed internationally, with roughly one-third of them winning medals at either World Championships or Olympic Games. To evaluate cross-national differences between the Swiss, Danish, and Polish samples, mean differences were calculated with separated one-way analysis of variances (ANOVAs). For categorical variables, chi-square tests were calculated, and proportions were reported.

Results

Concerning the *individual characteristics* and the variables related to their sports career, the most substantial difference was found in the level of education at the end of the sports career, with 85% of Polish athletes having obtained a higher educational degree (bachelor or master), compared to 62% of Danish and 39% of Swiss athletes. Polish athletes reported the highest athletic identity; they were most confident in their skills, perceived themselves as the most popular, and earned a greater portion of their income through their elite sports involvement. Swiss athletes had gathered more previous work experience compared to Danish and Polish athletes during their career, had earned the smallest portion of their income through sport, and had the lowest athletic identity scores. Danish athletes perceived themselves as less confident in their skills and as least publicly well known, despite being the sample with the relatively highest ratio of top-three rankings at major sports events. However, in comparison to the Swiss and Polish athletes, Danish athletes rated the general outcome of their elite sport involvement significantly more positively when comparing investments and benefits of their elite sports career.

Regarding the *career-end characteristics*, the findings suggested that a combination of several reasons influenced athletes' decisions to end their elite sports careers. The most prominent reasons, independent of the national context, were personal/motivational reasons, family-related reasons, and health-related reasons (e.g. injury). Job/educational reasons and sport-environmental reasons (e.g. conflict with coach or federation) were not amongst the influential reasons in any context. About two-thirds of the athletes reported that their decision to retire from elite sport was entirely voluntary. Analyses showed that 62% of the Swiss, 63% of the Danish, and 68% of the Polish athletes had made long-term plans for their time after elite sport. On average, athletes from all three countries started to plan for their career termination between 7 and 11 months before they actually retired. However, individual values ranged from 0 to 48 months in all three countries.

Regarding the variables related to the *quality of the transition*, results showed that the adaptation period was least problematic for Swiss athletes, who reported the lowest emotional, social, health, vocational, and financial adaptation difficulties and high transition satisfaction ($M = 4.45$, $SD = 0.65$, on a five-point scale). The transition was most problematic for Polish athletes who struggled with the financial and vocational adaptation and expressed significantly lower satisfaction with their transition ($M = 3.61$, $SD = 0.97$) process compared to the other athletes. Polish athletes accordingly perceived their career end as far more of a loss compared to the Swiss and Danish athletes. Danish athletes reported the highest social and emotional adaptation difficulties but rated their overall transition process as very satisfying ($M = 4.45$, $SD = 0.62$). In general, the averages of the adaptation difficulties were low to medium in all three countries, suggesting that the majority of the athletes faced minor problems during their transition out of elite sport.

When comparing the *adaptation to the post-sport life* in former athletes, both similarities and differences across contexts were found. Swiss athletes expressed the highest satisfaction with their current occupational situation and were highly satisfied with their lives. The former Polish athletes reported a significantly lower life satisfaction at the time of questioning compared to Swiss and Danish athletes. Compared to the general population, a relatively large proportion (21% of Swiss and Danish, 32% of Polish) of former athletes is self-employed after their sports career. Furthermore, many athletes reported having not only one main occupation but holding up to four jobs at the same time (e.g. coach, TV expert, mentor, working for a sponsor). On the other hand, significantly more Polish athletes (74%) worked in a sports-related job (e.g. coach, sports teacher, sport club administrator) than Swiss (35%) and Danish (31%) athletes. In addition, several significant differences were found regarding the factors that athletes considered important for obtaining their current job(s). Polish athletes rated their popularity and their professional network within the field of sport significantly more influential than their Swiss and Danish counterparts. In general, the former athletes considered their personality, the skills learned through elite sport, and their education as the most helpful factors for obtaining their current occupation(s).

Discussion

It is a rather new approach to investigate athletes' career trajectories and transitions across cultures. The results of this study revealed career and retirement patterns that are distinctive for Swiss, Danish, and Polish athletes. In general, when comparing the transition quality across the samples, the results revealed that the national context plays an important role in how well former athletes cope with the demands of the transition. The many differences in the variables related to life in elite sport indicate that athletes' sports careers are considerably influenced by the national context. Namely, the financial support athletes receive from their federation or the national sport governing body (De Bosscher et al., 2015) as well as the institutionalised support elite athletes receive for their dual-career efforts (Aquilina & Henry, 2010; Stambulova & Ryba, 2013).

As expected, Polish athletes expressed the highest vocational and financial adaptation difficulties and perceived their career end as far more of loss compared to the athletes from the other two countries. The negative perception of their career end may be related to the high athletic identity that the Polish athletes expressed since identity foreclosure has been shown to be related to higher adaptation difficulties during the transition (e.g. Grove, Lavallee, & Gordon, 1997; see also chapter 6). Another reason

16   *Andreas Küttel*

might be that the privileges connected with elite athlete status (e.g. special regulations for studying, salary from the federation/army, high public recognition; see Figure 1.1) end abruptly when Polish athletes retire. Similar reactions to retirement distress have been described amongst Russian and Lithuanian athletes (Alfermann, Stambulova, & Zemaityte, 2004). The athletes from these two countries also developed their sports careers in the more autocratic sports systems that are common in former communist countries, such as Poland or other Eastern European countries.

Many Swiss athletes completed a qualified vocational education course and were working part-time while active in elite sport. Hence, their pre- and post-environment concerning their working situation may not have been as different as it is for athletes from the other two nations. Accordingly, Swiss athletes reported the lowest vocational-related difficulties of the three samples. Having gathered relevant work experience before ending their elite sports career, a low employment rate, the generally good economic situation, and the high living standard in Switzerland are possible reasons why most Swiss athletes had a rather smooth transition out of elite sport and adapted successfully to the demands of the life after elite sport.

Danish athletes coped well with the transition concerning their vocational and financial adaptation, but they reported elevated distress levels concerning their emotional and social adaptation. This might be related to the Danish cultural value of equality, the so-called 'Jante law' (Sandemose, 1933), which emphasises 'being within the standard' (i.e. not higher, but also not lower than the majority of people) as a basis for personal satisfaction and self-esteem. This principle of equality stands in opposition to the notion of elite sport (i.e. to be the best and to achieve outstanding results) and might lead to a conflict of values in retiring Danish elite athletes. Swedish athletes (from a similar socio-cultural context such as Denmark) reported comparable adjustment difficulties, and it took them longer to find their social role and to adapt to the high living standards after ending their elite sports career (Stambulova, Stephan, & Jäphag, 2007).

When interpreting an elite sport career as a form of accumulated social capital (Bourdieu, 1986) or as a resource for an athlete's life career (Stambulova, 2010), previous research has shown that financial status, educational status, competencies, working experience, and top-sport success/popularity all have a potential positive effect on the adaptation to the post-sport life in a European context (e.g. Aquilina & Henry, 2010; Cecić Erpič et al., 2004; Conzelmann & Nagel, 2003; Dewenter & Giessing, 2014). However, the results of this chapter suggest that the socio-cultural context influences the usefulness of these different forms of social capital when athletes try to set a foothold in the job market. Accordingly, the former Polish athletes rated their professional network from sport, their popularity, and their connections to federations/clubs as more influential for obtaining their current employment than their Swiss and Danish counterparts, since most Polish athletes relocate within the sports domain.

Transition Out of Elite Sport in Europe 17

Ecological psychology (Bronfenbrenner & Morris, 2006) emphasises that human development is influenced by the respective context. The results of this chapter support the assumption that in order to understand the complex nature of the transition out of elite sport, researchers must look beyond the individual athlete and include the micro-, meso-, and macro-environment in their investigation. This study highlights that athletes from different countries have access to different athlete career services and follow diverse (dual) career trajectories. These diverse career patterns provide athletes with different educational levels and work experience before transitioning out of elite sport and starting their post-elite sport life. The national culture was also shown to be influential in terms of athletes' perception of their athletic identity, their status in society, and their perception of their career end. As such, athletes' careers and transition patterns are more culturally situated than we often tend to acknowledge. Moreover, the holistic perspective showed that both athletic and non-athletic factors influence the adaptation to post-sport life. Therefore, the combination of ecological and holistic (lifespan) perspectives in career research is needed to optimise athletes' career development environments (Stambulova & Ryba, 2013). Accordingly, the ecological framework for studying the transition out of sport displayed in Figure 1.1 can be used as a helpful orientation tool for both researchers and practitioners.

Implications for Practice

Athletes from Switzerland, Denmark, and Poland faced mostly emotional and social difficulties during the adaptation process of the transition out of elite sport. Therefore, and as previously recommended by other authors (e.g. Gordon, Lavallee, & Grove, 2005; Park et al., 2013; Stambulova et al., 2009), athletes need to be prepared for their transition, by both their sport (e.g. coaches, counsellors, sports psychologists) and private environments (e.g. partner, family, friends). Pre-retirement planning is one of the best predictors of successful career transitions out of sport and even enhances on-field performance (Lavallee, 2019). Schlossberg (1981) emphasised that any transition requires a corresponding change in one's behaviour and relationships. Thus, athletes need to be made aware that because life will be different after ending the elite sports career, the nature of close personal relationships may also change and need to be constantly worked at.

A positive perception of the career-end situation is amongst the strongest facilitators for a successful transition to the post-sport life (Kuettel, Boyle, & Schmid, 2017). Hence, preparing and assisting athletes to see their career end (voluntarily chosen or not) as a possible positive turn-around point in life, one that opens new opportunities, will increase the chances that individual athletes cope better with the transitional demands. To be able to disengage from the elite sports role in the transition process may help athletes to move on to the next stage of life and increase their well-being (Holding,

18   *Andreas Küttel*

Fortin, Carpentier, Hope, & Koestner, 2019). In addition, it is important to develop assistant programmes that are accessible and relevant to elite athletes. Current programmes, especially in Poland, seem to largely target elite athletes still competing, with little attention directed to recently retired athletes who find themselves in an 'in-between' social status (still perceived as an athlete yet trying to assume other social roles). This is a crucial time for continued intervention to influence the quality and development of an athlete into post-sport life and prevent the difficulties associated with the transition. Interestingly, however, are the findings of North and Lavallee (2004) showing that many athletes elect not to engage in intervention programmes during and after their sports career even when they have access to such services.

The ethos of helping athletes to make their athletic career a part of and a resource for their life career, and to prepare them for transitions and the life beyond elite sports, should be seen as the umbrella goal for career assistance. Therefore, and in line with the proposals of Stambulova and Wylleman (2014), this chapter advocates for the following principles of the athletes' career assistance professional culture:

- A *cultural-specific approach* to help athletes adjust within a particular sports system, society, and culture.
- A *whole-career approach* to help athletes cope with both normative and non-normative transitions throughout the whole course of an athletic career.
- A *whole-person approach* to help athletes deal with transitions in various spheres of life.
- A *developmental approach* to help athletes linking their past career experience, present situation, and the plans for their future.
- An *individual approach* to accommodate the athletes' perceptions of the transition and their distinctive resources and barriers for the transition(s).
- A *transferable skills approach* to teach athletes life skills that are applicable both in and outside sport and in the athletic and post-athletic career.

References

Alfermann, D., Stambulova, N., & Zemaityte, A. (2004). Reactions to sport career termination: A cross-national comparison of German, Lithuanian, and Russian athletes. *Psychology of Sport and Exercise, 5*(1), 61–75.

Andersen, D., & Morris, T. (2000). Athlete lifestyle programs. In D. Lavallee & P. Wylleman (Eds.), *Career transitions in sport: International perspectives* (pp. 59–80). Morgantown, WV: Fitness Information Technology.

Aquilina, D., & Henry, I. (2010). Elite athletes and university education in Europe: A review of policy and practice in higher education in the European union member states. *International Journal of Sport Policy, 2*(1), 25–47.

Bourdieu, P. (1986). The forms of capital. In J. Richardson (Ed.), *Handbook of theory and research for the sociology of education* (pp. 46–58). New York, NY: Greenwood.

Transition Out of Elite Sport in Europe

Bronfenbrenner, U., & Morris, P. A. (2006). The bioecolocical model of human development. In R. M. Lerner (Ed.), *Handbook of child psychology: Vol 1. Theoretical models of human development* (6th ed., pp. 793–828). New York, NY: Wiley.

Cecić Erpič, S., Wylleman, P., & Zupančič, M. (2004). The effect of athletic and non-athletic factors on the sports career termination process. *Psychology of Sport and Exercise, 5*(1), 45–59.

Conzelmann, A., & Nagel, S. (2003). Professional careers of the German Olympic athletes. *International Review for the Sociology of Sport, 38*(3), 259–280.

Côté, J. (1999). The influence of the family in the development of talent in sport. *The Sport Psychologist, 13*(4), 395–417.

De Bosscher, V., Shibli, S., Westerbeek, H., & van Bottenburg, M. (2015). *Successful elite sport policies: An international comparison of the Sport Policy factors Leading to International Sporting Success (SPLISS 2.0.) in 15 nations.* Maidenhead: Meyer & Meyer Sport.

Dewenter, R., & Giessing, L. (2014). *The effects of elite sports on later job success.* SOEP-paper No. 705. Retrieved from http://dx.doi.org/10.2139/ssrn.2532499

Esping-Andersen, G. (1990). *The three worlds of welfare capitalism.* Princeton, NJ: Princeton University Press.

Gordon, S., Lavallee, D., & Grove, J. R. (2005). Career assistance program interventions in sport. In D. Hackfort, J. Duda, & R. Lidor (Eds.), *Handbook of research in applied sport and exercise psychology: International perspectives* (pp. 233–244). Morgantown, WV: Fitness Information Technology.

Grove, J. R., Lavallee, D., & Gordon, S. (1997). Coping with retirement from sport: The influence of athletic identity. *Journal of Applied Sport Psychology, 9*(2), 191–203.

Hofstede, G., Hofstede, G. J., & Minkov, M. (2010). *Cultures and organizations: Software of the mind. Intercultural cooperation and its importance for survival* (3rd ed.). New York, NY: McGraw-Hill.

Holding, A., Fortin, J.-A., Carpentier, J., Hope, N., & Koestner, R. (2019). Letting go of gold: Examining the role of autonomy in elite athletes' disengagement from their athletic careers and well-being in retirement. *Journal of Clinical Sport Psychology (aop), 1*, 1–21.

Kuettel, A. (2017). *A cross-cultural comparison of the transition out of elite sport* (PhD Thesis). University of Southern Denmark, Odense.

Kuettel, A., Boyle, E., Christensen, M., & Schmid, J. (2018). A cross-national comparison of the transition out of elite sport of Swiss, Danish, and Polish athletes. *Sport and Exercise Psychology Review, 14*(1), 2–22.

Kuettel, A., Boyle, E., & Schmid, J. (2017). Factors contributing to the quality of the transition out of elite sports in Swiss, Danish, and Polish athletes. *Psychology of Sport and Exercise, 29,* 27–39.

Kuettel, A., Christensen, M. K., Zysko, J., & Hansen, J. (2020). A cross-cultural comparison of dual career environments for elite athletes in Switzerland, Denmark, and Poland. *International Journal of Sport and Exercise Psychology, 18*(4), 454–471.

Lavallee, D. (2000). Theoretical perspectives on career transitions in sport. In D. Lavallee & P. Wylleman (Eds.), *Career transitions in sport: International perspectives* (pp. 1–28). Morgantown, WV: Fitness Information Technology.

Lavallee, D. (2019). Engagement in sport career transition planning enhances performance. *Journal of Loss and Trauma, 24*(1), 1–8.

20 Andreas Küttel

North, J., & Lavallee, D. (2004). An investigation of potential users of career transition services in the United Kingdom. *Psychology of Sport and Exercise, 5*(1), 77–84.

Park, S., Lavallee, D., & Tod, D. (2013). Athletes' career transition out of sport: A systematic review. *International Review of Sport and Exercise Psychology, 6*(1), 22–53. doi :10.1080/1750984x.2012.687053

Ronglan, L. T. (2015). Elite sport in Scandinavian welfare states: Legitimacy under pressure? *International Journal of Sport Policy and Politics, 7*(3), 345–363.

Sandemose, A. (1933). *En flyktning krysser sitt spor [A refugee crosses his tracks]*. Oslo: Tiden Norsk Forlag.

Schlossberg, N. K. (1981). A model for analyzing human adaptation to transition. *The Counseling Psychologist, 9*(2), 2–15.

Sinclair, D. A., & Orlick, T. (1993). Positive transitions from high-performance sport. *Sport Psychologist, 7*, 138–150.

Stambulova, N. (2003). Symptoms of a crisis-transition: A grounded theory study. In N. Hassmén (Ed.), *SIPF Yearbook 2003* (pp. 97–109). Örebro: Örebro University Press.

Stambulova, N. (2010). Professional culture of career assistance to athletes: A look through contrasting lenses of career metaphors. In T. V. Ryba, R. J. Schinke, & G. Tenenbaum (Eds.), *Cultural turn in sport psychology* (pp. 287–314). Morgantown, WV: Fitness Information Technology.

Stambulova, N., Alfermann, D., Statler, T., & Côté, J. (2009). Career development and transitions of athletes: The ISSP position stand. *International Journal of Sport and Exercise Psychology, 7*(4), 395–412.

Stambulova, N., & Ryba, T. V. (2013). *Athletes' careers across cultures*. London: Routledge.

Stambulova, N., Stephan, Y., & Jäphag, U. (2007). Athletic retirement: A cross-national comparison of elite French and Swedish athletes. *Psychology of Sport and Exercise, 8*(1), 101–118.

Stambulova, N., & Wylleman, P. (2014). Athletes' career development and transitions. In A. G. Papaioannou & D. Hackfort (Eds.), *Routledge companion to sport and exercise psychology* (pp. 605–620). Hove: Routledge.

Storm, L. K. (2015). *"Coloured by culture": Talent development in Scandinavian elite sport as seen from a cultural perspective* (PhD Thesis). University of Southern Denmark, Odense.

Weissensteiner, J. R. (2017). How contemporary international perspectives have consolidated a best-practice approach for identifying and developing sporting talent. In J. Baker, S. Cobley, J. Schorer, & N. Wattie (Eds.), *Routledge handbook of talent identification and development in sport* (pp. 51–68). Oxon: Routledge.

Wylleman, P., Reints, A., & Knop, P. D. (2013). A developmental and holistic perspective on athletic career development. In P. Sotiriadou & V. De Bosscher (Eds.), *Managing high performance sport* (pp. 159–182). New York: Routledge.

2 Psychosocial Aspects of Sport Retirement Amongst Collegiate Student-Athletes in the United States

Ashley Brauer

Psychosocial Outcomes of Sport Retirement

More than 480,000 student-athletes compete in the National Collegiate Athletic Association (NCAA, 2019) within a given year. However, only a small percentage of those athletes advance to the professional level after college. In 2019, rates of collegiate athletes to advance to the professional level were 0.9% in women's basketball, 1.2% in men's basketball, 1.6% in American football, and 6.9% in men's ice hockey (NCAA, 2019). Consequently, the majority of collegiate athletes terminate competitive sport participation during or upon graduation from college. Although sport retirement amongst US collegiate athletes is understudied, research has demonstrated that significant variability exists in the trajectory and psychological outcomes associated with sport retirement. Some studies suggest that retired athletes have less psychological distress (Weigand, Cohen, & Merenstein, 2013). However, other studies have found acute distress upon retirement and, for some, the onset of mental health disorders (Kerr, DeFreese, & Marshall, 2014). Understanding psychological outcomes following sport retirement is imperative, given that collegiate sport termination coincides with a developmental age common to the onset of many mental health disorders (American Psychiatric Association, 2013).

Sport retirement is a multifaceted process consisting of a variety of emotional and psychological responses. Sport transitions may be accompanied by changes in identity, interpersonal relationships, schedules, and behavioural changes (Stephan, 2003; Murphy, 1995). Therefore, it is not uncommon for student-athletes to experience some degree of emotional or psychological distress when retiring from sport. In fact, a national-level survey conducted by NCAA indicated that three of four student-athletes reported difficulty transitioning out of collegiate sport (Brooks, 2016). Moreover, sport retirement has been identified as a risk factor for mental health concerns, such as depression (Wolanin, Gross, & Hong, 2015). Distinguishing between acute psychological distress and a mental health condition is essential to effectively helping individuals transition out of sport, at both the individual and organisational levels. Psychosocial outcomes following sport retirement can

22 *Ashley Brauer*

be broadly differentiated between (a) acute psychological distress, (b) mental health disorders, and (c) healthy adjustment.

Acute Psychological Distress

Acute psychological distress following sport retirement may be best under-stood in the context of stressful life events. Stressful life events, such as job transitions and family conflict, have been shown to predict the onset of mental health concerns, such as depression (Kendler, KarKowski, & Prescott, 1999). Sport retirement is a significant life event, and negative emotions are a common response to the transition. A systematic review conducted by Park, Lavallee, and Tod (2013) found that 86 of 126 studies demonstrated athletes experienced some degree of negative emotions due to sport transition. Moreover, 16% of athletes experienced acute adjustment difficulties characterised by negative emotions including grief and distress during the transition (Park et al., 2013). Acute psychological distress following sport retirement is time limited, can be managed effectively with support and coping skills, and does not significantly impair functioning in daily life. Transitioning out of sport is a stressful time period, but several studies have shown that athletes tend to report higher levels of life satisfaction with time after retirement (Douglas & Carless, 2009; Lally, 2007; Wippert & Wippert, 2008). For example, less perceived life stress was reported at three months following the transition compared to ten days after retirement (Wippert & Wippert, 2008). Although identifying and diagnosing mental health disorders is complex, psychological distress can be conceptualised on a continuum ranging from the absence of symptoms to severe illness (Clark, Cuthbert, Lewis-Fernández, Narrow, & Reed, 2017). Acute distress in response to an event is often time limited, with increasing severity, duration, and level of impairment signalling potential for the onset of a mental health disorder.

Mental Health Disorders

Although many athletes experience a healthy transition out of sport, a portion goes on to have more long-standing psychosocial difficulties. Approximately 20% of elite athletes endorse significant problems with sport retirement (Lavallee, Nesti, Borkoles, Cockerill, & Edge, 2000). Whilst minimal data exists on the prevalence of mental health disorders for retired US collegiate athletes, a few studies have been conducted on elite samples that include former collegiate athletes (Mannes et al., 2020). Most commonly studied mental health concerns among former athletes include depression, anxiety, and substance abuse (Esopenko et al., 2017; Kerr et al., 2014).

In the United States, rates of depression in retired athlete samples range from 10.4% in former collegiate athletes to greater than 20% in former professional athletes (Kerr et al., 2014; Esopenko et al., 2017). Moreover, retired athletes have endorsed moderate-to-severe depression at a rate two

Psychosocial Aspects of Sport Retirement 23

times higher than those active in competitive sport (Aston, Filippou-Frye, Blasey, Johannes van Roessel, & Rodriguez, 2020). These differences also appear to be evident between athletes and non-athletes as former collegiate athletes endorsed lower quality of life (e.g. depression, fatigue, sleep disturbances) compared to their non-athlete counterparts (Simon & Docherty, 2014). With regard to anxiety, approximately 16% of former Division 1 collegiate athletes have reported experiencing anxiety symptoms post-retirement (Kerr et al., 2014). Alcohol misuse has been shown in 5.8% of former collegiate student-athletes (Kerr et al., 2014). However, rates may be higher in some subsamples as evidenced by 31.5% of retired hockey players meeting criteria for alcohol dependence (Esopenko et al., 2017).

Whereas acute psychological distress tends to dissipate with time following the stressor, those with more long-standing mental health concerns may notice ongoing distress that impairs their ability to engage in one or more domains of daily life (APA, 2013). This distinction is important for those working with athletes pre- and post-retirement because it has implications for determining intervention needs. Given that definitions used to operationalise and study mental health concerns in the literature vary widely, an overview of diagnostic criteria for the common aforementioned mental health disorders is outlined in the subsequent sections.

Adjustment Disorder

Adjustment disorder is characterised by the onset of emotional or behavioural symptoms within three months of an identifiable stressor (e.g. sport retirement) and does not persist past six months after termination of the stressor. Adjustment disorder requires "marked distress that is out of proportion to the severity or intensity of the stressor, taking into account the external context and the cultural factors that might influence symptom severity and presentation" (APA, 2013, p. 286) and/or "significant impairment in social, occupational, or other important areas of functioning" (APA, 2013, p. 286).

Major Depressive Disorder

Major depressive disorder (MDD) is characterised by depressed mood and/or loss of interest and pleasure with the presence of five or more clinical depressive symptoms. Such symptoms may include fatigue, difficulties concentration, unintentional weight loss, insomnia, or hypersomnia. Symptoms are present for at least two weeks and impair functioning in daily life (APA, 2013).

Generalised Anxiety Disorder

Generalised anxiety disorder (GAD) includes excessive anxiety and worry about a number of events or activities (e.g. school, work) that is difficult to

24 *Ashley Brauer*

manage. Worry and anxiety with GAD occurs more days than not for at least six months. At least three of the following clinical symptoms are present: restlessness, easily fatigued, difficulty concentrating or mind going blank, irritability, muscle tension, or sleep disturbance (APA, 2013).

Substance-Use Disorders

Substance use disorder (SUD) includes a pattern of symptoms that results from ongoing intake of a substance (e.g. alcohol, cannabis, hallucinogens, opioids) despite experiencing problems. Examples of symptoms include taking the substance in larger amounts than intended, being unable to cut back on use despite wanting to, cravings or urges to use a substance, being unable to manage daily responsibilities because of use, and needing more of the substance to get intended effects. SUDs may be classified as mild, moderate, or severe based on the severity of use and the number of symptoms identified. Additional information on criteria for mental health disorder can be found in the *Diagnostic and Statistical Manual of Mental Disorders* (5th ed.; *DSM-5*; American Psychiatric Association).

Positive Adjustment

For collegiate athletes in the United States, sport retirement coincides with transitions in academics as they subsequently graduate college, relocate, and transition to their next academic or occupational endeavour. Despite this, many athletes have a positive experience whilst transitioning out of sport. A majority of student-athletes report believing that sport participation had a positive impact on their health during participation (85%; Theberge, 2007) and following retirement (Brooks, 2016). In addition, rates of mental health concerns such as depression have been found to be significantly higher in athletes currently active in sport compared with former student-athletes (Weigand et al., 2013). Self-esteem also has shown to improve following collegiate sport participation when individuals are well rounded across various domains of academics, athletics, and social involvement (Clark, 2008). These findings indicate that some student-athletes may experience a relief in psychological distress with sport retirement. In order to better understand the differing psychosocial outcomes of sport retirement, factors that moderate the relationship between retirement and psychosocial functioning should be considered.

Factors Impacting Psychosocial Outcomes of Sport Retirement

Voluntary Versus Involuntary Retirement

One of the most well-studied situational factors impacting sport transitions is whether a decision to retire is voluntary or involuntary (Wippert &

Wippert, 2010). Examples of involuntary decisions include age, career-ending injuries, and de-selection (Park et al., 2013). In contrast, athletes who voluntarily choose to retire tend to experience less negative outcomes. Involuntary sport retirement has been associated with greater psychological distress and shown to have a negative impact on mental health (Wippert & Wippert, 2010; Erpič, Wylleman, & Zupančič, 2004). It is promising that psychological distress following involuntary retirement was shown to decrease with time and that planning for sport retirement was associated with fewer negative emotional reactions compared to unplanned retirement (Wippert & Wippert, 2010; Alfermann, Stambulova, & Zemaityte, 2004). Through planning and cultivating agency over their decision, athletes may have the ability to perceive transitions as more voluntary than involuntary. This may be particularly helpful for collegiate athletes whose competitive sport career coincides with graduation from university. College student-athletes may perceive retirement as forced through loss of eligibility due to graduation, or as a choice to transition into their next academic or occupational endeavour.

Athletic Identity

The degree to which one identifies with their athletic identity is another well-known contributor to how an athlete experiences sport retirement. Identity foreclosure is defined by the experience of identifying with solely one identity without having explored other options (Murphy, Petitpas, & Brewer, 1996). Although former collegiate athletes have been shown to experience lower rates of depression than current collegiate athletes, it is likely that this finding does not hold true for individuals with exclusive athletic identity (Weigand et al., 2013). Athletes with strong and exclusive identities have shown to demonstrate greater levels of stress following sport retirement and may require more time to adjust to life following retirement (Grove, Lavallee, & Gordon, 1997). Similarly, those with strong athletic identities may be more prone to experience difficulties adjusting to changes in social roles and experience greater emotional difficulties with retirement overall (Baillie & Danish, 1992; Alfermann et al., 2004; Grove et al., 1997).

Social Roles and Transition

Athletes experience a significant shift in their social roles and environment upon retirement from collegiate sport. The loss of social support from their sport network, teammates, coaches, and athletic and academic personnel is associated with greater distress and mental health concerns (Gouttebarge et al., 2017; Gouttebarge, Frings-Dresen, & Sluiter, 2015; Vihjalmsson, 1993). However, athletes may perceive minimal loss of social support if they have other networks within or outside sport to engage in. Perception about one's level of social support is important to consider, given that perceptions

26 *Ashley Brauer*

of low social support are associated with greater depressive symptomatology (Aston et al., 2020). Additional social factors that may increase the risk of psychosocial difficulties include major life events, career dissatisfaction, and financial difficulties (Gouttebarge et al., 2015, 2017).

Health Status and Physical Activity

Rates of mental health disorders among former collegiate athletes have been observed at rates similar to those of the general US population (Kerr et al., 2014). However, those with health conditions or history of injury scored lower on scales of physical functioning and pain interference post-retirement, indicating that injuries during college may inhibit later functioning and quality of life (Kerr et al., 2014). This is problematic, given that collegiate athletes face unique stressors (e.g. playing time, scholarships) that may promote playing with injury or illness. Division 1 student-athletes endorsed practicing with injury or illness 2.1 times more than recreational athletes (Simon & Docherty, 2014). Unsurprisingly, former student-athletes have endorsed greater levels of pain than age-matched controls (Simon & Docherty, 2016). Moreover, a majority of student-athletes will become less active or inactive after sport retirement (Reifsteck, Gill, & Brooks, 2013). Pain, illness, and physical inactivity significantly impact physical functioning and mental health following sport retirement (Simon & Docherty, 2014; Simon & Docherty, 2016; Turner, Barlow, & Heathcote-Elliott, 2000). When combined, depressive symptoms and pain are predicative of poor sleep, relationship strain, and financial concerns, further increasing risk for difficulties with adjustment to sport retirement (Schwenk, Gorenflo, Dopp, & Hipple, 2007).

Head injuries and concussions can also significantly impact transition to sport retirement. Approximately 10,000 sport-related concussions occur annually in collegiate athletics, of which 1 in 11 is a recurrent concussion (Zuckerman et al., 2015). Although clinical recovery typically occurs within a week of injury, a subset of athletes will experience a prolonged recovery that may be accompanied by both ongoing symptoms and functional impairments (McCrea et al., 2013). Prolonged symptoms are associated with unconsciousness, post-traumatic amnesia, and severity of acute symptoms (McCrea et al., 2013). Literature on the impact of concussions on psychological functioning post-sport retirement is mixed. Some findings indicate no significant differences between the number of previous concussions and mental health concerns post-retirement (Kerr et al., 2014). However, others have demonstrated an increased likelihood of experiencing depressive symptoms with an increasing number of concussions (Didehbani et al., 2013; Kerr, Marshall, Harding, & Guskiewicz, 2012). Former elite athletes with a history of one or two concussions were 1.5 times more likely to diagnosed with depression; those with three or more concussions were three times more likely to be diagnosed with depression than those

Psychosocial Aspects of Sport Retirement 27

without a history of concussion (Guskiewicz et al., 2007). In addition, those with a history of concussion and depression endorsed greater impairment in daily physical functioning, more alcohol-related problems, and were more likely to be separated or divorced (Guskiewicz et al., 2007).

Interventions

In the absence of national-level programming in the United States, universities have begun to independently implement interventions to assist with sport retirement. Although sport retirement is a long-term process, transition programmes are often conducted in a focused and time-limited format, given the time constraints student-athletes face at US institutions. Programmes may target several transition aspects, including preparation and prevention, screening, and/or referrals to resources. In addition, programmes have also targeted different factors that impact psychosocial health following sport retirement. Two programmes have been published in peer-reviewed journals: one targeting psychological and emotional health (Hansen, Perry, Ross, & Montgomery, 2018) and another aimed at prompting a physically active lifestyle after sport (Reifsteck & Brooks, 2018).

The workshop developed by Hansen et al. (2018) targets psychological and emotional health. Content for the workshop was divided into four sections: (a) psychoeducation, (b) coping skills, (c) psychological processing of sport retirement and (d) referral sources (Hansen et al., 2018). Participants were provided with psychoeducation on factors that impact adjustment, as well as warning signs of maladjustment. Participants were also introduced to helpful coping techniques, including cognitive-behavioural skills such as reframing thoughts, behavioural activation, and adopting positive health behaviours (e.g. sleep, exercise). In addition, participants learned how to utilise their personal and athletic values to assist with goal setting and transferrable skills from athletics to post-retirement life. Finally, participants engaged in small and large group discussions aimed at facilitating time to begin processing their sport career. At the end of the workshop, participants were provided with optional relevant resources and referral sources. An example of workshop content adapted by Hansen et al. (2018) can be found in Table 2.1.

Physical activity and health have significant implications on an athlete's psychosocial functioning and adjustment following competitive sport. Therefore, it is important to cultivate programmes specifically targeting physical activity and positive health behaviours (e.g. nutrition). The Moving On! Program is one programme developed by researchers at an NCAA institution to target long-term health during sport retirement. This is an evidence-based programme that helps student-athletes in their final year of competition transition from competitive sport to lifestyle physical activity (Reifsteck & Brooks, 2018). The programme is brief, structured, and consists of four sessions: (a) an overview, (b) identity exploration,

28   *Ashley Brauer*

Table 2.1 Example structure of sport retirement workshop

Phase	Topic	Content
Psychoeducation	Understanding maladjustment	Introduction and overview
		Prevalence for target population
	Factors related to maladjustment	Voluntary (e.g. choice) and involuntary retirement (e.g. injury)
		The role of athletic identity
		Other identities and roles
		Health status
	Warning signs	Emotional
		Social
		Dysfunctional self-perceptions
		Behavioural
Facilitating a healthy adjustment	Part 1: Cognitive-behavioural techniques	Challenging and reframing thoughts
		Distress tolerance skills
		Behavioural activation and self-care
		Developing social support network
	Part 2: Reflective exercises	
	Values	Identifying values
		Linking values to behaviours and goals
		Identifying transferrable skills
	Identity	Identifying multiple roles and understanding of how they change
Processing sport retirement	Reflection of sport career	Identifying notable and important aspects of sport career
Additional resources	Referral sources	Organisations and clinics in the community
	Resources	Relevant websites, books, videos

(c) goal setting and action plans, and (d) planning ahead, which was later expanded to also target healthy eating (Reifsteck & Brooks, 2018; Reifsteck, Brooks, Newton, & Shriver, 2018). On average, student-athletes reported having increased knowledge and feeling more prepared to transition into a physically active lifestyle after retirement (Reifsteck & Brooks, 2018). In addition, research has indicated that student-athletes in their final year of competition reported positive changes in self-efficacy for healthy eating behaviours and nutrition-related self-efficacy (Reifsteck et al., 2018). By addressing the many factors impacting sport retirement early, sport personnel may be better able to assist athletes in preparing for the transition out of competitive sport.

Implications for Practice

Research on psychosocial aspects of sport retirement provides athletes and sport personnel a foundation of data to inform practice. Given the few evidence-based and organisational resources for student-athletes transitioning out of sport, this information can be utilised to tailor and develop programmes that meet the needs of athletes across institutions. In addition, the information provided will assist athletes and sport personnel in understanding the multitude of emotional responses that commonly occur during sport retirement, and how to appropriately differentiate between normative emotional responses and more significant mental health concerns. This information will help sport personnel screen and triage athletes to appropriate resources to meet their needs.

References

Alfermann, D., Stambulova, N., & Zemaityte, A. (2004). Reactions to sport career termination: A cross-national comparison of German, Lithuanian, and Russian athletes. *Psychology of Sport and Exercise, 5*(1), 61–75.

American Psychiatric Association. (2013). *Diagnostic and statistical manual of mental disorders* (5th ed.). Washington, DC: Author.

Aston, P., Filippou-Frye, M., Blasey, C., Johannes van Roessel, P., & Rodriguez, C. I. (2020). Self-reported depressive symptoms in active and retired professional hockey players. *Canadian Journal of Behavioural Science/Revue Canadienne Des Sciences du Comportement, 52*(2), 97–106.

Baillie, P. H., & Danish, S. J. (1992). Understanding the career transition of athletes. *The Sport Psychologist, 6*(1), 77–98.

Brooks, D. D. (2016). *Physical challenges of moving on! Student-athletes transition after sport.* Talk presented at 2016 NCAA convention, San Antonio, TX.

Clark, J. A. (2008). Retirement from competitive athletics: Key predictors of post-collegiate self-esteem in former division I athletes. *Dissertation Abstracts International: Section B: The Sciences and Engineering, 68*(8-B), 5562.

Clark, L. A., Cuthbert, B., Lewis-Fernández, R., Narrow, W. E., & Reed, G. M. (2017). Three approaches to understanding and classifying mental disorder: ICD-11, DSM-5, and the national institute of mental health's research domain criteria (RDoC). *Psychological Science in the Public Interest, 18*(2), 72–145.

Didehbani, N., Munro Cullum, C., Mansinghani, S., Conover, H., & Hart, J. (2013). Depressive symptoms and concussions in aging retired NFL players. *Archives of Clinical Neuropsychology, 28*(5), 418–424.

Douglas, K., & Carless, D. (2009). Abandoning the performance narrative: Two women's stories of transition from professional sport. *Journal of Applied Sport Psychology, 21*(2), 213–230.

Erpič, S. C., Wylleman, P., & Zupančič, M. (2004). The effect of athletic and non-athletic factors on the sports career termination process. *Psychology of Sport and Exercise, 5*(1), 45–59.

Esopenko, C., Chow, T. W., Tartaglia, M. C., Bacopulos, A., Kumar, P., Binns, M. A., . . . Levine, B. (2017). Cognitive and psychosocial function in retired professional hockey players. *Journal of Neurol Neurosurg Psychiatry, 88*(6), 512–519.

Gouttebarge, V., Frings-Dresen, M. H. W., & Sluiter, J. K. (2015). Mental and psychosocial health among current and former professional footballers. *Occupational Medicine, 65*(3), 190–196.

Gouttebarge, V., Jonkers, R., Moen, M., Verhagen, E., Wylleman, P., & Kerkhoffs, G. (2017). The prevalence and risk indicators of symptoms of common mental disorders among current and former Dutch elite athletes. *Journal of Sports Sciences, 35*(21), 2148–2156.

Guskiewicz, K. M., Marshall, S. W., Bailes, J., McCrea, M., Harding, H. P., Matthews, A., . . . Cantu, R. C. (2007). Recurrent concussion and risk of depression in retired professional football players. *Medicine & Science in Sports & Exercise, 39*(6), 903–909.

Grove, J. R., Lavallee, D., & Gordon, S. (1997). Coping with retirement from sport: The influence of athletic identity. *Journal of Applied Sport Psychology, 9*(2), 191–203.

Hansen, A., Perry, J., Ross, M., & Montgomery, T. (2018). Facilitating a successful transition out of sport: Introduction of a collegiate student-athlete workshop. *Journal of Sport Psychology in Action, 10*(1), 1–9.

Kendler, K. S., Karkowski, L. M., & Prescott, C. A. (1999). Causal relationship between stressful life events and the onset of major depression. *American Journal of Psychiatry, 156*(6), 837–841.

Kerr, Z. Y., DeFreese, J. D., & Marshall, S. W. (2014). Current physical and mental health of former collegiate athletes. *Orthopaedic Journal of Sports Medicine, 2*(8), 2325967114544107.

Kerr, Z. Y., Marshall, S. W., Harding Jr, H. P., & Guskiewicz, K. M. (2012). Nine-year risk of depression diagnosis increases with increasing self-reported concussions in retired professional football players. *The American Journal of Sports Medicine, 40*(10), 2206–2212.

Lally, P. (2007). Identity and athletic retirement: A prospective study. *Psychology of Sport and Exercise, 8*(1), 85–99.

Lavallee, D., Nesti, M., Borkoles, E., Cockerill, I., & Edge, A. (2000). Intervention strategies for athletes in transition. In D. Lavallee & P. Wylleman (Eds.), *Career transitions in sport: International perspectives* (pp. 111–130). Morgantown, WV: Fitness Information Technology.

Mannes, Z. L., Ferguson, E. G., Perlstein, W. M., Waxenberg, L. B., Cottler, L. B., & Ennis, N. (2020). Negative health consequences of pain catastrophizing among retired national football league athletes. *Health Psychology, 39*(5), 452–462.

McCrea, M., Guskiewicz, K., Randolph, C., Barr, W. B., Hammeke, T. A., Marshall, S. W., . . . Kelly, J. P. (2013). Incidence, clinical course, and predictors of prolonged recovery time following sport-related concussion in high school and college athletes. *Journal of the International Neuropsychological Society, 19*(1), 22–33.

Murphy, G. M., Petitpas, A. J., & Brewer, B. W. (1996). Identity foreclosure, athletic identity, and career maturity in intercollegiate athletes. *The Sport Psychologist, 10*(3), 239–246. doi:10.1123/tsp.10.3.239

Murphy, S. (1995). Transitions in competitive sport: Maximizing individual potential. In S. Murphy (Ed.), *Sport psychology interventions* (pp. 331–346). Champaign, IL: Human Kinetics.

Psychosocial Aspects of Sport Retirement 31

National Collegiate Athletics Association. (2019). *Estimated probability of competing in professional athletics.* Retrieved from www.ncaa.org/about/resources/research/estimated-probability-competing-professional-athletics

Park, S., Lavallee, D., & Tod, D. (2013). Athletes' career transition out of sport: A systematic review. *International Review of Sport and Exercise Psychology, 6*(1), 22–53. doi: 10.1080/1750984X.2012.687053

Reifsteck, E. J., & Brooks, D. D. (2018). A transition program to help student-athletes move on to lifetime physical activity. *Journal of Sport Psychology in Action, 9*(1), 21–31.

Reifsteck, E. J., Brooks, D. D., Newton, J. D., & Shriver, L. H. (2018). Promoting a healthy post-collegiate lifestyle: An evaluation of the moving on! Transition program for student-athletes. *Journal of Higher Education Athletics & Innovation, 4,* 54–76.

Reifsteck, E. J., Gill, D. L., & Brooks, D. L. (2013). The relationship between athletic identity and physical activity among former college athletes. *Athletic Insight, 5*(3), 271–284.

Schwenk, T. L., Gorenflo, D. W., Dopp, R. R., & Hipple, E. (2007). Depression and pain in retired professional football players. *Medicine & Science in Sports & Exercise, 39*(4), 599–605.

Simon, J. E., & Docherty, C. L. (2014). Current health-related quality of life is lower in former Division I collegiate athletes than in non—collegiate athletes. *The American Journal of Sports Medicine, 42*(2), 423–429.

Simon, J. E., & Docherty, C. L. (2016). Current health-related quality of life in former national collegiate athletic association division I collision athletes compared with contact and limited-contact athletes. *Journal of Athletic Training, 51*(3), 205–212.

Stephan, Y. (2003). Repercussions of transition out of elite sport on subjective well-being: A one-year study. *Journal of Applied Sport Psychology, 15*(4), 354–371.

Theberge, N. (2007). It's not about health, it's about performance. In J. Hargreaves & P. Vertinsky (Eds.), *Physical culture, power, and the body* (pp. 176–194). New York: Routledge.

Turner, A. P., Barlow, J. H., & Heathcote-Elliott, C. (2000). Long term health impact of playing professional football in the United Kingdom. *British Journal of Sports Medicine, 34*(5), 332–336.

Vihjalmsson, R. (1993). Life stress, social support, and clinical depression. *Social Science & Medicine, 37,* 331–342.

Weigand, S., Cohen, J., & Merenstein, D. (2013). Susceptibility for depression in current and retired student athletes. *Sports Health, 5*(3), 263–266.

Wippert, P. M., & Wippert, J. (2008). Perceived stress and prevalence of traumatic stress symptoms following athletic career termination. *Journal of Clinical Sport Psychology, 2*(1), 1–16.

Wippert, P. M., & Wippert, J. (2010). The effects of involuntary athletic career termination on psychological distress. *Journal of Clinical Sport Psychology, 4*(2), 133–149.

Wolanin, A., Gross, M., & Hong, E. (2015). Depression in athletes: Prevalence and risk factors. *Current Sports Medicine Reports, 14*(1), 56–60.

Zuckerman, S. L., Kerr, Z. Y., Yengo-Kahn, A., Wasserman, E., Covassin, T., & Solomon, G. S. (2015). Epidemiology of sports-related concussion in NCAA athletes from 2009–2010 to 2013–2014: Incidence, recurrence, and mechanisms. *The American Journal of Sports Medicine, 43*(11), 2654–2662.

3 The Professionalisation of Paralympic Sport and Implications for the Retirement Experiences of Paralympians

Andrea Bundon

Introduction

The Paralympic Movement has long pursued an agenda intended to raise the profile and prestige of the Paralympics through strategies that align with their mission of enabling athletes with disabilities to 'achieve sporting excellence' (IPC, 2019). This work is informed by an underpinning belief that Paralympic athletes can and should be seen as equal to their Olympic counterparts—that their training should be equally demanding, their events equally competitive and their medals equally valued. The professionalisation of Paralympic sport, that is the shift from being a pastime pursued by enthusiastic amateur athletes supported by largely volunteer coaches to a highly complex system that includes high-performance athletes and increasingly specialised staff, has largely been framed as 'progress' in this quest for equality. However, progress comes at a cost, and, in this chapter, I explore the consequences of the professionalisation of Paralympic sport as it pertains to the career transitions, and specifically the retirements, of elite para-athletes. Drawing on interviews with Paralympians at various stages in their careers, I discuss how the pathways to the Paralympics, the conditions surrounding training and competition, and the context of para-athlete retirements have changed. By bringing together literature and theorising from the sociology of sport, sport psychology and critical disability studies with empirical qualitative data, I demonstrate how the equal treatment of Paralympic athletes can and has contributed to unequitable outcomes in their sport retirements. This chapter concludes with recommendations for practices that can support the sport transitions of elite para-athletes.

The Rise of High-Performance Disability Sport

David Howe, a leading researcher on the cultural context of Paralympic sport, has written extensively on the evolution of the Paralympics. He identifies three moments in the history of the Paralympics: the early Games hosted in the wake of the Second World War focused on the rehabilitation of disabled veterans, the rise of the International Organisations of Sport for the Disabled that prioritised creating opportunities for people with disabilities to engage in sport, and the third and current moment—the age of high-performance disability sport (Howe, 2008). There is no definitive start to this moment, but it is possible to see a shift in the priorities and operations of the Paralympic Movement starting in the late 1980s and early 1990s when the International Paralympic Committee (IPC) and other stakeholders made a series of decisions to ensure that the Paralympics were a 'viable' sporting event (Howe, 2008). This included reducing the number of events (over concerns that the field was too diluted) and implementing rules to ensure that athletes had met certain athletic standards (Cashman & Darcy, 2008). The 2000 Sydney Games were also a landmark moment in the Paralympic Movement in that, for the first time, attention was paid to the 'spectacle' of the event. Tickets and merchandise were sold, the Opening Ceremonies and select events televised, and there was significant investment in the marketing of the Games (Cashman, 2008). This trend towards delivering a professional, marketable, elite sport event has been described as the 'Olympification' of Paralympic sport (Gérard, 2020). It was also around this time that the IPC and the International Olympic Committee (IOC) started to formalise their relationship and, in 2001, an agreement was signed stipulating that all future hosts would be required to deliver both Games. This agreement was followed by numerous initiatives that would further bind the fates of the IPC and the IOC (Purdue, 2013). While these arrangements were heralded as guaranteeing the ongoing financial and logistical feasibility of the Paralympics, they have also been widely criticised for making the IPC dependent upon the more powerful IOC. Concerns have been raised that "there is perhaps a tendency for the identity of the Paralympic Movement to become subsumed by the Olympic Movement" (Purdue, 2013, p. 8).

The Professionalisation of Paralympic Sport

The era of high-performance Paralympic sport is closely associated with the professionalisation of Paralympic sport. Although the term 'professionalisation' appears frequently in sport management literature, definitions of the term are few. Dowling, Edwards, and Washington (2014) explain that a review of the extant sport management research generally indicates the term is used to describe both the process by which sport organisations adopt more managerial and business-like orientations towards operations and the process of sport-related occupations becoming 'professions' and individuals pursuing these occupations becoming 'professionals.' Both operationalisations of the term professionalisation are evident in the current era of high-performance Paralympic sport.

The previously described changes in the 'field' of Paralympic sport (i.e. the closer ties with the IOC, the concerns about delivering a viable

34 *Andrea Bundon*

sport spectacle) are examples of *systemic* professionalisation (Dowling et al., 2014). However, systemic professionalisation goes hand in hand with *organisational* and *occupational* professionalisation (Dowling et al., 2014). For example, as collectively the Paralympic Movement adopted a high-performance agenda and sought to align more closely with the standards of the Olympics, this put pressure on the National Paralympic Committees and the ISODs to implement processes and policies able to deliver high-performance sport. The introduction of athlete quotas, the ongoing refinement of the classification system and the development of international standards all contributed to an ongoing formalisation of governance structures and operations (organisational professionalism). Carrying out these practices required individuals with specialised knowledge in sport management, sport science, coaching and more. The negotiation of broadcast rights and the acquisition of sponsors required media relations and marketing experts.[1] The result is an influx of paid, full-time sport managers into disability sport organisations that were previously dependent on volunteer labour and/or training existing volunteers to prepare them for their changing roles (occupational professionalisation).

In addition to the professionalisation of the field, there is also the professionalisation of the athlete role. As Howe (2004) writes, discussions of the distinction between amateur and professional often fall back on the argument that amateurs pursue something as a pastime or a passion whereas professionals derive their income from the activity. However, this fails to accurately capture the context in which the present-day sport is practiced. There are several ways in which an athlete might be compensated for their sport performance including salaries, sponsorship, prize money and training allowances. It is true that there are considerable discrepancies between athletes, but the amount of income received that is directly attributed to sport is only one part of the equation. The other part is understanding what other pursuits the athlete engages in, what alternative employment options exist, and whether or not the athletes consider themselves to be 'full-time.' In the case of Paralympic athletes, there is certainly evidence that they are earning more income compared to Paralympians of earlier eras albeit still significantly less than their Olympic counterparts. They are also more likely to be pursuing training on a year-round basis and to the exclusion of other pursuits compared to previous generations of Paralympians (Bundon, Ashfield, Smith, & Goosey-Tolfrey, 2018). It is on this basis that I claim there has been a professionalisation of the Paralympic athlete that has happened in concert with the professionalisation of the Paralympic field in the era of high-performance disability sport.

The Careers of Paralympic Athletes

My intent here is to explore the implications of professionalisation specifically as they pertain to how Paralympians experience sport career

Retirement Experiences of Paralympians   35

transitions. To accomplish this, I am drawing on multiple data sets that include qualitative interviews with Paralympians at different careers stages. Since 2008, I have been engaged in a programme of research largely organised around understanding the experiences of para-athletes and the inclusion/exclusion of people with disabilities in sport. I have conducted over 60 semi-structured interviews with athletes, coaches and managers involved in the Paralympics, and I have listened to and analysed many more by collaborators. To be explicit, only one project, conducted whilst a working at the Peter Harrison Centre for Disability Sport (see Bundon et al., 2018), focused on Paralympic athletes and career transitions. None were specifically about professionalisation. However, all contained some variation in asking athletes to 'tell me about your experiences in sport' and athletes shared stories of coming to sport, pursuing a sport career, and of leaving sport. Collectively, these interviews have provided rare first-hand accounts of changes in the Paralympic Movement over a period that spans 30 years (some athletes competed in Games in the 1980s, others are still competing) told by those most directly impacted by these changes. It is these interviews that provide the empirical basis for this chapter.

My analysis is underpinned by the understanding that athletes negotiate a number of transitions throughout their career, including normative and non-normative transitions (Wylleman & Lavallee, 2004). Although often triggered by an event (e.g. making a team) or non-event (e.g. deselection from a team), transition is a process of coping and not a particular moment (Stambulova, Engström, Franck, Linnér, & Lindahl, 2015). Whilst the research has often focused on sport retirement, as this is a period when athletes often struggle to cope, there is increasingly an awareness that how an athlete experiences and make sense of their retirement requires looking at their sport careers as a whole (Debois, Ledon, Argiolas, & Rosnet, 2012). With this in mind, I compare and contrast the stories of athletes from different 'eras' and at different points in their careers to demonstrate how the professionalisation of Paralympic sport has impacted their experiences.

From Hospitals to Paralympian Searches

The origin story of the Paralympics is well documented in other publications, but the short version is that Dr. Ludwig Guttman, a neurologist in charge of the Spinal Cord Injury unit at Stoke Mandeville Hospital in England, had the idea to implement sport as part of the therapeutic programming at the hospital (Anderson, 2003). His vision was that sport would be a vehicle not only to physically rehabilitate the patients but also to raise the profile of disabled people in broader society. The Stoke Mandeville Games were the precursor to the Paralympics, and the early organisers of the Games were almost exclusively medical professionals specialising in rehabilitation. The Paralympics are no longer hosted by hospitals, yet medical practitioners are still very much a part of the delivery of disability sport (Bundon, 2019).

One area where they are particularly visible is in the recruitment and initiation of people to disability sport. Throughout my research, Paralympians cited physicians, physiotherapists and occupational therapists working in rehabilitation facilities as essential in introducing them to disability sport:

> My physiotherapist—so they talked to me a lot about Paralympic sport and about how the opportunities to be competitive were still there and just kind of planted the seed because I wasn't really ready to hear any of that at that time. But they knew that I kind of came from a sport background so they sort of just gave me the lay of the land and stuff like that. She got me swimming right away.
>
> (*Competed in 1992, 1996, 2000 and 2004 Paralympics*)

Although the athlete quoted ultimately had a long career in wheelchair basketball, her experience of transitioning into disability sport via the pool is a common one. Swimming is a popular activity in rehabilitation facilities and often one of the first forms of exercise prescribed. Many interviewees who were injured in the 1980s and 1990s 'found' Paralympic sport this way.

Starting around the time of the 2000 Sydney Games, there was a shift in how athletes were recruited to Paralympic Sport. As previously described, Sydney raised the profile of disability sport through broadcast media. It is shortly after Sydney that we first observe nations seriously investing in Paralympic Sport and developing Paralympic athletes. For example, in 2006 in Canada, the first edition of 'No Accidental Champions' was published. This document built upon the Canadian Long Term Athlete Development framework and outlined unique considerations for recruiting people with disabilities and supporting their athletic development. Policy documents and published research suggest that other leading Paralympic nations were also starting to invest in talent development and talent identification in the first decade of the twenty-first century (see Baker, Lemez, Van Neutegem, & Wattie, 2017; Radtke & Doll-Tepper, 2014).

It is around this time that athletes started reporting that their initiation into sport was not happenstance but rather the result of strategic recruitment and talent identification processes:

> I was able-bodied until I was 15. I was always really active, I played a ton of sports for the school teams and things. I was never exceptional at one. So after I was poorly, I went back—out of the hospital—I used a wheelchair, I used prosthetic legs. And I actually started playing basketball and [the coach] tracked me down during a wheelchair session . . . then I got into wheelchair racing and I was the 4th UK male. And then I almost got headhunted by the GB Wheelchair Rugby Team. Tried it, loved it and that was about 2009—and then went to London 2012. So it was all a bit of a rollercoaster really.
>
> (*Competed in 2012 Paralympics*)

The increased investment in Paralympic sport meant that more sport managers and coaches were actively searching for the next Paralympic champion. In addition to scanning local programmes for recruits, some National Paralympic Committees implemented Paralympian Searches or Talent Identification events where people with disabilities participate in a battery of tests intended to identify those with the potential to succeed in sport at the highest level (Dehghansai & Baker, 2020). Athletes recruited via these routes were frequently connected directly to the national programme and placed on an accelerated career pathway. The increased investment in talent identification and talent development initiatives is a clear example of organisational professionalisation (and potentially occupational professionalisation if one assumes that delivering these initiatives requires new staff roles).

What is the impact of the professionalisation of talent identification on the transition into sport and subsequent careers of athletes? Paralympians identified via these channels tend to report very rapid transitions through careers stages—or perhaps more accurately a blurring of stages where initiation into sport, development and specialisation happen almost simultaneously. As described by one retired Paralympian who had since started coaching, one of the implications of accelerated pathways is that little time is invested in developing fundamental skills.

> We get athletes, especially new injuries, who are late-entry, good athletes before they got hurt, come to wheelchair sports. 'Oooh, there's a class one woman, we need her for the national team.' Boom, straight up there after, you know, one season in our domestic league. So they get jetted up to that level without the time to develop those fundamental skills. I've seen it happen in [other sport] too where they've gone and just plucked people out of [the grocery store] and say 'do you want to be on the national team?'
>
> (*Competed in four Paralympics and started coaching in 2012*)

Athletes commonly reported they had attended their first international competition only a short time after their first national event. Supporting this claim is an analysis by Dehghansai and Baker (2020) of participants in a Canadian Paralympian Search event that found, on average, athletes spent three years transitioning from local to international competition.

More Than a Hobby, Not Quite a Career

It is also important to consider structures that shape their experiences whilst in sport. Here also there was a dramatic increase in funding following Sydney. For example, UK Sport invested £10,075,602 in Summer Paralympic sports in preparation for Sydney and £72,786,652 in preparation for the 2016 Rio Paralympics (UK Sport, n.d.). For athletes whose careers spanned

38   *Andrea Bundon*

this time period, this resulted in several dramatic changes—changes in support they received and changes in how they perceived themselves. The following quote is from an athlete who started training for her sport in 2004 and it illustrates the slow but steady trend towards professionalisation of the athlete role:

> When I was at university it was literally—you just fit it in training when you can and hope that you do more than the other countries. It was just part time. Fit it in where you can at university, because it wasn't really fully funded and whilst we were committed to it, it was a bit more than a hobby but not quite a career. And then as we gradually got more funding, got Paralympic status and so on, it kind of, we kind of grew with that and it became more of a lifestyle then it did sort of a pastime.
>
> (*Competed in 2008 and 2012 Paralympics*)

The athlete went on to describe how the shift meant that she and her teammates had many more interactions with sport professionals:

> We got Paralympic status in 2005 [when] London had the bid for 2012—over those years it kind of changed into a sport where we were fully funded by the lottery, we had our own equipment, we had a coach, we had a performance coach, we had a weight coach, we had a physiotherapist, access to nutrition, psychology all of that.

Her description of multiple practitioners each with differentiated roles is indicative of the occupational professionalisation of Paralympic sport. She then describes when the team started sharing facilities with the Olympic athletes:

> I think in 2006 we started being integrated into the Olympic team, which was obviously a huge motivation, you know, cause we're like, 'oh my god,' we're with real people now, with the people who are amazing, who you see on tele all the time, and it was a huge inspiration for us to be part of that.

The aforementioned quotes illustrate the Olympification of Paralympic athletes and also the underpinning assumption that progress within the Paralympic Movement means being treated the 'same' as Olympic athletes. It also demonstrates how the role of the Paralympic athlete has changed since the turn of the century. That is not to suggest that previous Paralympians were less committed to their sport or training less rigorously. But few would have referred to sport as their career—simply because most were simultaneously pursuing other employment at the same time.

Retirement Experiences of Paralympians   39

Changing Investment, Changing Expectations

For many athletes, the increased investment in para-sport was a welcome change. Finally, they could focus exclusively on their sport.

> On a day to day basis it meant a switch in lifestyles really. . . . You could train and then you could rest. . . . You didn't have to go to work and then train or train and then go to work. . . . You were worked very hard but in a day to day setting you had time to rest and sit down and get the most of the training.
>
> *(Competed at the 2012 Paralympics)*

For other athletes, the professionalisation of para-sport meant a loss of agency. These athletes described how they had previously achieved significant sport success whilst balancing work, education and/or family responsibilities, but these circumstances became increasingly untenable. Athletes reported being told they had to quit their jobs, leave school or relocate to centralised training facilities if they wanted to continue in sport. Many felt that these demands were unnecessary, given that they had already proven they were able to compete at the highest level without these measures.

> I went into that meeting to tell the chief executive that it wasn't fair on me and it wasn't fair on my family. . . . I was one of the hardest working players on the team as well and the others weren't in the same circumstances as I was, weren't training as hard as I was, weren't as skint as I was—and I thought—at this point I was probably one of the fifth best players in the world—I was probably the third best! I had scored half of the team's points in the Paralympics [the previous year].
>
> *(Competed in 2012 Paralympics)*

A key critique heard from athletes who competed during the period that ranges from 2010 to 2016 was that they felt the professionalisation and Olympification of para-sport had gone too far. Whilst they acknowledged that winning at the Paralympics was also their goal, they felt constricted by the structures of professionalisation.

> The culture in [my national sport governing body] is incredibly results oriented. Of course, in competition that is expected but on almost one level it takes the human factor out of it completely. And for me with the way the structure of the coaching set up, the rigidity of the coaching set up—this took the fun and excitement out of the sport completely. I felt like I was just a number on the spreadsheets. And it suddenly wasn't about myself. It was about getting results for other people, people I didn't like.
>
> *(Competed in 2012 Paralympics)*

40   *Andrea Bundon*

Not only did this athlete disagree with decisions that were being made, but he specifically referenced that it was his impression that modelling the Paralympic programme off of the Olympic programme was doing more harm than good.

> I think the coaches mirrored themselves on the able-bodied squad a lot. It was sort of like the able-bodied squad coaches are their peers as well as their colleagues. They kind of look up to them an awful lot and if they kind of do something right then it must be right for absolutely everybody else. There wasn't enough adaptation if you like for disability. For different people's needs.

One particular concern with systems that failed to adapt for individual athletes was that the supply of para-athletes does not support this approach. As previously described, para-athletes are often identified through targeted approaches because they have the 'right' impairment to be competitive in an event. This is very different from the Olympic system that is predicated on an assumption that athletes are numerous and that one's position is never secure because there are always others vying for the spot. Instead, many Paralympians described a situation where the national teams were desperate to find enough para-athletes to justify the resources being spent in the programme and yet were not valuing the athletes they had:

> Who is going to fill those spots? And eventually if nobody's filling those spots, then well, there's no jobs for anybody. And not that that is their priority—I know the coaches well and I know that they care about the athletes, they care about developing good humans. They care about performances. There are really good people that are behind the machine in the [sport], but they also understand the priorities of what they need to deliver in order to keep their programme alive.
>
> (*Competed in the 2010 and 2014 Paralympics*)

Another athlete described it as a shift within the culture from wanting to win games because that is what athletes do, to needing to win to ensure that the coaches were not fired, or the programme defunded. Whilst there is rarely a single reason that athletes leave sport, the lack of agency, increased restrictions on how and where they trained, and the sense that their values no longer aligned with those of their sport organisations was a key factor for many of the athletes who left sport in the years following Vancouver, London, Sochi and Rio.

Readiness to Leave Sport

What happens to these athletes once they leave sport? The first concern raised by many athletes when discussing retirement was that the current

Retirement Experiences of Paralympians 41

structures designed to 'support' athletes were in fact infantilising and contributing to a generation of para-athletes are ill-prepared to leave sport:

> I think that might be one of the challenges that athletes face now that maybe athletes of my generation didn't have to face is that during my [sport] career nobody did anything for me. There was no physio paid for, there was no English Institute of Sport, there was no strength and condition coach. I had a swimming coach but everything else, the food on my table, my rent and everything I had to sort out. And so you can't be anything other than proactive. It was great when people did pay for my sport and I did get a physio and all that stuff, it was absolutely fantastic, and it made life easier but there is a generation of athletes out there now who are being spoon fed. And I know it's positive for them as athletes but it's not necessarily positive for them as adults when they retire.
>
> *(Competed at 1988, 1992, 1996, 2000, 2004)*

Another athlete stated:

> You have a governing body of the sport and they take all the stress and the pressure off the players because their goal is high-performance. But the thing of high-performance is unfortunately that in the real world they expect you to do for yourself. . . . They are not going to create opportunities for themselves because they have been spoon fed for years and years.
>
> *(Competed in 2012 Paralympics)*

The aforementioned statements could equally apply to Olympic athletes, but this trend towards 'doing-for' athletes is particularly problematic in the context of para-sport. There is a long history of infantilising people with disabilities and positioning them as dependent (Shakespeare, 2000). Whilst the Paralympic Movement states that empowering people with disabilities is central to their mission, structures that deny athletes opportunities to act in an agentic manner—and this includes having responsibility for their own sport training—are not empowering. The professionalisation of Paralympic sport has reinforced this trend by creating more jobs in disability sport, but not necessarily more opportunities for people with disabilities to be involved outside the athlete role.

A second consideration related to retirement is whether or not the services that have been introduced to prepare athletes for transitions out of sport are really catering to their needs. Although many nations have introduced initiatives to assist athletes to plan for their post-sport careers (e.g. Canada's 'Game Plan' that provides support to national team athletes), to my knowledge, none of these programmes have been specifically designed with a 'disability lens.' Para-athletes will face different barriers to employment and education compared to their able-bodied counterparts.

42 *Andrea Bundon*

As described by this athlete, a 'one-size-fits-all' approach rarely works for people with disabilities:

> I do think it needs to be more tailored and individualised and especially so the Paralympians—because again that added complication and barriers such as, well studying is a lot harder, harder for me to do my degree with a visual impairment than it was you know—than my friends I was on course with. Yeah, everything's harder or can potentially be harder. So yeah. Definitely see more focus on tailored, individualised support program as opposed to the one-size fits all approach.
>
> *(Competed in the 2008 and 2012 Paralympics)*

The final consideration raised references how few opportunities there are for people with disabilities to work in sport after their careers as athletes. Because para-athletes are often recruited directly to national teams, they have generally smaller networks in sport and spend less time in local programmes. Secondly, there is an assumption that a retiring Paralympian is only interested in or only capable of working in para-sport. It is rarely considered that they might want to coach able-bodied athletes or have the ability to manage an able-bodied programme. The result is that they lack the networks needed to find employment in sport, not have access to mentorship to pursue employment in sport, and/or not be considered for roles. The following quote is from an athlete who, after a very successful Paralympic career, found very few opportunities to coach:

> What does that look like for me? Does that mean that I'm only going to be coaching adaptive athletes? Can I build my criteria so that I can coach able-bodied? And I would never limit myself so I would say 'yes, yes, sure, why not?' But what are those streams and how do I access them? And who do I mentor under? Who do I learn from? And it may be that the system might already be there, but it's not visible, I haven't seen it.
>
> *(Competed in the 2010 and 2014 Paralympics)*

Implications for Practice

What are some practical considerations for supporting Paralympic athletes approaching retirement? As stated at the start of this chapter, retirement is only part of the story and how athletes retire is heavily predicated on their many other experiences throughout their careers. Just as it is important to take a lifespan approach to understanding retirement, it is critical that support of the athlete be integrated throughout the entire career and not implemented only once an athlete has been identified as retiring.

Create Opportunities to Connect and Grow Networks

Prior research has shown that para-athletes benefit from having extended networks that include close relations from others with impairments because these connections provide information on how to navigate the world as a person with a disability (Bundon & Hurd Clarke, 2015). Retiring athletes can also benefit from connections with others without impairments who can provide other forms of mentorship—for example, they may be working in a field that the athlete is considering. One practical suggestion is to develop mentorship programmes that do not rely on a single mentee and a single mentor but consist of groups of four or five individuals each at different stages of their athletic and post-sport careers and that include individuals with and without impairments. This can assist to counter the effect of the previously discussed 'accelerated' pathways that result in athlete going directly to national programmes and thereby having less time to grow their networks.

Build Practical Skills That Foster Agency

The trend towards the professionalisation of Paralympic sport has also reinforced the notion that athletes should 'just focus on sport.' Whilst this freedom from the stress of managing all the other logistics that go into sustaining an elite sport career is in many ways beneficial, it can also be disempowering. Athletes can and should be supported to take responsibility for their own sport careers. There is also a long history of athletes with disabilities self-organising and engaging in advocacy. Supporting athletes to take an interest in the operations of their teams, to have meaningful roles on boards, or to contribute to projects related to fundraising or marketing can not only benefit the sport organisation but also create opportunities to develop skills that will assist them when they retire.

Don't Be Afraid to Discuss Disability

The Olympification of Paralympic sport is a trend that will continue. One consequence is that it tends to dismiss disability by portraying Paralympians as the same as Olympians. It fails to acknowledge that people with disabilities still do face barriers and discrimination and that they may need different accommodates to participate equally in society. Para-athletes need to be able to discuss and explore these points of difference with athlete service providers. This could include discussions about their finances after leaving sport (Will they receive any government-related disability assistance? What does this mean for their employment options?). They could have concerns about facing discrimination in the workforce where and the same injury that made them a desirable 'recruit' for sport could have very different implications for them when hunting for a job. Given the rapid transition

44 *Andrea Bundon*

that many athletes make from rehabilitation hospitals to national teams, it is possible that some will never have navigated the 'real world' with a disability. Practitioners need to be able to have open discussions with athletes about what they are facing when they leave sport, and this means not assuming that all athletes are 'the same.' This is also a reason to create and develop teams of practitioners that are also diverse as they can bring different perspectives and experiences to the role.

Note

1. This is consistent with Howe (2004) and Allison (2001), who remark that commercialisation is a key driver of professionalism as sport responds to market demands and those within sport demand to profit from the spectacle they produce.

References

Allison, L. (2001). *Amateurism in sport: An analysis and a defence.* London: Routledge.

Anderson, J. (2003). Turned into taxpayers': Paraplegia, rehabilitation and sport at Stoke Mandeville, 1944–56. *Journal of Contemporary History, 38*(3), 461–475.

Baker, J., Lemez, S., Van Neutegem, A., & Wattie, N. (2017). Talent development in parasport. In J. Baker, S. Cobley, J. Schorer, & N. Wattie (Eds.), *Routledge handbook of talent identification and development in sport* (pp. 432–442). New York: Routledge.

Bundon, A. (2019). Injury, pain and risk in the Paralympic movement. In K. Young (Ed.), *The suffering body in sport: Shifting thresholds of pain, risk and injury* (pp. 71–87). Bingley: Emerald Publishing Limited.

Bundon, A., Ashfield, A., Smith, B., & Goosey-Tolfrey, V. L. (2018). Struggling to stay and struggling to leave: The experiences of elite para-athletes at the end of their sport careers. *Psychology of Sport and Exercise, 37*, 296–305.

Bundon, A., & Hurd Clarke, L. (2015). Unless you go online you're on your own: Blogging as a bridge in para-sport. *Disability and Society, 30*(2), 185–198.

Cashman, R. (2008). The benchmark games. In R. Cashman & S. Darcy (Eds.), *Benchmark games: The Sydney 2000 Paralympics* (pp. 56–73). Sydney: Walla Walla Press.

Cashman, R., & Darcy, S. (2008). Paralympic benchmarks before 2000. In R. Cashman & S. Darcy (Eds.), *Benchmark games: The Sydney 2000 Paralympics* (pp. 35–54). Sydney: Walla Walla Press.

Debois, N., Ledon, A., Argiolas, C., & Rosnet, E. (2012). A lifespan perspective on transitions during a top sports career: A case of an elite female fencer. *Psychology of Sport and Exercise, 13*(5), 660–668.

Dehghansai, N., & Baker, J. (2020). Searching for Paralympians: Characteristics of participants attending "search" events. *Adapted Physical Activity Quarterly, 37*(1), 129–138.

Dowling, M., Edwards, J., & Washington, M. (2014). Understanding the concept of professionalisation in sport management research. *Sport Management Review, 17*(4), 520–529.

Gérard, S. (2020). The best of both worlds? In D. Chatziefstathious, B. García, & B. Séguin (Eds.), *Routledge handbook of the Olympic and Paralympic games* (pp. 84–97). New York: Routledge.

Howe, P. D. (2004). *Sport, professionalism, and pain: Ethnographies of injury and risk.* London: Routledge.

Howe, P. D. (2008). *The cultural politics of the Paralympic movement: Through an anthropological lens.* New York: Routledge.

International Paralympic Committee. (2019). *Strategic plan 2019–2022.* Retrieved from www.paralympic.org/sites/default/files/document/190704145051100_2019_07+IPC+Strategic+Plan_web.pdf

Purdue, D. E. (2013). An (in)convenient truce? Paralympic stakeholders' reflections on the Olympic—Paralympic relationship. *Journal of Sport and Social Issues, 37*(4), 384–402.

Radtke, S., & Doll-Tepper, G. (2014). *A cross-cultural comparison of talent identification and development in Paralympic sports: Perceptions and opinions of athletes, coaches and officials.* Berlin: Freire Universitat [Berlin, Germany: Free University Press].

Shakespeare, T. (2000). The social relations of care. In G. Lewis, S. Gewirtz, & J. Clarke (Eds.), *Rethinking social policy* (pp. 52–65). London: Sage.

Stambulova, N. B., Engström, C., Franck, A., Linnér, L., & Lindahl, K. (2015). Searching for an optimal balance: Dual career experiences of Swedish adolescent athletes. *Psychology of Sport and Exercise, 21*, 4–14.

UK Sport (n.d.). *Historical funding figures.* Retrieved July 11, 2017, from www.uksport.gov.uk/our-work/investing-in-sport/historical-funding-figures

Wylleman, P., & Lavallee, D. (2004). A developmental perspective on transitions faced by athletes. In M. R. Weiss (Ed.), *Developmental sport and exercise psychology: A lifespan perspective* (pp. 503–524). Morgantown, WV: Fitness Information Technology.

4 Considering the Connections Between Doping and Transitions Out of Sport

Desperate Times and Desperate Measures?

Laurie Patterson

The Definition and Prevalence of Doping

Doping refers to engaging in one or more of eleven anti-doping rule violations (ADRVs) outlined in the World Anti-Doping Code ('the Code', World Anti-Doping Agency [WADA], 2020); these include possession, administration and trafficking of prohibited substances or methods, as well as complicity in any of these activities, prohibited association with anyone who has been found to have committed an ADRV, and acts to discourage or retaliate against anyone who reports doping-related information to authorities. Amongst the violations, the most commonly seen is the *presence* of a prohibited substance or its metabolites or markers in an athlete's blood or urine sample, which is established via testing (often referred to as doping control). According to WADA's (2019) most recently published annual testing statistics, there were 1,459 (53%) confirmed analytical ADRVs (i.e. presence) among the samples collected in 2017. By comparison, a total of 345 non-analytical cases were recorded. Demonstrating the widespread nature of doping, the analytical ADRVs came from 89 sports/disciplines and 111 nationalities, and the non-analytical ADRVs were from 317 athletes of 47 nationalities from 41 sports.

Testing statistics likely show only a fraction of the true number of athletes doping. This is due to the limited number of athletes who are tested compared to the total number of athletes participating across all sports, nations and levels of competition, as well as the limited period of time that many substances remain in the body and can be detected by tests and the fact that the science of testing is usually lagging behind the science of pharmacological advances (i.e. the creation of new substances and methods) (de Hon, Kuipers, & van Bottenburg, 2015). Thus, a growing body of research indicates that doping may be more prevalent than indicated by testing statistics. As an example, de Hon et al. (2015) reviewed different methods of estimating prevalence, such as self-report and Randomised Response Technique questionnaires, and concluded that rates of intentional doping among elite adult athletes are between 14% and 39%. Of course, much

Doping and Transitions Out of Sport   47

like testing, some of the alternative methods of measuring prevalence that were included in this review also have limitations. For instance, self-report research is vulnerable to social desirability and/or misinterpretation of questions (de Hon et al., 2015).

Whether utilising prevalence rates from testing statistics, other forms of measurement or even anecdotal accounts, there is convincing evidence that doping happens. And, since doping is against the rules of sport, it should be addressed. What is more, the harmful consequences that an individual may experience due to doping, including legal, financial, social, emotional and self-imposed sanctions, which means that doping *must* be addressed. The experienced consequences of individuals who have engaged in doping behaviours are covered later in this chapter, but, in short, they likely include being banned from sport, loss of contract/sponsorship, condemnation and negative physical and/or mental health effects. Of particular importance to this chapter, doping can act as a catalyst for athlete retirement. Before this is considered in greater depth, let us consider what might lead an athlete to dope in the first place.

Factors Associated With Doping Behaviours

In order to devise effective strategies to address doping, social scientists have conducted research to better understand the risk and protective factors that may influence athlete doping behaviours (for a review, see Backhouse, Whitaker, Patterson, Erickson, & McKenna, 2016). At an *individual* level, influential factors include (lack of) knowledge of anti-doping rules and regulations (e.g. Johnson, Butryn, & Masucci, 2013), a belief that doping is (un)acceptable (e.g. Woolf & Mazanov, 2017) and a perception that doping is (not) necessary to cope with the demands of the sport (Didymus & Backhouse, 2020) or to achieve one's goals (e.g. Teetzel & Weaving, 2014). Notably, the importance placed on achieving sporting goals in relation to other goals outside sport can also play a part (e.g. Lentillon-Kaestner & Carstairs, 2010). Furthermore, individuals who defined success in self-referenced terms, i.e., focusing on their own performance as opposed to outcomes such as winning, are at a lesser risk of doping (Erickson, Backhouse, & Carless, 2017).

Building on this notion, doping is more likely if winning is emphasised by people around the athlete, and if the structure of the sport (e.g. funding) reinforces this emphasis (e.g. Kirby, Moran, & Guerin, 2011). Indeed, important *environmental* influences include the climate or culture within which individuals reside. The country in which an individual competes (e.g. Overbye, 2016), the sport they are involved with (e.g. Chan et al., 2014) and the level of competition they participate at (e.g. Weaving & Teetzel, 2014) can all increase or decrease the likelihood that an athlete might dope. From a social perspective, there is strong evidence that individuals who are close to the athlete play a significant role in increasing

48 *Laurie Patterson*

or decreasing risk of doping (e.g. Chan et al., 2014). This includes fellow athletes, coaches, parents, family members and friends. These people may influence an athlete directly, through explicit instruction or pressure (e.g. Kegelaers, Wylleman, De Brandt, Van Rossem, & Rosier, 2018), as well as indirectly, if the athlete perceives that the significant other(s) would accept or reject doping behaviours (e.g. MacNamara & Collins, 2014).

Significantly, doping behaviours appear to be often dependent upon a complex interaction of individual and environmental factors, in that doping happens if an athlete finds themselves feeling a particular way (e.g. low in confidence) in a particular environment (e.g. high external pressure). Evidence shows that specific situations individuals find themselves in are pivotal. In particular, doping is more likely when an athlete experiences injury (e.g. Didymus & Backhouse, 2020; Whitaker, Backhouse, & Long, 2017) and/or performance dips (e.g. Mazanov & Huybers, 2010). In addition, doping behaviours can be triggered by transitions between different training environments (e.g. Kirby, Moran, & Guerin, 2011) or from one stage of development to another (or the level of competition to the next) (e.g. Lentillon-Kaestner & Carstairs, 2010). Providing the rationale for this chapter, retirement from sport has been highlighted as a critical moment of athlete vulnerability to doping.

Doping to Avoid Retirement From Sport

Previous research has indicated that individuals may be at an increased risk of doping if they are preparing to transition out of sport. Maquirriain and Baglione (2016) associated the risk of doping during later stages of an athlete's career with age, when they examined doping offences (N=47) committed in tennis between 2003 and 2014. They found that the average age of players who had committed offences was 26.40 (±3.48) years, and they commented that most violations are, therefore, after the age at which a tennis player 'peaks' (at approximately 24 years old). Consequently, they concluded that likelihood of doping is related to players being in the "decline phase" of their careers and referred to this as an "end-game effect" (p. 1061). Further support for the connection between age/stage of career and doping is provided by Piffaretti (2011), who reported a similar average age amongst doping-sanctioned athletes (27.6±3.95 years), with three out of eleven interviewees being over 30 years of age. Likewise, Aubel and Ohl (2014) discovered that 45% of cyclists sanctioned between 2005 and 2012 were 30–35 years old and 13% were over 35 years old. Given that cyclists in these age groups made up only 21% and 4% of the total rider population in the top two divisions of cycling in the world (on which their analysis was based), this equates to 24% and 9% over-representation, respectively.

Aubel and Ohl (2014) suggested that elite cyclists' vulnerability to doping might, in part, be explained by their 'precarious' working conditions,

Doping and Transitions Out of Sport 49

where cyclists live with substantial amounts of uncertainty due to the short length of contracts and careers. Supporting their suggestion, they reported the average career length of a cyclist was 4.7 years (3–7 years range for 50% of the rider population). They concluded that cyclists might "need drugs in order to keep their jobs" (p. 1101) and "the hope of extending careers might explain why [older riders] are more readily than younger riders to cross the line" (p. 1098). In a rare study involving "admitted dopers" (N=5), Kirby et al. (2011) also established that doping occurred later in athletes' careers and this was driven by a desire to stay in the sport as long as possible. Several interviewees reported being outperformed and suggested their doping was initiated to "keep up, rather than surpass" (Kirby et al., 2011, p. 212). Athlete vulnerability was often underpinned by, or related to, a series of poor performances and/or coming back from injury or time off. Aligned with Aubel and Ohl's suggestion that doping risk may be related to precarious working conditions, some admitted dopers also suggested that their behaviours were, to some extent, caused by their wages being connected to their performances and wanting to establish a stable financial situation to support their family (Kirby et al., 2011). Yet, this was not the case for everyone; other admitted dopers identified the perceived potential financial damage (i.e. losing one's income in the long term due to not being as employable after serving a ban) as a deterrent to doping (Kirby et al., 2011), and the reality of this is discussed in the next section.

Retirement From Sport Due to Doping

In addition to being a risk factor for doping, as briefly mentioned previously, there is some indication that retirement may also be a consequence of doping. In one of very few studies that explored this explicitly, Maquirriain and Baglione (2016) concluded that a ban from sport may accelerate retirement. They found that 12% of (N=46) players who committed doping offences (N=47) in tennis between 2003 and 2014 did not return to professional tennis. In addition, average time to retirement after a doping sanction was under 3 years (35.7±31.03 months). In terms of understanding why the players retired, the authors presented data to show that players were unable to achieve the same levels of performance as before their suspension. Specifically, only 27.65% of players reached their highest ranking in their career after being sanctioned with an ADRV (Maquirriain & Baglione, 2016). This is interesting, as the average length of sanction was relatively short (11.13±9.20 months), which means that the players (on average) did not spend as much time away from their sport as they might if were sanctioned post-2015, when the 'standard' doping sanction was increased from 2 to 4 years. If this research were to be replicated across more recent sanctions, it would be interesting to see if the percentage of players not returning increases (above 12%). The connection between sanction length and likelihood of continuing/retiring is something that has

50 Laurie Patterson

been suggested previously (Hong, Henning, & Dimeo, 2020), but is yet to be thoroughly investigated. In a study by Maquirriain and Baglione (2016) specifically, aside from sanction length, the players' capacity to attain previous performance levels (and general decision to not return to sport) could be connected to their age, because those receiving sanctions were typically older, and beyond their 'peak' for tennis, as discussed previously.

Whilst age, performance capacity and length of time away from sport are sensible explanations for athletes retiring after being sanctioned for doping, the response athletes receive from the sporting community likely has an important role to play. In fact, it has been proposed that the combination of social, psychological and financial consequences brought about by doping-related bans from sport makes them the component of anti-doping policy that has the greatest impact on athlete well-being (Elbe & Overbye, 2015) in general, not just on decisions to retire. With regard to finance, even before engaging in banned practices, individuals interviewed by Kirby et al. (2011) had acknowledged that if they were not 'accepted' back into the sport, they would not be an appealing prospect to an employer or a sponsor. In fact, admitted dopers discussed their fear of losing income as a deterrent to doping. Ultimately, some of these fears were realised, as well as several of the interviewees experiencing a negative public reaction (i.e. the social and psychological consequences).

These findings are corroborated by Georgiadis and Papazoglou (2014), who interviewed five elite Greek athletes who had tested positive during the previous year. They concluded that doping led to significant career disruption; the athletes described being 'ditched' by sports organisations (e.g. losing income, having to leave athlete accommodation) and media coverage causing their achievements to be "annihilated in the eyes of the people" (p. 66). Combined with the sanction already requiring them to take several years out of sport, these experiences often left athletes with no choice but to retire. One athlete illustrates,

> In the morning, I woke up just to find myself trembling with fear; not so much due to what I would deal with in sports, but with what I would face later in the future. What would I do from that point on? Back in the old days, it was different. I was certain that when I would stop competing there would be some open doors waiting. But after that [the positive doping sample], I only see closed doors everywhere.
> (Athlete A; Georgiadis & Papazoglou, 2014, p. 68)

The athletes recounted an emotional rollercoaster, filled with uncertainty and condemnation. Georgiadis and Papazoglou (2014) likened the psychological consequences of doping experienced, including the loss of athletic identity, to those associated with career termination. Furthermore, the emotions the athletes described were compared to those reported by athletes whose careers have been *involuntarily* terminated due to injury (e.g. shock, anger). However, in addition, the athletes in this study—who each claimed they had not doped intentionally—also had to process feelings of fear and shame that came from the social stigma and thoughts of losing family and friends.

Dimeo and MØller (2018) dedicated an entire chapter of their book, *The Anti-Doping Crisis in Sport. Causes, Consequences, Solutions*, to discussing the social stigma attached to doping. They presented a number of example cases to illustrate, what they termed, the devastating consequences that athletes who have been associated with doping have experienced. These included isolation/ostracism (i.e. being shunned by fans, teammates) and being branded with an association with doping forever (e.g. increased scrutiny, public humiliation and/or criticism by the media). Dimeo and MØller (2018) also presented evidence of serious mental health issues among athletes who have doped, such as suicide/suicide attempts and depression. Of course, they acknowledge that some of the athletes found to have committed doping offences could have been experiencing mental health issues prior to the violation; in fact, they suggest that doping behaviour might itself have been indicative of the need for support. Nonetheless, their insights, which were based on collated media coverage and athlete autobiographies, corroborated interview research conducted with admitted dopers (Kirby et al., 2011) and sanctioned athletes (Georgiadis & Papazoglou, 2014; Piffaretti, 2011). Taken together, existing evidence signals the importance of considering the impact that a sanction can have on an athlete's ability to return to sport, as well as their capacity to continue living, after doping.

Support Available for Individuals Sanctioned for Doping

The risk of an athlete retiring from sport due to a doping sanction could perhaps be minimised if appropriate support were in place. Backhouse (2015) proposed that timely interventions are necessary to ensure that substance (or method) use does not escalate, in the first instance, followed by longer term support with processing the consequences. Athletes interviewed by Georgiadis and Papazoglou (2014) identified the need for counselling to cope with the entire experience, from the point of testing positive to where they were at the time of being interviewed and beyond. Similar calls for counselling were made by Dimeo and MØller (2018), who questioned the anti-doping system for predominantly focusing upon the act of doping rather than the person engaging in doping behaviours. Specifically, they suggested that very little consideration is given to how challenging the situation must be that athletes find themselves in prior to and after doping. They proposed that a more 'person-centred' lens must be adopted, where the 'suffering' of individuals is acknowledged and people are afforded empathy, or at least respect, for the fact that they have lost their job and their income and face real uncertainty about their future employment (Dimeo & MØller, 2018).

52 Laurie Patterson

This sentiment echoed those of Piffaretti (2011), who signalled an urgent need for primary, secondary and tertiary intervention to be introduced. Based on interviews with sanctioned athletes (N=11, all male), he identified three phases that most athletes progress through following notification of their violation. In the 'acute phase' (the first 2–3 weeks), most athletes found it challenging to come to terms with what had happened, reporting distress, anger and denial. This was typically followed by a 'realisation phase', as athletes confronted the situation. Here, it was common for athletes to experience great sadness, disappointment and regret, at the loss of career opportunities and the impact their circumstances were having on others (e.g. family). Despite this, athletes were able to begin to manage their emotions to some degree. In the third stage, which Piffaretti (2011) referred to as 'acceptance', many athletes experienced progressively less emotional upset; most athletes were even able to 're-organise' themselves personally and/or professionally to create a 'new life' (e.g. having a baby, finding a new job/career). This type of growth was one of a number of positives that the majority of the athletes (9/11) were able to identify. Other positives seemed to revolve around gaining perspective, such as being less concerned with what people think, money not being as important as it had been previously, and a higher value being placed on relationships with those close to them. However, it is important to note it could take 18 months for athletes to reach this point, and some athletes had still not achieved this level of 'recovery' from the sanction by the time they were interviewed. Notably, how athletes experienced their sanction and their recovery from it, Piffaretti proposed, seemed to be related to their interpretation of the event, e.g., accepting it as the right consequence for their own actions versus seeing it as unfair and exaggerated because the doping was unintentional.

The athletes interviewed by Piffaretti (2011) highlighted a lack of support from 'official structures'. This is something that Dimeo and MØller (2018) have more recently commented on, positing that little, if any, support appears to be available for individuals associated with doping. Providing evidence of this, Hong and colleagues (2020) investigated the support provided across organisations, using a combination of web searches and a survey. Fifty organisations were contacted, primarily National Olympic Committees (NOCs), and 22 (44%) provided information across five (out of six) continents. Most organisations reported that they did not currently have a support programme in place for athletes associated with doping. Across the support that was provided, Hong et al. (2020) attempted to identify the components of the Holistic Athletic Career (HAC) Model (Wylleman, Reints & Deknop, 2013, cited in Hong et al., 2020); only psychological (i.e. counselling, access to a sport psychologist) and financial support (i.e. funding to pay for judicial processes) were present, and these types of support were mentioned by only two and one organisation, respectively. Outside the components of HAC, some 'informative support' was offered,

Doping and Transitions Out of Sport 53

which comprised anti-doping education being accessible; but limited details of exact content were provided by survey respondents. Overall, the authors concluded that organisations did not provide support for athletes related to coping with being suspended from sport for doping, including the myriad consequences they would likely experience (Hong et al., 2020).

Though there is currently limited support specific to helping athletes to rehabilitate from doping and, in turn, avoid retirement from sport, it was positive to see that some organisations expressed an interest in learning what other organisations provide. Hong et al. (2020) suggested this was a sign that organisations might be willing to learn from others' best practice to develop a programme of their own in the future. In addition, the IOC reported having a scheme in development, as they 'recognise the importance of this matter' (Hong et al., 2020). In this vein, it must not be forgotten that a number of programmes are available to aid career transitions generally, such as the IOC Athlete Career Programme (Athlete365 Career+) and the International Paralympic Committee (IPC) Adecco Career Programme. Beyond this, career support is also provided by a number of sports institutes (e.g. English Institute of Sport's Performance Lifestyle Advisors and 'More2Me' campaign) and players' associations (e.g. Professional Cricketers' Association Personal Development and Welfare Programme).

Implications for Practice

Piffaretti (2011) suggested that sanctioned athletes should be offered 'systemic follow-up' to aid their rehabilitation, comprising psychological-, physical- and occupationally oriented provision. Addressing some of the main consequences discussed earlier in this chapter, psychological support from a certified professional could help athletes process the sanction, including understanding what may have contributed towards their doping behaviour and what will happen in the coming months (e.g. procedures/legal advice, changes to social environment, media coverage) (Piffaretti, 2011). Under this umbrella, Piffarretti (2011) proposed that athletes could be put in touch with others who have experienced a similar situation, who might be able to empathise with the athlete's circumstances. Physical provision related primarily to enabling athletes to continue training, in order to minimise any challenges they would face when returning to competitive sport (e.g. lack of fitness/practice) (Piffaretti, 2011). In addition, helping athletes to maintain some level of normalcy with their training might mitigate some of the negative psychological consequences if it provides structure and purpose (Piffaretti, 2011). To accommodate this type of support, sport science support and coaching staff would be required—but it is important that their involvement is permitted by WADA, otherwise these individuals may be liable to the Prohibited Association violation. Lastly, occupational support would help athletes, who might have limited experience with employment beyond sport, to identify appropriate opportunities and plan

54 *Laurie Patterson*

for their future (Piffaretti, 2011). This type of support might go some way to addressing the financial concerns that sanctioned athletes report experiencing (Piffaretti, 2011).

Of course, prevention is better than cure! Therefore, effort must be invested into supporting athletes who are vulnerable to doping due to upcoming retirement, *before* they take the decision to engage in doping behaviours. Here, adopting the three-pronged approach of psychological, physical and occupational support suggested by Piffaretti (2011) for rehabilitation would likely be preventative, addressing some of the main risk and protective factors. From a physical perspective, it is important that athletes have confidence in their ability to perform and/or achieve their goals (Erickson, McKenna, & Backhouse, 2015; Ntoumanis, Ng, Barkoukis, & Backhouse, 2014). Therefore, athletes can benefit from access to facilities and trained staff (e.g. coaches, sport scientists, medical professionals) that can aid them with their development, including providing athletes with individualised nutritional plans and strength training programmes (Whitaker & Backhouse, 2016).

In addition to providing this type of practical support, staff working with athletes can aid doping prevention efforts by establishing social norms that make it clear that doping is not accepted. For example, research into protective factors for doping has shown that coaches can have a positive influence by instilling participants with a sense of right and wrong (Erickson et al., 2015; Ntoumanis et al., 2014). This is not to say that staff working with athletes need to adopt a controlling or threatening stance. Rather, they should be clear about the values they hold and wish to see in others. Such values can be introduced formally through contracts or codes of conduct and should be regularly reinforced through verbal and non-verbal communications. However, an issue to be overcome in this regard is that many individuals in the athlete support network, such as coaches, do not feel well-prepared to engage in anti-doping efforts (Patterson & Backhouse, 2018; Patterson, Backhouse, & Lara-Bercial, 2019). Therefore, more must be done to support the support network through appropriate provision of learning opportunities.

Whilst on the topic of staff learning opportunities, those working with athletes could be provided with education around recognising moments of vulnerability including career termination explicitly, but also other critical incidents that might be associated with career termination such as injury, (de-)selection, contract/funding renewal, performance dips and difficulty achieving a goal or coping with demands. In order for staff to feel confident taking action once vulnerabilities are recognised, they could be trained in having difficult conversations around performance development and age/ stage of development, with transparency and sensitivity. Understandably, some practitioners may still feel uncomfortable working with athletes in relation to matters that might be emotionally charged or sensitive. Therefore, in an ideal world, professional psychological support for athletes should

Doping and Transitions Out of Sport 55

also be available. Services such as counselling are especially important for those who experience challenges throughout their athletic career. Whilst it is difficult for some sporting contexts to implement this level of support due to restricted resource, there may be avenues that can be explored with charities or athlete foundations/associations.

The suggestion for psychological support aligns well with recent developments in the United Kingdom, where there are plans to introduce new Professional Standards for Personal Development Practitioners,[1] whose role will include supporting athletes throughout transitions, including beyond their sporting career. This type of service, which also encapsulates occupational support, can aid doping prevention efforts as research into protective factors for doping has shown that some protection from engagement in doping behaviours is provided by athletes developing life skills (i.e. resilience, coping, self-control/regulation) and an identity beyond sport (Erickson et al., 2015; Ntoumanis et al., 2014). However, such development should be intentional, rather than assumed to happen naturally as a consequence of other activities. Furthermore, activities that aid athletes in developing their life skills and exploring the employment opportunities that may be available to them beyond their sporting careers will require organisational support, through structures and funding systems, within national federations and other sporting organisations.

Note

1. www.eis2win.co.uk/article/new-professional-standards-for-personal-develop ment-practitioners/

References

Aubel, O., & Ohl, F. (2014). An alternative approach to the prevention of doping in cycling. *International Journal of Drug Policy, 25*(6), 1094–1102. doi:10.1016/j. drugpo.2014.08.010

Backhouse, S. H. (2015). Anti-doping education for athletes. In V. Møller, I. Waddington, & J. Hoberman (Eds.), *Routledge handbook of drugs and sport* (pp. 322–336). Routledge. doi:10.4324/9780203795347.ch19

Backhouse, S. H., Whitaker, L., Patterson, L., Erickson, K., & McKenna, J. (2016). *Social psychology of doping in sport: A mixed-studies narrative synthesis.* Montreal, Canada: World Anti-Doping Agency. Retrieved from www.wada-ama.org/sites/default/files/resources/files/literature_review_update_-_final_2016.pdf

Chan, D. K., Hardcastle, S. J., Lentillon-Kaestner, V., Donovan, R. J., Dimmock, J. A., & Hagger, M. S. (2014). Athletes' beliefs about and attitudes towards taking banned performance-enhancing substances: A qualitative study. *Sport, Exercise, and Performance Psychology, 3*(4), 241. doi:10.1037/spy0000019

de Hon, O., Kuipers, H., & van Bottenburg, M. (2015). Prevalence of doping use in elite sports: A review of numbers and methods. *Sports Medicine, 45*(1), 57–69. doi:10.1007/s40279-014-0247-x

56 *Laurie Patterson*

Didymus, F. F., & Backhouse, S. H. (2020). Coping by doping? A qualitative inquiry into permitted and prohibited substance use in competitive rugby. *Psychology of Sport and Exercise*. Advance online publication. doi:10.1016/j.psychsport.2020.101680

Dimeo, P., & MØller, V. (2018). *The anti-doping crisis in sport. Causes, consequences, solutions.* Abingdon, Oxon: Routledge.

Elbe, A., & Overbye, M. (2015). Implications of anti-doping regulations for athlete well-being. In V. Møller, I. Waddington, & J. Hoberman (Eds.), *Routledge handbook of drugs and sport* (pp. 322–336). Routledge. doi:10.4324/9780203795347.ch26

Erickson, K., Backhouse, S., & Carless, D. (2017). Doping in sport: Do parents matter? *Sport, Exercise and Performance Psychology, 6*(2). doi:10.1037/spy0000081

Erickson, K., McKenna, J., & Backhouse, S. (2015). A qualitative analysis of the factors that protect athletes against doping in sport. *Psychology of Sport and Exercise, 16*(2), 149–155. doi:10.1016/j.psychsport.2014.03.007

Georgiadis, E., & Papazoglou, I. (2014). The experience of competition ban following a positive doping sample of elite athletes. *Journal of Clinical Sport Psychology, 8*(1), 57–74. doi:10.1123/jcsp.2014-0012

Hong, H. J., Henning, A., & Dimeo, P. (2020). Life after doping—A cross-country analysis of organisational support for sanctioned athletes. *Performance Enhancement & Health*, 100161. doi:10.1016/j.peh.2020.100161

Johnson, J., Butryn, T., & Masucci, M. A. (2013). A focus group analysis of the US and Canadian female triathletes' knowledge of doping. *Sport in Society, 16*, 654–671. doi:10.1080/17430437.2012.753522

Kegelaers, J., Wylleman, P., De Brandt, K., Van Rossem, N., & Rosier, N. (2018). Incentives and deterrents for drug-taking behaviour in elite sports: A holistic and developmental approach. *European Sport Management Quarterly, 18*(1), 112–132. doi:10.1080/16184742.2017.1384505

Kirby, K., Moran, A., & Guerin, S. (2011). A qualitative analysis of the experiences of elite athletes who have admitted to doping for performance enhancement. *International Journal of Sport Policy and Politics, 3*, 205–224. doi:10.1080/19406940.201 1.577081

Lentillon-Kaestner, V., & Carstairs, C. (2010). Doping use among young elite cyclists: A qualitative psychosociological approach. *Scandinavian Journal of Medicine and Science in Sports, 20*, 336–345. doi:10.1111/j.1600-0838.2009.00885.x

MacNamara, Á., & Collins, D. (2014). Why athletes say no to doping: A qualitative exploration of the reasons underpinning athletes' decision not to dope. *Performance Enhancement and Health, 3*, 145–152. doi:10.1016/j.peh.2015.09.001

Maquirriain, J., & Baglione, R. (2016). Doping offences in male professional tennis: How does sanction affect players' career? *SpringerPlus, 5*(1), 1059–1062. doi:10.1186/s40064-016-2765-5.

Mazanov, J., & Huybers, T. (2010). An empirical model of athlete decisions to use performance-enhancing drugs: Qualitative evidence. *Qualitative Research in Sport and Exercise, 2*(3), 385–402.

Ntoumanis, N., Ng, J. Y., Barkoukis, V., & Backhouse, S. (2014). Personal and psychosocial predictors of doping use in physical activity settings: A meta-analysis. *Sports Medicine, 44*(11), 1603–1624. doi:10.1007/s40279-014-0240-4

Overbye, M. (2016). Doping control in sport: An investigation of how elite athletes perceive and trust the functioning of the doping testing system in their sport. *Sport Management Review, 19*, 6–22. doi:10.1016/j.smr.2015.10.002

Patterson, L. B., & Backhouse, S. H. (2018). "An important cog in the wheel", but not the driver: Coaches' perceptions of their role in doping prevention. *Psychology of Sport and Exercise, 37*, 117–127. doi:10.1016/j.psychsport.2018.05.004

Patterson, L. B., Backhouse, S. H., & Lara-Bercial, S. (2019). Examining coaches' experiences and opinions of anti-doping education. *International Sport Coaching Journal, 6*(2), 145–159. doi:10.1123/iscj.2018-0008

Piffaretti, M. (2011). *Psychological determinants of doping behaviour through the testimony of sanctioned athletes.* World Anti-Doping Agency. Retrieved from www.wada-ama.org/sites/default/files/resources/files/learning_about_determinants_m.piffaretti_final_report_6.2011def.pdf

Teetzel, S., & Weaving, C. (2014). From silence to surveillance: Examining the aftermath of a Canadian university doping scandal. *Surveillance and Society, 11*, 481–493. doi:10.24908/ss.v11i4.4758

Weaving, C., & Teetzel, S. (2014). Getting jacked and burning fat. *Journal of Intercollegiate Sport, 7*, 198–217. doi:10.1123/jis.2014-0094

Whitaker, L., & Backhouse, S. H. (2017). Doping in sport: An analysis of sanctioned UK rugby union players between 2009 and 2015. *Journal of Sports Sciences, 35*(16), 1607–1613. doi:10.1080/02640414.2016.1226509

Whitaker, L., Backhouse, S. H., & Long, J. (2017). Doping vulnerabilities, rationalisations and contestations: The lived experience of national level athletes. *Performance Enhancement & Health, 5*(4), 134–141. doi:10.1016/j.peh.2017.06.001

Woolf, J., & Mazanov, J. (2017). How athletes conceptualise doping, winning, and consequences: Insights from using the cognitive interviewing technique with the Goldman dilemma. *Qualitative Research in Sport, Exercise and Health, 9*, 303–320. doi:10.1080/2159676X.2016.1272480

World Anti-Doping Agency. (2019). *2017 Anti-doping rule violations (ADRVs) report.* Montreal, Canada: World Anti-Doping Agency. Retrieved from www.wada-ama.org/sites/default/files/resources/files/2017_adrv_report.pdf

World Anti-Doping Agency. (2020). *World Anti-Doping Code.* Montreal, Canada: World Anti-Doping Agency. Retrieved from www.wada-ama.org/sites/default/files/resources/files/2021_wada_code.pdf

5 Exploring Transitions in UK Professional Football

Alan Tonge

Introduction

This chapter presents a series of contextual professional football 'player voice' case studies. The challenging impact of retirement is examined as well as some of the transitional challenges that players face within their journey through the professional game. The aim is to present and discuss a range of issues which players typically have to confront and how these can be underpinned by relevant sport psychology theory. One of the difficulties when presenting work around psychology and professional football is the low amount of insight and academic research undertaken within this traditionally hard-to-access environment. Early work conducted by Parker (1995) investigated youth trainee experiences and following this there have been studies on sport psychology and coaches (Pain & Harwood, 2007), deselection and identity of youth players (Brown & Potrac, 2009) and professional football organisations (Relvas, Littlewood, Nesti, Gilbourne, & Richardson, 2010). Although interesting and informative, the main critique with some of these studies is that the demands and pressures within the professional game and the culture associated with youth and youth development are very different indeed (Richardson, Relvas, & Littlewood, 2013).

To place a fresh and exciting lens on the topic area of transitions, this chapter presents a series of case studies, which employ a professional player's voice. This is currently an underrepresented method of presenting data within transitions-based research. Calvin (2017) stated that only a small amount of players coming through the current system will ever reach and accrue first-team appearances, so this insight is from a unique and original angle. Playing the game to a high level personally and interviewing contemporary professional players about their experiences via my own research has allowed me to consider and examine current psychological topics such as transitions and how these are experienced and can impact a player within professional football. This has led me to consider and suggest which psychological support would be most beneficial within the environment and culture of professional football. The information provided in this chapter shines a light on the topic of understanding transitional related

Exploring Transitions in UK Professional Football   59

challenges as players' journey through the professional game, rather than within the developmental and supportive culture found at an academy level (Richardson et al., 2013).

The five semi-fictional case studies that ensue highlight experiences of transitions and how they potentially impact professional football players and their mental health. The case studies are put together employing real experiences within professional football and through communications with other professional football players. The case studies will present differing contextual scenarios with a professional football player (P) and a sport psychologist (SP). To satisfy confidentiality, all of the players have been kept anonymous.

Practical Experiences of Transitions—Case Study 1

The player had been at the club since a teenager and had transitioned through the various stages to become involved with the first team on a regular basis. Tragically, he had sadly suffered a really bad injury. After two operations, the consultant informed him he faced a huge battle to get back to full fitness. This was a massive shock as he was only in his early 20s. The player was also having difficulties of the field due to the strain of it all. After a long rehabilitation, and attempting to move forward, the consultant told him the heartbreaking news that his career was over. The player decided to speak to a sport psychologist a while later. He had a trusting relationship with the psychologist as he had worked with them for a period of time over his career. This was some of the dialogue taken from the meeting.

PLAYER: 'how could football do this to me? I've been in a nightmare since this injury. I've been totally reckless, a loose cannon, I have been done for drink driving, I got a year and a half ban, the same week I got a restraining order from my ex against her, police coming round. . . . [B]oth of them happened in a week and you're thinking what on earth is going on to me. This isn't me.

SP: 'I am very sorry to hear this. It sounds like it has been a horrific time over this recent period for you. When you say, 'this isn't me', what is you?'

PLAYER: 'I have always been fun, I liked a laugh and a joke, but I started drinking a lot and then started to get nasty with the drink and I know everyone's different with it but I just got really, really selfish and I didn't care about anything'

SP: 'have you had support, or spoken about this to your close family?'

PLAYER: 'my Mum and Dad have been up here and they have been worried like hell about me, even they couldn't get through to me and that makes you shiver and you think that was actually my behavior. I suppose everyone in their life has their moments, and I have been depressed

60   Alan Tonge

and I have tried tablets to help the depression and I came off them, because they made me worse.

SP: 'have you had any other means of support to help you through this difficult time?'

PLAYER: 'The kids. The kids. I thought you know what and this hit me hard, what role model am I to my kids here? I took the relationship breakdown really bad as I'm not a person who likes to be on their own. I would say c'mon what are you doing, you're better than this, wake yourself up, what will the kids think of this you being a waste of time, that's how it was. However, I've now got a job with the club in their community projects and I'm coaching youngsters and I am a patron for lads who come out of the army and I'm slowly getting through it and can see light at the end of the tunnel'

It has been proposed within academic research that athletes can have differing experiences when having to transition out of professional sport. Some may see the move as a positive experience and some may have an incredibly difficult experience (Stambulova, 2000). Every experience has to be taken on context. The player in this particular case study has been at the club since they were young and has dedicated themselves to becoming the best they can be. This journey will have formed a key part to their identity (Nesti, 2010). It is clear that through the circumstances of a devastating injury tragically curtailing a career, the player lost a sense of meaning and purpose. From the dialogue, the player has become a shadow of their former selves and parts of their life spiralled into turmoil. The player mentioned they had been treated for depression and had been suffering for a number of months. The player struggled to cope after the transition out of professional football had been made.

Getting this level of dialogue, openness and information from an elite-level football player requires trust, and a complete understanding that anything said is fully confidential and will not go anywhere else (Nesti, 2004). This is a crucial area of sport psychology practice, and it can be extremely difficult to achieve this in the modern world where players are distrustful of outsiders and may be unsure where the dialogue will go or end up.

The transition of life after sport is probably the toughest thing that an athlete has to face up to and deal with. Quick fixes and temporary solutions serve no purpose whatsoever within this context (Corlett, 1996a). If the injury happens as a young player, or in the middle of a career, there could be potential difficult issues with lack of planning or financial implications. According to the Professional Footballers' Association, there could be as much as a loss of 70% of income when coming out of the game and many football players go bankrupt within 5 years of finishing playing (PFA, 2019).

When elite-level football players have had the heartbreaking news of having to face retirement through injury, some players can have huge problems of filling the void. The adulation and joy of playing has been lost, and this

Exploring Transitions in UK Professional Football   61

challenges their sense of meaning and purpose. As well as alcohol abuse, there have been reported issues with gambling and even drugs use. These are clear indications that all is not well and that the player has completely lost meaning, or an important part of their identity has been obliterated. Courageously, the player in the case study admitted to the sport psychologist he had issues with depression. The player had been under intense pressure, and an important source of his identity was being directly threatened. Freud theorised that depression is aggression turned inwards, and it seems that this individual's frustrated feelings of loss, co-existing with anger and confusion, may have turned to short-term fixes such as drinking, gambling and drugs. If an identity lacks or has only weak core values, that is does not possess a deep and clear sense of meaning based on the truth, then when temporary things of the world were taken from him or end (his football career) then he ended. To anaesthetise the pain of this existential oblivion, he abused alcohol to lose himself in a temporary buzz and stimulation. Sadly, when the temporary buzz and stimulation wears off, the player can face meaninglessness again and even hate themselves for cowardice. This led to him becoming clinically depressed. At the end of the dialogue, the player was seeing light at the end of the tunnel and was channelling their efforts into a new opportunity. This is consistent with Frankl (1984), who suggested that when we are no longer able to change a situation, we are challenged to change ourselves. A few months on when he had a chance to deeply re-examine his identity and what he wanted to become, he managed to find meaning again within community projects, coaching youngsters and broader things away from being a professional football player (Corlett, 1996a). This was an extremely positive outcome from a destructive situation. To attempt to move his life on and accept a new identity for himself took courage (Corlett, 1996b). This involved movement from a secure place (being a professional football player) to something yet to unfold (doing something new). Even a professional football player who has accrued a number of first-team appearances can quickly lose their way and need to consider future steps and options. Coaches can be very supportive in this process, however; meeting confidentially with a sport psychologist who understands broader contexts (and recognises that the player is a person too!) can help the player examine their identity, who they are and what they stand for. Through dialogue and careful consideration, the player can find solutions and potential ways forward to overcome the difficult moments they are currently facing.

Practical Experiences of Transitions—Case Study 2

The player had been at an elite-level club for a number of seasons and had been making good progress through the youth teams and the reserves. Towards the end of the season, he had been on the bench a few times and then made his debut, before playing in the last few games of the season. As

62   Alan Tonge

the new season commenced, a few of the first-team squad who had been injured returned to fitness and competition was starting to become fierce. The player had hardly been involved within the pre-season fixtures, and this was a concern to him. The manager called the player in to his office and said it would be in his best interests to go out on loan and in his words 'get some proper game time.' The player dropped down a couple of levels from the Premier League to League One. Halfway through this move, the sport psychologist managed to meet with the player when he was back up in the area.

SP: 'how are you getting on? How is your loan move going?'

PLAYER: 'although the results have been a bit mixed, I'm managing to get plenty of game time in, so this is positive and the club are really looking after me, but there are a few things that are really concerning me at the moment'

SP: 'ok, what are those?'

PLAYER: 'firstly, I feel some of that the other players don't respect the manager as much as they should do and secondly I honestly believe that some players are not giving him 100%'

SP: 'why do you feel like this?'

PLAYER: 'well, in the changing room, a few players only seem to be bothered about what horses are running in the afternoons and I have noticed that one player in particular keeps turning up to training worse for wear. To be honest, it has disgusted me because there is no way this would happen where I have come from'

SP: 'I'm sorry to hear this. What are your options and what can you do?'

PLAYER: 'I will play my way through it and keep battling away for the club because that is all I know. Because I have arrived from a big club, I have felt that the other players have looked to me to do something or sort things out. I am only fairly young myself so it's been a steep learning curve for me. On occasions I have sensed that there's a resentment from some of the players as well. I have definitely felt that, so all in all, it hasn't been an amazing loan spell so far, but my resilience is a big part of who I am, and when you've had a tough youth coach and a tough manager tucking into you as I've come through the system, you build that up and get through it'

The transition that the player faced of going out on loan from a big club to a smaller club involved anxiety (Nesti, 2010). There were issues cropping up that they were not used to and this was causing some angst. This provided an opportunity to develop courage and attempt to think about what they wanted in order to move forward (Corlett, 1996b). This is a difficult thing to do as ultimately, through choice, the player will not know what the outcome will be and whether the choice that they make will be a productive or an unproductive move. Within the meeting, the

Exploring Transitions in UK Professional Football   63

sport psychologist guided the player to consider options and freedom to choose as these will always be available (Frankl, 1984). The choices that the player faced were that he could have ended his loan spell and move back to his club, he could have gone and spoke to the manager about issues in the dressing room, or he even could have ignored what was going on and let fate take its course. By speaking to the sport psychologist and confronting the issues that were bothering him, the player had the opportunity to grow as both a person and a player. If the player had decided to ignore the situation, and passed the decision over to fate and what will be, it may have caused a stunted person centre (Buber, 1999). A stunted person centre refers to the development and growth of a person and his means that the player would be less likely to confront difficult situations in the future by deciding not to choose or even ignoring the issue in the hope that it would go away. Ignoring issues such as this within day-to-day existence can cause problems in relation to mental health and well-being.

Practical Experiences of Transitions—Case Study 3

The player had been bought into the club for a reasonable fee and had gone straight into the first team. For the first few months, everything had been going really well and the team had been achieving plenty of good results. However, a couple of key players had got injured and had to serve suspensions and now the team had found themselves in the midst of a bad spell. Results had turned and were going poorly. The player had become aware of severe criticism from fans, social media was rife with vitriol, and even the manager had directed negative comments directly to the player in question. He came to see the sport psychologist as this had started to affect him.

PLAYER: 'I am finding the going a bit tough all of a sudden. A number of people including the Gaffer have been having a right go and it seems to be directed at just me for some reason. This is starting to rankle me and hammer my confidence'

SP: 'What do you feel about this and what is your view?'

PLAYER: 'well I feel I am a solid pro, I have been for a number of years, I always give my best and am totally dedicated to helping the team get some good results again. I know what is required of me and what I need to do. I know my job.'

SP: 'what are those things that you need to do?'

PLAYER: 'well to keep believing in myself, to keep working hard in training, to keep standing up and being counted and to help other younger players through this tough time. I have been in the game for many years and have seen these issues time and time again. Professional football can be fickle and it is crucial to stay grounded and humble in the good

64   *Alan Tonge*

times and also crucial to stay grounded and humble through the bad times too.'

SP: 'and how do you feel about people pointing fingers at you including the Gaffer'

PLAYER: 'it's been tough that. The fans were great a few weeks ago, and now I'm becoming aware of some heavy criticism especially on social media and the Gaffer had a right go at me in the dressing room over my performance on Saturday'

SP: 'how did this make you fee and what can you do about that?'

PLAYER: 'I was a bit p****d off to be honest. I know I'm a good pro, I've been through many battles before and I get my rest in, behave well away from the training and playing environment and look after myself off the field. I've seen others hitting the booze after bad performances, shrinking, or hiding when they get serious verbal attacks off the Manager, or even worse they start acting as though it hasn't bothered them. It just fires me up and I want to get out there and show him what I can do and help the team find wins again. I'm a good professional on and off the field. You simply can't exist as two different people in that world. It will find you out.

This case study brings to light how an issue in elite professional football such as criticism from the media, fans, other players, coaches or manager can bring a player to examine deeply who they truly are (i.e. their identity). The dialogue between the sport psychologist and player allowed an encounter to take place where the player could look hard at themselves and the issue they are facing and attempt to bring some clarity to it. The conversation 'with a purpose' sought to remind the player that they were not only an elite-level professional football player but that they had another important part to their identity outside their job. The player patiently thought about what he needed to do and how he needed to act and behave in order to gain the maximum chance of success from his role in helping the team get some positive results again. This was based around the differing identities that the player had, which made up his whole identity. Without this re-visit to where he had come from, who he was and what he was striving towards, he admitted that it would be very difficult to find his performance level again and continue surviving in the ever-changing, ruthless and brutal culture of elite-level professional football. To go and see a sport psychologist and get his level of dialogue can be hard to achieve in a football club, especially when you are consistently around other players and the Manager. The player could potentially open themselves up to banter, possibly appear weak in front of the other players, coaches or the manager or show that the criticism had affected them in any way. Being mentally resilient is a huge part of the journey to, into and away from elite-level professional football. Quite simply, a mental skills training approach for this issue would not be enough as it has been reported by Nesti (2010) that player mental skills are usually fairly good when they reach professional level (imagery, self-talk, concentration, goal setting etc.). In this context, the player needed someone who they could trust, open up to; someone who would listen; someone who could understand topics such as identity, anxiety and transitions; and someone who had played the game to some sort of level and had a feel for the sport. Even though the majority of coaches are a great help and can be very supportive, this dialogue is better served to a sport psychologist in order to achieve the maximum understanding, outcome and the best ways forward.

Practical Experiences of Transitions—Case Study 4

The player had been at the club since they were very young and had transitioned through the different developmental stages to finally achieving their dream and playing in the first team. The player had gained caps at youth international level, and the start of lengthy career in the game was looking promising. In the middle of the season, the player had picked up a small injury, which had kept them out for a few weeks. The player though that they would come straight back into the team, but this was not happening due to other players performing well and results being strong. The player decided to come and see the sport psychologist.

SP: 'how are you, are you fully recovered after your injury?'

PLAYER: 'I feel great to be honest, my fitness is good but the manager is simply not picking me in the starting eleven and it is starting to bother me. I know I am good enough to be starting, but this is the 3rd week I have been put on the bench now and I am starting to get frustrated'

SP: 'that must be difficult for you at the moment. How does that make you feel?'

PLAYER: 'I was playing really well before my injury and the results were going well, and I honestly thought I'd come back into the first team. It's a bit concerning to be honest. I thought I was rated higher than this.'

SP: 'so what are your options. What are you going to do?'

PLAYER: 'I may have to go and see the Gaffer to ask why I am not getting a start. If this keeps happening, I might have to look at other options. I want to play, I feel I am good enough to play and I'm not spending time sat on the bench, or hardly playing. It's really disappointing this because I was doing well prior to the injury.

SP: 'How has this made you feel?'

PLAYER: 'It's starting to affect my confidence. I've started start questioning my ability and my worth in this team. It's really hard this because I want the team to do well, but if other players are doing well and contributing to getting good results, the manager won't change his line ups and I won't get a look in'

66 *Alan Tonge*

SP: 'have you had moments like this before in your career and how have you reacted to them?'

PLAYER: 'I got sent off in a youth match a few seasons back and had to serve a 3 match ban so I've had experience of not being involved. I have also been sub on certain occasions especially when I was coming through and trying to break into the reserve side as a youth player, but I have taken feedback on board from the coaches, reflected, dug in and worked hard and managed to get back into the side. I know my attitude is strong. I just want to be the best I can be but things move fast in football and I simply want to play. My attitude has been a huge part of me getting into the first team and is a substantial part of who I am as a person, to keep going, fighting and never give up.'

Within the dynamic, fast-paced, ever-changing world of contemporary professional football, players may be faced with this situation as they progress in the game and it can potentially impact on their mental health if not managed correctly. If communication lines are not strong within the culture, the player can become confused, frustrated, angry and de-motivated. At professional level, especially it is really important to stay visible and be involved with the first-team squad. If not, others, such as fans and the media, may start to question attitude, or whether the player is doing enough to get back into the frame for selection. For the player, this can be an anxiety-ridden and uncomfortable experience, and the only option can be to demonstrate calmness, patience and see what unfolds. In the dialogue, the sport psychologist nudged and coaxed the player to reflect on whether this issue had been experienced before in their career and how it had been previously dealt with. However, this was when the player was in the academy and the youth team. The culture and environment was very different (Richardson et al., 2013). Now he had transitioned out of that environment and had gained recognition as a first-team player and even represented the under 21's international side it was a different scenario. The player openly admitted in the worst-case scenario he would have to sit down with the manager to discuss where he stood and even consider the option of moving somewhere else. This would be a particularly hard choice as he had been at the club a long time and had experienced a tough road to getting to the top. By considering and weighing up the differing options and deciding to speak with the manager and then potentially play for his life to get back in the team, the player has demonstrated courage and their ability to cope with a challenging situation. This was a constructive step forward.

Practical Experiences of Transitions—Case Study 5

The player had been rewarded with a 2-year deal at his club, had broken into the first team and had started to gain more and more appearances. The results were mixed, however, and the team had settled in the middle of

Exploring Transitions in UK Professional Football 67

the table. About 6 months into the second year of his contract, the player had found himself out of the team due to loss of form and being out of favour. However, due to injuries, the player got a chance in a cup match away from home. In the run up to this match, the player had picked up a troubling back injury in training, and, by the morning of the game, this had developed into quite a sore injury. The game was very important to the player in an attempt to get visible again, as his contract was coming up for renewal. As opposed to go and telling the physio, the player decided to speak to the sport psychologist about this transition back into the first-team environment.

SP: 'are you ok?'
PLAYER: 'I can't believe it, I've been out of the side for ages, I get a recall and I've picked up a bloody back injury'
SP: 'so what does this mean for you?'
PLAYER: 'well I could go and see the physio and tell him to go and tell the manager that I'm not quite right, but I've had an issue like this before in my career. I see myself as resilient, courageous and this is a moment that's presented itself to grit my teeth and dig in. Sometimes, you have to put needs first. It's hugely important that I get back into the 1st team and put a decent performance in as my contract is up and I need to get a decent appearance in'
SP: 'are you sure this is the right course of action for you?'
PLAYER: 'it sounds mad and it probably is, but if I can get some deep heat rubbed on it and warm up properly, I'll be ok. I can move ok, it's just that it gets sore when I move in a certain way. It's more a niggle than anything and if I tell the physio and I don't play, I'm not sure what the manager will say, and I may not even get a chance again. This could be disastrous for a new contract as, quite simply I may not get one.'
SP: 'I know this is a very difficult scenario for you, but ultimately it's your choice'
PLAYER: 'thanks for listening, I'll be ok, I just needed to get this off my chest and tell someone as its been bothering me'

The task in this piece of dialogue was for a sport psychologist to assist the only being on the planet that holds a measure of free will to make a choice. The transitional opportunity of getting back into the first team was clearly causing the player angst due to a sore injury. The main objective was for the sport psychologist to ask some challenging questions to help the player understand themselves in more depth and to closely look at their identity and whether the decision they were set to make was the right one. Mental skills training such as visualisation, positive self-talk or goal setting would not have served any purpose in this. This was really about getting the player to think about what they were aspiring to and whether they had faced similar issues in their career in the past and what they had done about them.

68   *Alan Tonge*

The player's reaction was commendable as they were prepared to analyse and demonstrate character, as this was an important component of the core of their personal identity as well as their athletic identity and is a huge factor in elite-level sport. In relation to their mental health however, the concern and question taken away from this particular meeting was an issue that the player was clearly not right, but was fearful of reporting himself as not right. This potentially suggests that the culture of the club at the time was not sympathetic to issues such as this and was seen by the player as harsh, ruthless and closed. The importance of being visible and playing in the first team and striving to acquire a new contract was over-riding the concerning issue that the player was not 100% right. This may need further investigation and enquiry around the culture and the ethical constructs of operating in elite-level professional football and whether players can be fully open about how they are feeling without being judged as weak or 'not up for it.'

Summary and Conclusions

The transitional issues presented within this chapter align with the reflective musings of Nesti (2010), who detailed his applied experiences when having 1–1 meetings with first-team players operating at Premier League level. Many of the psychological challenges reported by players in professional football cannot be addressed by the approaches and applications of mental skills training. Put simply, first-team–level football is not an extension of academy-level football. Although not refuting its worth, mental skills training tends to offer a narrow, quick-fix approach and not a long-term one (Corlett, 1996a). More often than not, hard-hitting dialogue, deeper care and patience for the player in front of you would be a better option. Getting the player to open up and feedback where and how they see themselves at that particular moment in time would be a much more productive option (Nesti, 2004). Mental skills training still tends to hold popularity in many football-based educational packages and university courses within the United Kingdom. This chapter has highlighted some of the transitional-based issues that players face when operating at first-team level and added to the ongoing debate of whether mental skills training is fit for purpose at this level. This chapter is designed to offer sport psychology educators and course writers with the evidence to consider a different angle when supporting professional players as they navigate their way through the game, specifically around the topics of transitions, identity and mental health challenges. The five contextual issues gave the players an opportunity to consider who they were at that particular moment and deeply examine the options they faced and with the help of a sport psychologist. These included common issues in professional football such as dealing with retirement (Case Study 1), the challenges of going out on loan (Case Study 2), facing the pressures at a new club when results are not

Exploring Transitions in UK Professional Football 69

working out (Case Study 3), the difficulties of deselection (Case Study 4) and playing through an injury to try and win a new contract (Case Study 5). These types of moments within a professional football players career have the potential to affect performance and enjoyment, and by recognising these, a much-needed approach of existential psychology (beyond the traditional, dominant cognitive-behavioural paradigm of mental skills training) is suggested for contemporary sport psychology practitioners to utilise and apply (Nesti, 2010).

Implications for Practice

Professional football players will face a wide range of psychological challenges on their journey and differing transitions through the sport.

1) These challenges can often provide a threat to a player's identity and create copious amounts of anxiety.
2) To deal with the challenges that crop up, a broader psychological approach may be needed.
3) Many professional football players will already possess high-quality mental skills and be competent with certain approaches that have been taught within the academy (i.e. imagery, concentration, goal setting). Something else would be useful.
4) An existential sport psychology approach can help fill this gap. This approach can help the player consider who they are at a particular moment in time and consider a range of choices, both narrow and broad, in order to help progress and move forward.

References

Brown, G., & Potrac, P. (2009). 'You've not made the grade, son': Deselection and identity disruption in elite level youth football. *Soccer and Society, 10*(2), 143–159.

Buber, M. (1999). *Martin Buber on psychology and psychotherapy: Essays, letters, and dialogue* (J. B. Agassi, Ed.). Syracuse, NY: Syracuse University Press.

Calvin, M. (2017). *No hunger in paradise: The players. The journey. The dream.* London: Random House.

Corlett, J. (1996a). Sophistry, Socrates, and sport psychology. *The Sport Psychologist, 10*, 84–94.

Corlett, J. (1996b). Virtue lost, courage in sport. *Journal of the Philosophy of Sport, 23*, 45–57.

Franck, A., Stambulova, N. B., & Ivarsson, A. (2018). Swedish athletes' adjustment patterns in the junior-to-senior transition. *International Journal of Sport and Exercise Psychology, 16*(4), 398–414.

Frankl, V. (1984). *Man's search for meaning: An introduction to Logotherapy.* New York: Simon & Schuster.

Nesti, M. (2004). *Existential psychology and sport: Theory and application.* London: Routledge.

Nesti, M. (2010). *Psychology in football: Working with elite and professional players.* London: Routledge.

Pain, M., & Harwood, C. (2007). The performance environment of the England youth soccer teams. *Journal of Sports Sciences, 25,* 1307–1324.

Parker, A. (1995). Great expectations: Grimness or glamour? The football apprentice in the 1990s. *The Sports Historian, 15,* 107–126.

The PFA. (2019). Retrieved from www.thepfa.com/wellbeing/mental-health-and-football/wellbeing-introduction

Relvas, H., Littlewood, M., Nesti, M., Gilbourne, D., & Richardson, D. (2010). Organisational structures and working practices in elite European professional football clubs. *European Sport Management Quarterly, 4,* 195–214.

Richardson, D., Relvas, H., & Littlewood, M. (2013). Social and cultural influences on player development. In M. A. Williams (Ed.), *Science and soccer.* London: Routledge.

Stambulova, N. B. (2000). Athlete's crises: A developmental perspective. *International Journal of Sport Psychology, 31,* 584–601.

6 Athlete Identity and Career Transition

Implications for Retirement Outcomes

Suzanne M. Cosh

It is well established that retirement from sport can be distressing and lead to the onset or exacerbation of psychological disorders (Park, Lavallee, & Tod, 2013; Wylleman, Alfermann, & Lavallee, 2004). Whilst a range of factors influence transition outcomes, athlete identity has widely been reported to play a seminal role (Park et al., 2013). Athlete identity became an area of focus in sport psychology throughout the 1990s and is considered to be a theoretically and practically important construct for understanding athletes' experiences. Athlete identity has been linked with a variety of outcomes, including adjustment to transition (Brewer, Van Raatle, & Linder, 1993).

In early athlete identity work, identity was conceptualised within a role theory framework, typically utilising survey methods. More recently, the field has seen growth in diverse methods and epistemological approaches to examining athlete identity; in particular, there has been growth in qualitative and interpretive approaches (Ronkainen, Kavoura, & Ryba, 2016a). These evolutions in identity research have expanded understanding of athlete identity in relation to career transition experiences. This chapter reviews work from across theoretical approaches and highlights key findings regarding athlete identity and retirement as well as providing implications for practice and directions for future research.

Post-Positivism and Role Theory

The construct of athlete identity was initially conceptualised by Brewer and colleagues (Brewer, 1993; Brewer et al., 1993). Athlete identity was understood as an individual's level of identification with the athlete role, and the *Athlete Identity Measurement Scale* (AIMS) was developed for the systematic study of identity (Brewer et al., 1993). The AIMS has formed the basis of much athlete identity and career transition research, with survey methods (including other developed identity surveys) initially the most common approach to exploring identity and retirement.

The extant literature has shown that athlete identity influences adjustment to retirement (e.g. Grove, Lavallee, & Gordon, 1997; Lotysz & Short,

72 *Suzanne M. Cosh*

2004). According to a recent review, high athletic identity has consistently been associated with poorer transition outcomes and taking longer to adjust (Park et al., 2013). High athlete identity has been linked to depression (Sanders & Stevinson, 2017) and anxiety (Giannone, Haney, Kealy, & Ogrodniczuk, 2017) following retirement. Such patterns are observed across performance levels and are also seen amongst para-athletes and in retirement from disability sports (Marin-Urquiza, Ferreira, & Van Biesen, 2018).

A number of reasons for the relationship between athlete identity and transition outcomes have been proposed. Firstly, the transition out of sport constitutes a disruption to what have become self-defining activities (Blinde & Stratta, 1992; Lotysz & Short, 2004). Consequently, athletes frequently experience loss of identity upon retirement (Lally, 2007), which can trigger identity crises, and these crises are typically experienced as distressing (Blinde & Stratta, 1992; Lotysz & Short, 2004). A lack of alternate identities outside sport also delays identity shifts into retirement, prolonging distress (Park et al., 2013). The notion of identity foreclosure (or an exclusive athlete identity) has thus also been examined in relation to transition outcomes. Foreclosure occurs when identity is formulated solely in terms of the athlete role without engagement or exploration of alternatives (Brewer & Petitpas, 2017). Identity foreclosure renders athletes more vulnerable to experiencing retirement difficulties including stress and anxiety, with these athletes typically taking longer to adjust to retirement (Grove et al., 1997).

Forming an identity exclusively in terms of the athlete role, especially when this occurs from a young age, has also been suggested to limit opportunities for the development of other aspects of life (Horton & Mack, 2000; Murphy, Petitpas, & Brewer, 1996). Those strongly identifying as athletes tend not to explore other possible roles and career options, resulting in career immaturity and delayed alternate career development (Brewer et al., 1993; Murphy et al., 1996). Identity foreclosure has also been associated with limited career knowledge, vocational skills and career optimism, as well as with higher levels of career indecisiveness and dysfunctional attitudes towards alternative careers (Albion & Fogarty, 2005; Brewer & Petitpas, 2017). Accordingly, upon retirement, these athletes are ill-equipped to pursue alternate careers or pursuits and often lack appropriate skills or feelings of competence in activities other than sport (Sinclair & Orlick, 1993). A delayed ability to enter an alternate career or gain a sense of competence in alternative lifestyles after sport causes and prolongs retirement distress. Conversely, programmes aimed to reduce identity foreclosure, such as Athlete Career and Education (ACE), have been shown to increase motivation for career planning and decision-making (Albion, 2007), facilitating smoother transitions.

Furthermore, it has also been proposed that bodily changes into retirement further impact the relationship between identity and retirement outcomes. The body is central to athletes' sense of self and identity (Saint-Phard, Van Dorsten, Marx, & York, 1999). Thus, changing bodies after retirement can contribute to identity disruption, thereby being a further source of distress and loss of self-esteem (Stephan, Torregrosa, & Sanchez, 2007). Notably, for retired athletes whose physical fitness remained high into retirement, limited changes in athlete identity were observed (Hadiyan & Cosh, 2019). Thus, body changes following retirement may compound identity losses and crises in retirement.

Interpretative Approaches

Over the past decade, alongside growth of cultural praxis within sport psychology, an emerging body of athlete identity research has been undertaken within an interpretative paradigm (Ronkainen, Kavoura et al., 2016a). These approaches, underpinned by relativism and constructionism, consider that cultural and social practices shape people's experiences (McGannon & Smith, 2015). Accordingly, identity cannot be considered in isolation from the cultural and discursive practices within which they are located. Interpretative approaches have thereby broadened conceptualisation of identity from a stable unified inner essence, to identities as shifting, fluid, multiple and necessarily constituted by and within the broader cultural and discursive context.

Accordingly, interpretative approaches have furthered understanding of athlete identity and the way athlete identity shapes retirement experiences (Ronkainen, Kavoura, & Ryba, 2016b). For example, using an interpretative phenomenological analytic approach, Lavallee and Robinson (2007) showed how dedicating lives to sport from an early age resulted in identities being based only on athletic performance, rendering the athletes lost and helpless upon retirement. Further, a constructionist thematic analysis demonstrated that the sporting identity continued into retirement, with limited alternatives (Agnew & Drummond, 2015). Such limited construction was shown to be problematic upon retirement as athletes struggled to redefine their lives and identities outside sport (Agnew, 2016). The body of interpretative research into identity and retirement has largely utilised qualitative approaches and has most commonly drawn on narrative inquiry and discursive psychology (Ronkainen, Kavoura et al., 2016b). These approaches are outlined in the subsequent sections.

Narrative Approaches to Identity

From a narrative approach, athlete identity is understood as an evolving set of storylines or narratives of the athletic self. The narrative of the self is constructed from available cultural stories or narrative resources (Ronkainen, Kavoura et al., 2016b; Smith & Sparkes, 2009) that people use to make sense of their experiences; and it is these stories that constitute identity

74 *Suzanne M. Cosh*

(Douglas & Carless, 2009). Thus, people's identity is viewed as constructed and developed within the complex interplay of individual agency and the narratives and cultural resources available (Smith & Sparkes, 2009), with some narratives less 'tellable' or accepted within a given culture (Cavallerio, Wadey, & Wagstaff, 2017). Most commonly in the narrative athlete identity and retirement literature, a life story interview method has been used (Ronkainen, Kavoura et al., 2016b).

Narrative Research in Identity and Retirement

Early narrative research demonstrated that retirement marked a rupture in the life stories and narratives of athletes (Gearing, 1999; Sparkes, 1998). These studies also concluded that athletes had limited resources outside hegemonic masculine narratives with which to make sense of their lives. Availability of only few narrative resources has been identified as problematic upon retirement. For example, limited narrative resources have been argued to 'lock' athletes in to an athlete identity, subsequently limiting coping and career decision-making into retirement (Stambulova, 2010). Where athletes were able to transfer their existing self-narrative into their post-retirement roles—such as the 'celebrity' narrative for those who moved into the entertainment industry—transition was smoother (Ferriter, 2008) as athletes did not encounter, to the same extent, a lack of narratives with which to make sense of their new lives.

Further, a performance narrative that emphasises achievement is dominant within elite sport (Douglas & Carless, 2009). This narrative shapes athletes' identity around prioritising winning above all else. However, when this performance narrative ceases to be relevant upon retirement, athletes struggle with having no alternate narrative by which to guide their life stories (Carless & Douglas, 2009). Indeed, an absence of achievement and detachment from the star performer identity in retirement has been shown to render a retired athlete vulnerable to depression (Jewett, Kerr, & Tamminen, 2019). Thus, the dominance of a performance narrative, which limits identity, may be problematic for transition. It has further been shown that Finnish female athletes relied strongly on performance narratives in constructing their identities, yet there was a tension between the performance narrative and cultural narratives around femininity. As such, challenges in identity construction and a lack of narrative resources saw female athletes terminating their athletic career earlier than males (Ronkainen, Watkins, & Ryba, 2016).

Further, an entangled narrative has also been identified, whereby those with exclusive athlete identities were unable to develop a new identity in retirement, which impacted wellbeing (Cavallerio et al., 2017). An entangled narrative leading to distress has likewise been demonstrated within Australian Rules Football (Demetriou, Jago, Gill, Mesagno, & Ali, 2018). Contrastingly, those taking up forward-going narratives were better able to develop multiple and new identities into retirement (Cavallerio et al., 2017). Notably, performance-based narratives became marginalised upon retirement, thereby marginalising the entangled narrative, which also functioned to silence retired athletes with regard to their post-retirement distress. Therefore, from a narrative perspective, athlete identity can largely be understood as part of a performance self-narrative. As such, psychological distress into retirement is viewed as the loss of this achievement and drive coupled with an absence of new and alternative life stories (Ronkainen, Kavoura et al., 2016b), with distress then silenced.

Discursive Approaches to Identity

From a discursive psychological perspective, identity is viewed as located within language. That is, identity is produced, ascribed and accomplished within discursive/language practices, and it is these versions that constitute the reality of our lived experience (Hepburn & Potter, 2003). Identity is viewed as governed by cultural and historical factors that constrain and limit the identities available, with some favoured, normalised or problematised (Davies & Harré, 1990). Although narrative approaches rely on the individual to make sense of and report their own identity, it has been argued that people cannot necessarily be treated as informants on their own identity; rather, identities are products of discourse and social interactions (Antaki & Widdicombe, 1998). Thus, there is a shift to examining naturally occurring data (i.e. talk and text that are produced without the researchers' involvement) in discursive psychology (Potter & Shaw, 2018), especially to examine the practices in which identities are produced. Therefore, the discursive literature examining identity and retirement has predominantly analysed naturally occurring media data in order to ascertain the patterns of cultural (re)production of athlete identities.

Discursive Examinations of Identity and Retirement

Analysis of the Australian newsprint media has demonstrated that limited identity positions are available for athletes during their careers and into retirement, with athletes positioned such that choice around both playing and retiring is constrained (Cosh, Crabb, & LeCouteur, 2013; Cosh, LeCouteur, Crabb, & Kettler, 2013). Retirements occurring due to age or injury were privileged, whereas other motivators for retirement were problematised (Cosh, Crabb et al., 2013). Thus, athletes were positioned such that they are expected to continue playing sport whilst physically able (Cosh, LeCouteur et al., 2013). These constructions functioned to ascribe athletes with the narrow identity position of needing to devote life to sport, which necessarily limited alternate pursuits and identities. Athletes were then positioned as needing to retire when a precise point is reached (Cosh,

76 *Suzanne M. Cosh*

Crabb et al., 2013), yet alternate identity positions are not made available upon retirement (Cosh, Crabb, & Tully, 2015).

An examination of retired Olympians highlighted that athletes continued to be ascribed the identity of champion athlete years into retirement, with limited alternatives (Cosh et al., 2015). Continuing to construct retired athletes using athletic identities also rendered their post-retirement career distress as inappropriate behaviour. Indeed, the only other identity position ascribed was that of the 'fallen champion', which functioned to stigmatise experiences of, and help-seeking for, retirement difficulties, thereby also silencing the commonality of transition difficulties.

Summary and Conclusions

A breadth of methodological and theoretical approaches has been used to contribute to knowledge of the implications of athlete identity for retirement. The growth in interpretive studies has also broadened understanding of athlete experiences within the cultural and discursive milieu, complementing research exploring identity within the individual. The diverse approaches used have allowed for unique and valuable insights to be gained, which together can guide and inform the scope of practice in order to best support transitioning athletes.

Research findings across epistemological and methodological positions coalesce around exclusivity of identity during a sporting career—be it an internalised narrow identity, due to limited subject positions and narrative resources, or the marginalisation of certain versions and stories—as problematic for retirement success. An exclusive identity, with athletes dedicating their whole lives to sport, does not allow room for alternate identities to be avowed or developed. In foreclosing their identity, athletes often fail to explore alternate pursuits and, as such, fail to develop skills and knowledge outside sport, which can leave athletes ill-prepared for life after sport and alternate careers (McGillivray & McIntosch, 2006; Sinclair & Orlick, 1993).

In addition to limited identities being available, the performance narrative remains dominant, and this also limits alternative storylines for athletes into retirement. Further, upon retiring, athletes continue to be viewed only as athletes with limited alternative positions made available (Agnew & Drummond, 2015; Cosh et al., 2015). Thus, whilst a going-forward narrative is privileged (Cavallerio et al., 2017), this is potentially challenging for retiring athletes to actually access. Notably, both discursive and narrative approaches have also identified that post-retirement distress is silenced through the marginalising of the 'fallen champion identity' or the 'entangled' athlete (Cavallerio et al., 2017; Cosh et al., 2015). Where stories are silenced or only limited versions made available, stigma can be perpetuated (Lafrance, 2007). Thus, the cultural, narrative and discursive practices surrounding retired athletes may have implications for stigma reproduction.

Stigma is a barrier to help-seeking and, notably, seeking help was further marginalised through being embedded within the 'fallen champion' identity. As such, limited alternative identities and narrative resources silencing distressed athletes may further compound transition difficulties through reducing access to support.

Implications for Practice

The repeated finding that a lack of identity outside sport was problematic for transition success points to a need to create and promote multiple and broader identities throughout athletes' careers. This may be achieved through development of interventions to promote the breadth of the person. Creating diverse stories and discursive practices, especially within sporting contexts, may also allow for alternative and broader identity positions. Therefore, the body of work linking athlete identity with transition outcomes underscores the need for interventions and supports focused at the a) athlete level, b) sporting organisations and c) the broader cultural level.

Where athletes are able to prepare for and divest identity prior to retirement, transition can be smoother (Lally, 2007). Therefore, engaging athletes throughout their careers to broaden their identities may play a critical role in promoting transition success. This is especially seminal given that involuntary and unexpected retirements are common and do not allow for intervention specifically prior to retirement. Accordingly, an emphasis on allowing athletes to engage in alternate activities or pursuits in addition to sport, as well as helping athletes to identify strengths, interests and talents outside the sporting environment may aid athletes to diversify their identities (Martin, Fogarty, & Albion, 2014). Further, an emphasis on the whole-person rather than just performance outcomes—thereby potentially decreasing the dominance of the performance narrative in identity construction—might also facilitate development of a less goal-oriented athlete identity. Recent shifts in some sporting contexts to provide holistic support and better guide dual-career development (Torregrosa, Reguela, & Mateos, 2020) may valuably assist in broadening athlete identity and ultimately facilitating smoother retirements. How to best engage athletes with these services and with a need to broaden identity during their careers remains an area in need of further consideration.

It should be noted, however, that support from sporting organisations is typically highest whilst athletes are at the peak of their careers, with a substantial decrease in support post-retirement (Alfermann & Stambulova, 2007). An increased focus on providing support into transition for athletes experiencing distress may be warranted. Provision of narrative therapy interventions for athletes might be valuable. Narrative therapy allows for exploration of how storylines of the self have been co-produced within the dominant societal discursive practices (White, 2007). This approach

78 *Suzanne M. Cosh*

allows for stories and identities to be explored and re-authored and may thus aid athletes in developing alternative storylines and identities into retirement.

Yet, working to develop alternate aspects of athletes' identities, in practice, may be limited by the broader socio-cultural context, specifically the available discursive practices and narratives. Enhancing understanding of the socio-cultural context in which identities are ascribed and made available may help sport staff to be aware of how they are (or are not) reproducing dominant discourses/narratives in everyday practice with athletes. It has long been argued that the limited range of dominant discursive practices can only be addressed by making diverse stories available within sport settings (Carless & Douglas, 2009). Thus, sporting bodies may benefit from a focus on expanding the available narrative/discursive practices that are deployed within everyday interaction in order to enhance flexibility of narratives and diversify available identities (Cosh, Crabb et al., 2013; Smith & Sparkes, 2009). That is, rather than work with individual athletes to build new or broader identities, sport staff may be able to reproduce alternate or broader versions of athlete identity in the everyday interactions through which identities are ascribed and constructed. Such a shift may make alternate identity positions more accessible and create a flexible array of narrative resources upon which to draw.

Redressing the silencing of retirement difficulties and the marginalisation of the distressed athlete identity may also be integral for supporting transitioning athletes (Cosh et al., 2015). Thus, allowing space for multiple storylines into transition may be especially critical to negate the silencing of the entangled narrative (Cavallerio et al., 2017). This, in turn, may provide narrative and discursive space for athletes to experience distress and seek help rather than have help-seeking marginalised as a 'fallen champion.' Promoting broader shifts in discursive/narrative resources at cultural levels and promulgation of a diversity of narratives might also better allow space for athletes to negotiate broader identities and storylines both during and after athletic careers and may especially allow athletes to re-position themselves upon retirement.

Future Research Directions

Although substantial understanding regarding athlete identity and retirement has been gained, there remains much to learn. Although expanding athlete identities may be protective upon retirement, to date, intervention studies to assess effectiveness of strategies to promote and support diverse identity development remain limited. An increased focus on how to best promote successful transition through a range of identity interventions is also needed. Such intervention research would best be targeted across the individual athlete as well as the sporting body and socio-cultural practices. Effectiveness of individual interventions for transition outcomes, as well as

Athlete Identity and Career Transition   79

how to best promote broader organisation and cultural change, requires ongoing examination.

Evolutions in theoretical and methodological approaches have added to our understandings of athlete identity and retirement. Recent increases in qualitative methods have complemented quantitative findings, although additional growth in pluralism in qualitative research may further benefit the field to provide synthesis across approaches and generate more holistic understanding (Frost et al., 2010). To date, the majority of qualitative studies have used interview data. Benefit may come from examination of naturally occurring data sources to explore how narrative and discursive practices occur in situ, especially within sport settings. Analysis of interactions taking place in sport environments, as well as analysis of cultural discursive and narrative practices (e.g. media accounts), would further understanding of how identities are constructed and reproduced in practice. Such analyses are likely to be best poised to inform interventions for sporting bodies and socio-cultural contexts regarding how it might be possible to expand the positions and resources available for athletes during their careers and into retirement.

Whilst the growth in cultural explorations of identity in retirement has provided valuable insights, the majority of literature regarding athlete identity and retirement remains located within Western (most commonly English-speaking) cultures. Whilst there has been some growth in inter-cultural studies and transition difficulties are seen globally, there remains a dearth of exploration of the ways in which athletic identities impact transition across cultures and contexts.

There is increasing awareness of mental health concerns amongst elite athletes including into retirement (Henriksen et al., 2019); however, athletes may be inhibited from seeking mental health support by the continuation of athlete identity and the marginalisation of the entangled and fallen champion. Further exploration and understanding of the stigmatisation of athletic identities in retirement difficulties may thus be beneficial. Such research may guide practices around stigma reduction and subsequently promote help-seeking amongst retired athletes. Likewise, how to engage athletes in support for identity during their careers and for identity crises in retirement requires ongoing exploration.

References

Agnew, D. (2016). Becoming a star: Life as an elite Australian footballer, identity construction and withdrawal from the spotlight. In M. Drummond & S. Pill (Eds.), *Advances in Australian football: A sociological and applied science exploration of the game* (pp. 90–100). Hindmarsh: Australian Council for Health, Physical Education and Recreation.

Agnew, D., & Drummond, M. (2015). Always a footballer? The reconstruction of masculine identity following retirement from elite Australian football.

Qualitative Research in Sport, Exercise and Health, 7(1), 68–87. doi:10.1080/21596 76X.2014.888588

Albion, M. J. (2007). *Restoring the balance: Women's experiences of retiring from elite sport.* Paper presented at the Paper presented at the International Women's Conference: Education, Employment and Everything: The Triple Layers of a Woman's Life, Queensland, Australia.

Albion, M. J., & Fogarty, G. J. (2005). Career decision making for young elite athletes: Are we ahead on points? *Australian Journal of Career Development, 14*(1), 51–62.

Alfermann, D., & Stambulova, N. (2007). Career transitions and career termination. In G. Tenenbaum & R. C. Eklund (Eds.), *Handbook of sport psychology* (pp. 712–736). New Jersey: Wiley.

Antaki, C., & Widdicombe, S. (1998). Identity as an achievement and as a tool. In C. Antaki & S. Widdicombe (Eds.), *Identities in talk* (pp. 1–14). London: Sage.

Blinde, E. M., & Stratta, T. M. (1992). The 'sport career death' of college athletes: Involuntary and unanticipated sport exits. *Journal of Sport Behavior, 15*(1), 3–20.

Brewer, B. (1993). Self-identity and specific vulnerability to depressed mood. *Journal of Personality, 61*(3), 343–364.

Brewer, B., & Petitpas, A. J. (2017). Athletic identity foreclosure. *Current Opinion in Psychology, 16*, 118–122. doi:10.1016/j.copsyc.2017.05.004

Brewer, B., Van Raatle, J., & Linder, D. (1993). Athletic identity: Hercules' muscles of Achilles heel? *International Journal of Sport Psychology, 24*, 237–254.

Carless, D., & Douglas, K. (2009). 'We haven't got a seat on the bus for you' or 'all the seats are mine': Narratives and career transition in professional golf. *Qualitative Research in Sport and Exercise, 1*(1), 51–66. doi:10.1080/1939844080 2567949

Cavallerio, F., Wadey, R., & Wagstaff, C. R. D. (2017). Adjusting to retirement from sport: Narratives of former competitive rhythmic gymnasts. *Qualitative Research in Sport, Exercise and Health, 9*(5), 533–545. doi:10.1080/21596 76X.2017.1335651

Cosh, S., Crabb, S., & LeCouteur, A. (2013). Elite athletes and retirement: Identity, choice, and agency. *Australian Journal of Psychology, 65*(2), 89–97. doi:10.1111/j.1742-9536.2012.00060.x

Cosh, S., Crabb, S., & Tully, P. J. (2015). A champion out of the pool? A discursive exploration of two Australian Olympic swimmers' transition from elite sport to retirement. *Psychology of Sport and Exercise, 19*, 33–41. doi:10.1016/j. psychsport.2015.02.006

Cosh, S., LeCouteur, A., Crabb, S., & Kettler, L. (2013). Career transitions and identity: A discursive psychological approach to exploring athlete identity in retirement and the transition back into elite sport. *Qualitative Research in Sport, Exercise and Health, 5*(1), 21–42. doi:10.1080/2159676x.2012.712987

Davies, B., & Harré, R. (1990). Positioning: The discursive production of selves. *Journal of the Theory of Social Behaviour, 20*, 43–65.

Demetriou, A., Jago, A., Gill, P. R., Mesagno, C., & Ali, L. (2018). Forced retirement transition: A narrative case study of an elite Australian rules football player. *International Journal of Sport and Exercise Psychology*, 1–15. doi:10.1080/16121 97X.2018.1519839

Douglas, K., & Carless, D. (2009). Abandoning the performance narrative: Two women's stories of transition from professional sport. *Journal of Applied Sport Psychology, 21*(2), 213–230. doi:10.1080/10413200902795109

Ferriter, M. (2008). Heroes and zeroes: Extending celebrity athlete narratives beyond retirement. *Football Studies, 10*(1).

Frost, N., Nolas, S.-M., Brooks-Gordon, B., Esin, C., Holt, A., Mehdizadeh, L., & Shinebourne, P. (2010). Pluralism in qualitative research: The impact of different researchers and qualitative approaches on the analysis of qualitative data. *Qualitative Research, 10*(4), 1–20.

Gearing, B. (1999). Narratives of identity among former professional footballers in the United Kingdom. *Journal of Aging Studies, 13*(1), 43–58. https://doi.org/10.1016/S0890-4065(99)80005-X

Giannone, Z. A., Haney, C. J., Kealy, D., & Ogrodniczuk, J. S. (2017). Athletic identity and psychiatric symptoms following retirement from varsity sports. *International Journal of Social Psychiatry, 63*(7), 598–601. doi:10.1177/0020764017724184

Grove, J. R., Lavallee, D., & Gordon, S. (1997). Coping with retirement from sport: The influence of athletic identity. *Journal of Applied Sport Psychology, 9*(2), 191–203.

Hadiyan, H., & Cosh, S. (2019). Level of physical and motor fitness post retirement and maintenance of athletic identity within active retired athletes. *Journal of Loss and Trauma, 24*(1), 84–95. doi:10.1080/15325024.2018.1540206

Henriksen, K., Schinke, R., Moesch, K., McCann, S., Parham, W. D., Larsen, C. H., & Terry, P. (2019). Consensus statement on improving the mental health of high performance athletes. *International Journal of Sport and Exercise Psychology*, 1–8. doi:10.1080/1612197X.2019.1570473

Hepburn, A., & Potter, J. (2003). Discourse analytic practice. In C. Seale, D. Silverman, J. Gubrium, & G. Gobo (Eds.), *Qualitative research practice* (pp. 180–196). London: Sage.

Horton, R. S., & Mack, D. E. (2000). Athletic identity in marathon runners: Functional focus or dysfunctional commitment? *Journal of Sport Behavior, 23*(2), 101–119.

Jewett, R., Kerr, G., & Tamminen, K. (2019). University sport retirement and athlete mental health: A narrative analysis. *Qualitative Research in Sport, Exercise and Health, 11*(3), 416–433. doi:10.1080/2159676X.2018.1506497

Lafrance, M. N. (2007). A bitter pill: A discursive analysis of women's medicalized accounts of depression. *Journal of Health Psychology, 12*(1), 127–140. doi:10.1177/1359105307071746

Lally, P. (2007). Identity and athletic retirement: A prospective study. *Psychology of Sport and Exercise, 8*(1), 85–99. doi:10.1016/j.psychsport.2006.03.003

Lavallee, D., & Robinson, H. K. (2007). In pursuit of an identity: A qualitative exploration of retirement from women's artistic gymnastics. *Psychology of Sport and Exercise, 8*(1), 119–141. doi:10.1016/j.psychsport.2006.05.003

Lotysz, G. J., & Short, S. E. (2004). 'What ever happened To. . . .' The effects of career termination from the national football league. *Athletic Insight: Online Journal of Sport Psychology, 6*(3).

Marin-Urquiza, A., Ferreira, J. P., & Van Biesen, D. (2018). Athletic identity and self-esteem among active and retired Paralympic athletes. *European Journal of Sport Science, 18*(6), 861–871. doi:10.1080/17461391.2018.1462854

82 *Suzanne M. Cosh*

Martin, L. A., Fogarty, G. J., & Albion, M. J. (2014). Changes in athletic identity and life satisfaction of elite athletes as a function of retirement status. *Journal of Applied Sport Psychology, 26*(1), 96–110. doi:10.1080/10413200.2013.798371

McGannon, K. R., & Smith, B. (2015). Centralizing culture in cultural sport psychology research: The potential of narrative inquiry and discursive psychology. *Psychology of Sport and Exercise, 17*(Suppl C), 79–87. https://doi.org/10.1016/j.psychsport.2014.07.010

McGillivray, D., & McIntosch, A. (2006). 'Football is my life': Theorizing social practice in the Scottish professional football field. *Sport in Society, 9*, 371–387.

Murphy, G. M., Petitpas, A. J., & Brewer, B. W. (1996). Identity foreclosure, athletic identity, and career maturity in intercollegiate athletes. *The Sport Psychologist, 10*(3), 239–246.

Park, S., Lavallee, D., & Tod, D. (2013). Athletes' career transition out of sport: A systematic review. *International Review of Sport and Exercise Psychology, 6*, 1.

Potter, J., & Shaw, C. (2018). The virtues of naturalistic data. In U. Flick (Ed.), *The Sage handbook of qualitative data collection* (pp. 182–199). London, UK: Sage.

Ronkainen, N. J., Kavoura, A., & Ryba, T. V. (2016a). A meta-study of athletic identity research in sport psychology: Current status and future directions *International Review of Sport and Exercise Psychology, 9*(1), 45–64. doi:10.1080/1750984X.2015.1096414

Ronkainen, N. J., Kavoura, A., & Ryba, T. V. (2016b). Narrative and discursive perspectives on athletic identity: Past, present, and future. *Psychology of Sport and Exercise, 27*, 128–137. https://doi.org/10.1016/j.psychsport.2016.08.010

Ronkainen, N. J., Watkins, I., & Ryba, T. V. (2016). What can gender tell us about the pre-retirement experiences of elite distance runners in Finland? A thematic narrative analysis. *Psychology of Sport and Exercise, 22*, 37–45. https://doi.org/10.1016/j.psychsport.2015.06.003

Saint-Phard, D., Van Dorsten, B., Marx, R. G., & York, K. A. (1999). Self-perception in elite collegiate female gymnasts, cross-country runners, and track-and-field athletes. *Mayo Clinic Proceedings, 74*(8), 770–774. doi:10.4065/74.8.770

Sanders, G., & Stevinson, C. (2017). Associations between retirement reasons, chronic pain, athletic identity, and depressive symptoms among former professional footballers. *European Journal of Sport Science, 17*(10), 1311–1318. doi:10.1080/17461391.2017.1371795

Sinclair, D. A., & Orlick, T. (1993). Positive transitions from high-performance sport. *The Sport Psychologist, 7*(2), 138–150.

Smith, B., & Sparkes, A. C. (2009). Narrative analysis and sport and exercise psychology: Understanding lives in diverse ways. *Psychology of Sport and Exercise, 10*(2), 279–288. doi:10.1016/j.psychsport.2008.07.012

Sparkes, A. C. (1998). Athletic identity: An Achilles' heel to the survival of self. *Qualitative Health Research, 8*(5), 644–664. doi:10.1177/104973239800800506

Stambulova, N. (2010). Professional culture of career assistance to athletes: A look through contrasting lenses of career metaphors. In T. V. Ryba, R. Schinke, & G. Tenenbaum (Eds.), *Cultural turn in sport psychology* (pp. 285–314). Morgantown, WV: Fitness Information Technology.

Stephan, Y., Torregrosa, M., & Sanchez, X. (2007). The body matters: Psychophysical impact of retiring from elite sport. *Psychology of Sport and Exercise, 8*(1), 73–83. doi:10.1016/j.psychsport.2006.01.006

Torregrosa, M., Reguela, S., & Mateos, M. (2020). Career assistance programs. In D. Hackfort & R. Schinke (Eds.), *The Routledge international encyclopedia of sport and exercise psychology* (Vol. 2). London, UK: Routledge.

White, M. (2007). *Maps of narrative practice.* New York: Norton and Co.

Wylleman, P., Alfermann, D., & Lavallee, D. (2004). Career transitions in sport: European perspectives. *Psychology of Sport and Exercise, 5*(1), 7–20. doi:10.1016/s1469-0292(02)00049-3

7 Retirement Through Injury

A Case Study Approach Exploring Mental Health Issues and the Retirement Experiences of Two Ex-English Premier League Footballers

Thomas A. Buck

Introduction

Research in the past has often found links between engaging in regular physical activity and improvements in our own psychological well-being (Schuch, Dunn, Kanitz, Delevatti, & Fleck, 2016; Schuch, Vancampfort et al., 2016). To extend this further, researchers have explored the links between regular physical activity and its positive effects in treating existing mental health issues (Kvam, Kleppe, Nordhus, & Hovland, 2016; Stanton & Reaburn, 2014), suggesting moderate-to-vigorous levels of exercise act as an effective treatment for depression. It is interesting that when we begin to delve deeper into these topics surrounding physical activity and its positive influence over both our physical and psychological well-being that, within the confines of professional sport athletes train regularly, are expected to be in peak physical condition and rigorous physical testing conditions are commonplace. However, when an athlete is injured, there is suddenly a much greater likelihood of dealing with a mental health issue as they face life without their sport (Gulliver, Griffiths, Mackinnon, Batterham, & Stanimirovic, 2015), or certainly being unable to cope adaptively with the sudden loss of their sport (Lally, 2007). So, whilst it is interesting to see the benefits exercise can have on not only preventing mental health issues but also treating them, it is arguably much more intriguing to investigate what happens when a professional athlete, whose livelihood is structured around sport, is suddenly left without it. With this in mind, this chapter explores some of the more common antecedents, or factors associated with leading to/causing mental health issues within professional athletes across a range of sports.

There are many different antecedents associated with mental health issues, varying across individuals and experiences alike, but certainly within a professional sporting-context, we can see common trends and themes associated with athletes' experiences linked with mental health issues, such as long-term/career-ending injuries (Gouttebarge, Backx, Aoki, & Kerkhoffs,

2015), identity loss (Carless & Douglas, 2013a, 2013b), transitions (Wylleman, Alfermann, & Lavallee, 2004)—particularly within the context of forced, or involuntary transitions into retirement—and maladaptive coping mechanisms (Papathomas & Lavallee, 2014), largely surrounding the use of illicit/prescription drugs (Rice et al., 2016), alcohol and excessive gambling.

These numerous links surrounding mental health issues and professional sportspeople have more commonly been associated with the amount of injuries an athlete is likely to suffer within their career. For example, Hawkins and Fuller (1999) discussed the issue of professional footballers being 1,000 times more likely to suffer with a career-related injury than other industrial occupations deemed in a 'high-risk' category. Furthermore, Le Gall et al. (2006) estimated 11.2 injuries were suffered in 1,000 match hours and 3.9 injuries suffered per 1,000 training hours. The increased likelihood of suffering injuries within professional football, due in large to the enhanced level of practice, warm-up, cool-down and day-to-day rigours of competing in professional football has only increased over the years as the game has progressed. It is, therefore, reasonable to assume the same can be said for a variety of professional sports, and it is necessary to investigate the likely associated links of coping and dealing with injuries if an athlete is unable to regularly participate within their chosen sport. As a result of this, researchers (Gouttebarge, Aoki, & Kerkhoffs, 2015; Gouttebarge, Frings-Dressen, & Sluiter, 2015; Gouttebarge, Kerkhoffs, & Lambert, 2016; Gouttebarge, Tol, & Kerkhoffs, 2016; Gouttebarge et al., 2017) have conducted extensive research into the possible antecedents of mental health issues associated with injuries, as well as athletes' ability to deal with mental health issues. Specifically, suffering with an injury has been reported to be significantly more likely to lead to a common mental disorder (CMD) than other causes (including eating disorders and other maladaptive coping strategies) within a professional footballer (Gouttebarge, Backx et al., 2015). However, what is more intriguing is the *how* and the *why* athletes are more likely to suffer with a CMD when dealing with an injury.

Park, Tod, and Lavallee (2012) investigated such an association in their research surrounding loss of identity when dealing with retirement transitions. Whilst not directly linked to coping with injury, the two areas of research can certainly overlap as they both posit that when an athlete suffers a loss of their sport, i.e. an inability to participate in any capacity, it could then be argued that they are more likely to suffer a loss of identity or an identity crisis if they are unprepared for retirement from their sport (Lally, 2007; Wylleman et al., 2004). This could then highlight the risk of dealing with mental health issues when an athlete is 'forced' to retire through injury, or if they are unable to actively plan for their retirement (Park & Lavallee, 2015) and adjust their identity to life without sport (Lally, 2007; Wylleman et al., 2004). These have been referred to as normative or non-normative transitions (Wylleman et al., 2004), in which either an athlete voluntarily moves on to the next stage of their career/life, or this is a non-voluntary decision that has been forced upon them, i.e. a long-term injury or career-ending injury leading to retirement, thus facilitating a loss of identity.

Identity itself is described as something that can be multifaceted, but it is possible for one dimension of ourselves to become more dominant; for instance, a professional athlete is likely to typically narrow their identity to a more athletic sense of self in order to benefit this more dominant role (Lally, 2007). Something which is necessary in order to succeed in high-level sport is the need to excel, often being the case where athletes have reported a single-mindedness to achieve professional status, enhancing the need to win and consistently succeed at the highest elite level. It has been argued that in some cases it is almost a prerequisite to have a narrow athletic identity in order to be successful within professional sport (Carless & Douglas, 2013a, 2013b), even to the extent of an athlete manipulating their public image, and covertly managing their personal identities in order to sustain excellence in their respective sport. This could pose a danger to athletes who have narrow athletic identities or focus intently on elements of perfectionism, fear of failure, or measure their own self-worth versus their own success, as this has been shown to correlate with a higher likelihood of dealing with mental health issues, such as depression, anxiety and low levels of self-worth (Houltberg, Wang, Qi, & Nelson, 2018). It is important to remember then that these individuals are indeed people with their own lives, commitments and expectations as well as being elite-level athletes, and thus this comes with its own challenges, which they must face. Of course, as spectators, we only see the on-field performances and we can only speculate as to how they are able to cope with such high demands and expectations, not only from coaching staff, and spectators, but also from themselves. This being said, there has been much more academic literature published surrounding athlete's ability to cope within professional sport, and it is certainly of greater interest when we consider how athletes must also be able to cope with the notion of retiring from a sport they have (up until that point) invested their whole lives towards betterment in.

Coping strategies, much like mental health issues, are often unique to the individual. Yes, they may share similar experiences and have similar hobbies, or interests, but these change from individual to individual as we all experience things differently from one another. However, as literature has developed over the past few decades, we can see that coping strategies— whilst being unique to an individual in an experiential manner—can share similar themes and trends with others, and this provides us with a much greater depth of understanding as to how athletes are able to cope, or in some cases not cope in their respective sport. This development in research has explored how athletes are able to cope within their respective sport, investigating help-seeking behaviours (Gulliver, Griffiths, & Christensen, 2012; Gulliver et al., 2015; Tahinen & Kristjansdottir, 2018), social support

(Morris, Tod, & Eubank, 2017; Yang et al., 2014) as well as both adaptive—positively focused interventions/strategies (Slimani et al., 2018; Turner, 2016) and maladaptive—negatively focused coping strategies (Arvinen-Barrow et al., 2015; Doherty, Hannigan, & Campbell, 2016), which can include illicit/prescription drug abuse, alcoholism, eating disorders and gambling addiction, amongst others.

Considering how athletes are able to cope, and how they manage to develop adaptive coping strategies to deal with their sport's pressures and expectations through these effective strategies, as well as effective social support (Morris et al., 2017), it must then also be considered how athletes deal with the retirement transition from their professional careers once this professional/social support is no longer available through the channels they have become accustomed to. It has been discussed by previous researchers that athletes should be encouraged to develop a 'pre-retirement plan' (Park & Lavallee, 2015; Park et al., 2012) in advance of retirement in order to ease this transition. Similar studies by Carless and Douglas (2013a, 2013b) have also made recommendations regarding addressing athletic identity in order to broaden interests and reduce the likelihood of suffering with a CMD, or loss of identity (which could be argued to lead to a CMD if left unsupported) upon retirement. Certainly, the study by Park and Lavallee (2015) examining the career transition out of sport also highlighted the risk athletes face of losing their social support networks if they have not already established positive networks of family and friends in order to aid the transition experience. Recommendations from the study suggest a greater need to encourage pre-retirement planning; developing strong, adaptive coping strategies, broadening identities in preparation of life without professional sport; and encouraging a wider social support network outside the sporting environment.

Case Study Background

Having reviewed some of the previous literature surrounding the retirement transition in sport, mental health issues and their related antecedents, the remainder of the chapter now explore the experiences of two ex-English Premier League footballers and how this will provide a unique insight into a range of topics related to elite-level footballers. The small study was conducted via an exploratory case study approach in which both participants were interviewed and discussed their experiences of being a Premier League footballer, their subsequent retirement from the sport due to injury, as well as then dealing with their mental health issues as a result of the injury and a loss of identity now they were unable to participate in the sport.

It was important to gain a clear understanding of their respective experiences and explore how both had come to reflect and evaluate their journey through developmental youth phases, into senior-level football. Similar to

88   *Thomas A. Buck*

experiences mentioned earlier in this chapter, both individuals faced varying experiences throughout their professional and personal journeys up to retirement, but it was the study's aim to find some common links and associations in these journeys in order to explore the potential antecedents leading to mental health issues upon retirement from professional sport. From this, the study explored the topic of mental health issues with participants, querying their understanding and general literacy of mental health issues, the possible education of mental health within professional football, as well as their own awareness of their own mental well-being and the presence or absence of professional support provision, and any social support networks available to the participants during their career and upon retirement.

Both participants ($n = 2$), now referred to as '*David*' and '*Alan*,' are former Premier League footballers, having a combined 17 years' playing experience at the senior professional level. Using Swann, Moran, and Piggott's (2015) definition of elite-level status, both participants could be categorised as '*Successful Elite Athletes*,' with both competing at the highest elite level and having also had experience of success (i.e. winning the league and/or a Domestic/European cup competition), albeit infrequently. The study achieved ethical clearance from the institution prior to commencement of data collection. Both participants were recruited purposively for the study, having confirmed that both of them either suffered or were indeed still coping with a CMD and agreed to participate in a one-to-one interview. Overall, the case study accounted for over three hours of interview data, which was transcribed verbatim.

Analysis

The study was simple in its design and data collection method, using a qualitative approach, incorporating a relativist ontology and a subjective epidemiological design (Sparkes & Smith, 2014). It was important to maintain this in order to allow participants to freely discuss and recall their experiences throughout the interview process using a semi-structured interview method, allowing the interviewer to pose questions and offering the ability to probe and follow-up on responses. This provided a much more relaxed and flexible interview process for participants to freely recall and discuss their experiences without the risk of feeling pressured or coerced into responding in a way that would suit the agenda of the researcher, which ultimately gave the interviewee a sense of control when disclosing sensitive information regarding their mental health.

Following this, the study was analysed using the six phases of thematic analysis (Braun & Clarke, 2006) in order to produce codes and identify emerging themes within the interview data. Four main themes were found across the data, with various sub-components which ultimately informed the main themes. All four of the themes were associated with Adverse Mental Health literacy, relating to awareness, understanding, education, support networks and professional support provision. These were as follows:

1) Injuries—Reoccurring, Long-Term and Career-Ending.
2) Transitions—Youth-to-Senior, Retirement and Normative/Non-Normative.
3) Identity—Athletic, Personal and Dual-Identity.
4) Coping Strategies—Professional Support Provision, Social Support, Adaptive and Maladaptive.

The data revealed these four themes, which provided an insight into mental health experiences alongside playing careers and the retirement transition. Interestingly, all themes began to show interlinking associations with each other as mental health issues were discussed in increasingly greater depth by participants throughout the interviews, providing some suggestion that themes 1–4 can have a significant effect on one's mental well-being. The themes, alongside excerpts and previous literature, are discussed in further detail in the subsequent section.

Themes

The analysis of the raw data using Braun and Clarke's (2006) six phases of thematic analysis provided the themes illustrated in Figure 7.1. The

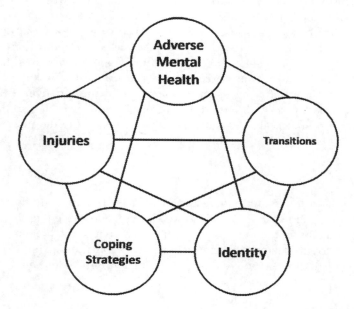

Figure 7.1 Illustration of themes. All themes were found to link to Adverse Mental Health within participants and shared links with other related themes within the analysis

90　*Thomas A. Buck*

relative definitions, whilst all emerging in their own separate theme, were also all found to share links with each other. In this sense, some of the main themes were discussed to share causality with each other. For example, Injuries were discussed in relation to both Adverse Mental Health and Coping Strategies and Identity. The theme of Injuries was also then linked to Transitions when participants discussed experiences of being forced to retire from their sport due to the injury sustained whilst playing.

Interestingly, participants both discussed how their transition out of sport, their loss of identity, their ability to cope effectively as well as the injury they had suffered was all a detriment to their mental health. In both cases, it was discussed that the injury itself had been the leading antecedent in facilitating a CMD, which supports previous findings in this area (Gouttebarge, Aoki et al., 2015; Gouttebarge, Frings-Dressen et al., 2015; Gouttebarge, Kerkhoffs et al., 2016; Gouttebarge, Tol et al., 2016; Gouttebarge et al., 2017). Similarly, a disparity emerged within each of the participants during the early phases of their retirement and their respective identities.

The following themes provide some insight into the participants' lives, drawing on their experience as professional footballers as they reflected on their transition into retirement.

Injuries

Injuries were a prominent theme discussed by both participants in detail. This was to be expected due to their forced retirement from professional football, much of the early discussions centred around the initial reactions dealing with the injury and their desire to return to play. However, after many struggles, both participants were dealt severe blows to their return with multiple reinjuries, leading to subsequent operations and rehabilitation, which would ultimately force them to retire as a pro-footballer. As you can see from the following excerpts the levels of support from coaching staff in particular were absent, and both participants were left to manage their own psychological needs during—what they both highlighted as—one of the most difficult times of their lives.

David

You'd be coming into training and my leg's been snapped in half, I'm on crutches, and he (The First-Team Manager) made a rule that the injuries had to be in for quarter past 9, but had to be out of the building for half past 10 for first team training. Had to get away from the place and it was like I was—like you had some sort of a disease that he didn't want you to pass on.

Alan

My dream was slowly diminishing before my very eyes and no one had anything to say to me or any kind of support, any kind of guidance

Retirement Through Injury 91

or help, or even to give me 10 minutes of their time. It got to a stage where it was that bad that I wasn't sleeping. I carried guilt around with me, frustration and a longing that I wasn't going to play again. What was I going to do next? How was I going to get a career for myself? What life would I have? How fulfilled would I be in the future? I've gone from having that adulation from playing in front of 40,000 fans, being made captain for a team I supported as a kid, it doesn't get much better than that.

The excerpts provide further support for previous literary findings surrounding injuries in professional sport and the increased likelihood of developing a CMD (Gouttebarge, Backx et al., 2015; Gouttebarge et al., 2017), placing an onus on enhanced support systems from professional support provisions for younger players (Richardson, Littlewood, Nesti, & Benstead, 2012), but certainly just as much for those who are close to retirement, or have indeed already retired, as well as a need to manage athletes' anxiety and low moods at the risk of re-injury during their playing careers (Walker, Thatcher, & Lavallee, 2010).

Transitions

Transitions in sport are an extensively researched topic area (Drew, Morris, Tod, & Eubank, 2019; Lally, 2007; Morris et al., 2017; Pummell & Lavallee, 2019; Park et al., 2012; Wylleman et al., 2004), with authors investigating a range of within-career and retirement transitions. The following are excerpts from the transcripts detailing the participants' experiences with their end-of-career transitions, revealing the immediate issues professional footballers may face when coming to terms with retiring from professional sport.

David

Footballers like to be told what to do, when to do it, how to do it, what to wear, what to eat, what time to be there, etc, etc. They don't like thinking for themselves, so on their first day when they wake up and they've got no club to go into, they've got to think for themselves, and they've got the time to think in the day. That's when they struggle, when they really struggle.

Alan

No. I don't think I've ever been content within myself, for me personally, ever since I retired. I'd go as far as to say that because of how my transition wasn't managed and wasn't supported. . . . The legacy that I have till I leave this mortal coil will be—I'd go as far to say that it has impacted on my life ever since then (retirement), and not in a positive way.

92 *Thomas A. Buck*

The current case study investigates the retirement transition and how this was managed by the athletes. Being forced to retire suddenly from their sport caused a severe dissonance within each of their identities, causing a reaction similar to grief/loss as they struggle to come to terms with a new reality outside their sporting environments. This shows a much greater need for a pre-retirement plan (Park et al., 2012), and developing a broader identity beyond being a 'footballer,' to avoid suffering a critical identity loss upon retirement (Lally, 2007).

Identity

The discussion surrounding transitions was further strengthened as both participants discussed the effects a forced retirement transition had on their identity as a person. However, it was '*Alan*' who discussed in detail the impact this had on their own sense of self-worth and the lasting impact it has had on their mental health.

> *Alan*
>
> I had no identity and I had no purpose. What happened as well was because I wasn't supported and I had no identity, you're always striving to try and find something that will give you that sense of worth and value. . . .
>
> I used to do that every day when I used to go into the club—I'd put a front on. I've always had gaps in not finding something that was for me, I never felt fulfilled, I never felt truly valued and my self-worth now still fluctuates between happy and content to something's missing, something's not right.

This provides an enhanced sense of appreciation for encouraging athletes to seek support both within their careers and into retirement when dealing with psychological issues (Mitchell et al., 2014). It is then necessary to build on the elements that '*Alan*' has discussed here as there is the possibility for clubs, and thereby National Governing Bodies within the sport, to place a greater value on mental health literacy and educating footballers about the dangers of CMDs and preventing future mental health issues by incorporating greater onus on broader identities and pre-retirement planning.

Coping Strategies

Lastly, coping strategies was a lesser discussed theme in both interviews, and it was interesting to hear that both participants had not been fully aware of their inability to cope effectively. There were also issues discussed surrounding culture of football in reference to gambling, which was referenced by '*David*' to be a problem within professional football in England. Drinking, which was quickly dismissed to being much less commonplace in more recent generations of footballer in the United Kingdom, but alas, it was still discussed as a maladaptive method of coping in the case of '*David*' when he suffered his career-ending injury.

David

You'd have a drink and it made you feel better, and you'd think; 'Oh, I want to feel better again', so you'd have another drink and you'd feel even better, and then you'd have another drink, and then (claps hands), before you know it you're going through the floor. It's just a coping mechanism, just coping, you're just surviving basically.

'*Alan*' provided a lesser-known view on the use of prescription drugs in sport, and due to the volume of medication he was required to take, he had formed a dependency on it beyond that which it was prescribed for.

Alan

I was taking anti-inflammatory as if they were bloody sweets which is not good for you. You could probably argue that I was addicted to them but it was the fact that it was just the pain that I was in, just to get through the day sometimes I had to take them to take the edge off it, so that was a frustration.

This is a lesser-known area that has very little understanding across the literature and is arguably a topic that should be examined further. However, '*Alan*' was happy to discuss the more positive methods of coping which they were able to develop once they had sought support from a counsellor. It was highlighted that this was post-career, and there was a stigma attached to help-seeking whilst he was still in the environment of his club, which again provides further support for pre-existing research which has explored the reluctance to help-seeking behaviours within professional sport, as they are often perceived as a 'weakness' (Newman, Howells, & Fletcher, 2016; Wood, Harrison, & Kucharska, 2017).

Alan

There are things that I learned by going to counselling to really give me the coping mechanisms to go and deal with—and how to find that part of me to fill that gap, the void, and to get what life is all about and then find some self-worth and some value, and some purpose. To be able to find what normal is, what normal looks like, and what normal should be for you. It takes a lot of unpicking and as I say, these are the mechanisms and the strategies that you can develop all the time.

94 *Thomas A. Buck*

Implications for Practice

This chapter has aimed to provide some insight into the experiences of ex-English premier League footballers from a unique perspective as they have provided a detailed account of their experiences as athletes, but also their experiences of being forced to retire unexpectedly from a sport they had dedicated their lives towards being successful in. This chapter provides a novel exploration of mental health issues and how the retirement transition can not only lead to developing a mental health issue but may also exacerbate pre-existing psychological issues that may have gone untreated during their playing careers. Similar to previous studies, this chapter has offered further support for the need of enhanced professional support provision from staff working within the club, or at the least enhancing the support available at National Governing Body level in order to increase the availability of support.

This provides some practical applications for managing transitions within professional football environments, but also offering some insight as to how the mental well-being of professional footballers can also be better managed. This not only indicates a drive towards better professional and social support networks but enhancing the levels of mental health literacy across the sport on a national scale. This can lead to increased awareness, understanding, prevention and ultimately a reduction in the stigma associated with mental health issues and help-seeking behaviours of professional footballers. As other sources of literature have attested to, the need for a reduction in help-seeking behaviours in athletes is paramount to receiving the proper support from professionals (Gulliver et al., 2012, 2015).

To summarise, the practical applications of this chapter offer recommendations of enhancing the understanding of experiences within a Premier League footballer, providing greater depth of knowledge to developing programmes that will introduce the concept of a pre-retirement plan for athletes to prepare for life without sport. This may also seek to incorporate the elements of developing broader identities in footballers to facilitate the success of a smoother transition into retirement, adding further support for existing recommendations of retirement-transition interventions (Wylleman et al., 2004). This should be coupled with the effective development of improved mental health literacy programmes, which not only aid the reduction of stigma associated with CMDs, but also encourage help-seeking behaviours whilst also offering an insight into the dangers of poor psychological well-being if left untreated.

References

Arvinen-Barrow, M., Clement, D., Hamson-Utley, J. J., Zakrajsek, R. A., Lee, S. M., Kamphoff, C., . . . Martin, S. B. (2015). Athletes' use of mental skills during sport injury rehabilitation. *Journal of Sport Rehabilitation, 24*, 189–197.

Braun, V., & Clarke, V. (2006). Using thematic analysis in psychology. *Qualitative Research in Psychology, 3*, 77–101.

Carless, D., & Douglas, K. (2013a). Living, resisting, and playing the part of the athlete: Narrative tensions in elite sport. *Psychology of Sport and Exercise, 14*, 701–708.

Carless, D., & Douglas, K. (2013b). "In the boat" but "selling myself short": Stories, narratives, and identity development in elite sport. *The Sport Psychologist, 27*, 27–39.

Doherty, S., Hannigan, B., & Campbell, M. J. (2016). The experiences of depression during the careers of elite male athletes. *Frontiers in Psychology, 7*, 1069. doi:10.3389/fpsyg.2016.01069

Drew, K., Morris, R., Tod, D., & Eubank, M. (2019). A meta-study of qualitative research on the junior-to-senior transition in sport. *Psychology of Sport & Exercise, 45*, 1–20.

Gouttebarge, V., Aoki, H., & Kerkhoffs, G. (2015). Symptoms of common mental disorders and adverse health behaviours in male professional soccer players. *Journal of Human Kinetics, 49*, 277–286.

Gouttebarge, V., Backx, F. J. G., Aoki, H., & Kerkhoffs, G. M. M. J. (2015). Symptoms of common mental disorders in professional football (soccer) across five European countries. *Journal of Sports Science and Medicine, 14*, 811–818.

Gouttebarge, V., Frings-Dressen, M. H. W., & Sluiter, J. K. (2015). Mental and psychosocial health among current and former professional footballers. *Occupational Medicine*, 1–7.

Gouttebarge, V., Jonkers, R., Moen, M., Verhagen, E., Wylleman, P., & Kerkhoffs, G. (2017). The prevalence and risk indicators of symptoms of common mental disorders among current and former Dutch elite athletes. *Journal of Sports Sciences, 35*(21), 2148–2156.

Gouttebarge, V., Kerkhoffs, G., & Lambert, M. (2016). Prevalence and determinants of symptoms of common mental disorders in retired professional Rugby Union players, *European Journal of Sport Sciences, 16*(5), 595–602.

Gouttebarge, V., Tol, J. L., & Kerkhoffs, G. M. M. J. (2016). Epidemiology of symptoms of common mental disorders among elite Gaelic athletes: A prospective cohort study. *The Physician and Sports Medicine, 44*(3), 283–289.

Gulliver, A., Griffiths, K. M., & Christensen, H. (2012). Barriers and facilitators to mental health help seeking for your athletes: A qualitative study. *BMC Psychiatry, 12*(157), 1–14.

Gulliver, A., Griffiths, K. M., Mackinnon, A., Batterham, P. J., & Stanimirovic, R. (2015). The mental health of Australian elite athletes. *Journal of Science and Medicine in Sport, 18*, 255–261.

Hawkins, R. D., & Fuller, C. W. (1999). A prospective epidemiological study of injuries in four English professional football clubs. *British Journal of Sports Medicine, 33*, 196–203.

Houltberg, B. J., Wang, K. T., Qi, W., & Nelson, C. S. (2018). Self-narrative profiles of elite athletes and comparisons on psychological well-being. *Research Quarterly for Exercise and Sport, 89*(3), 354–360. doi:10.1080/02701367.2018.1481919

Kvam, S., Kleppe, C. L., Nordhus, I. H., & Hovland, A. (2016). Exercise as a treatment for depression; A meta-analysis. *Journal of Affective Disorders, 202*, 67–86.

Lally, P. (2007). Identity and athletic retirement: A prospective study. *Psychology of Sport and Exercise, 8*, 85–99.

96 *Thomas A. Buck*

Le Gall, F., Carling, C., Reilly, T., Vandewalle, H., Church, J., & Rochcongar, P. (2006). Incidence of Injuries in elite French youth soccer players. *The American Journal of Sports Medicine, 34*(6), 928–938. doi:10.1177/0363546505283271

Mitchell, T. O., Nesti, M., Richardson, D., Midgley, A. W., Eubank, M., & Littlewood, M. (2014). Exploring athletic identity in elite-level English youth football: A cross-sectional approach. *Journal of Sports Sciences, 32*(13), 1294–1299. doi:10.1080/02640414.2014.898855

Morris, R., Tod, D., & Eubank, M. (2017). From youth team to first team: An investigation into the transition experiences of young professional athletes in soccer. *International Journal of Sport and Exercise Psychology, 15*(5), 523–539. doi:10.1080/1612197X.2016.1152992

Newman, H. J. H., Howells, K. L., & Fletcher, D. (2016). The dark side of top-level elite sport: An autobiographic study of depressive experiences in elite sport performers. *Frontiers in Psychology, 7*, 868. doi:10.3389/fpsyg.2016.00868

Papathomas, A., & Lavallee, D. (2014). Self-starvation and the performance narrative in competitive sport. *Psychology of Sport & Exercise, 15*, 688–695.

Park, S., & Lavallee, D. (2015). Roles and influences of Olympic athletes' entourages in athletes' preparation for career transition out of sport. *Sport and Exercise Psychology Review, 11*(1), 3–19.

Park, S., Tod, D., & Lavallee, D. (2012). Exploring the retirement from sport decision-making process based on the transtheoretical model. *Psychology of Sport and Exercise, 13*, 444–453.

Pummell, E. K. L., & Lavallee, D. (2019). Preparing UK tennis academy players for the junior-to-senior transition: Development, implementation, and evaluation of an intervention program. *Psychology of Sport & Exercise, 40*, 156–164.

Rice, S. M., Purcell, R., De Silva, S., Mawren, D., McGorry, P. D., & Parker, A. G. (2016). The mental health of elite athletes: A narrative systematic review. *Sports Medicine, 46*, 1333–1353. doi:10.1007/s40279-016-0492-2

Richardson, D., Littlewood, M., Nesti, M., & Benstead, L. (2012). An examination of the migratory transition of elite young European soccer players to the English premier league. *Journal of Sport Sciences, 30*(15), 1605–1618.

Schuch, F. B., Dunn, A. L., Kanitz, A. C., Delevatti, R. S., & Fleck, M. P. (2016). Moderators of response in exercise treatment for depression: A systematic review. *Journal of Affective Disorders, 195*, 40–49.

Schuch, F. B., Vancampfort, D., Richards, J., Rosenbaum, S., Ward, P. B., & Stubbs, B. (2016). Exercise as a treatment for depression: A meta-analysis adjusting for publication bias. *Journal of Psychiatric Review, 77*, 42–51.

Slimani, M, Bragazzi, N. L., Znazen, H., Paravlic, A., Azaiez, F., & Tod, D. (2018). Psychosocial predictors and psychological prevention of soccer injuries: A systematic review and meta-analysis of the literature. *Physical Therapy in Sport*, 293–300.

Sparkes, A. C., & Smith, B. (2014). *Qualitative research methods in sport, exercise and health: From process to product.* Oxon: Routledge.

Stanton, R., & Reaburn, P. (2014). Exercise and the treatment of depression: A review of the exercise program variables. *Journal of Science and Medicine in Sport, 17*, 177–182.

Swann, C., Moran, A., & Piggott, D. (2015). Defining elite athletes: Issues in the study of expert performance in sport psychology. *Psychology of Sport and Exercise, 16*, 3–14.

Tahinen, R. E., & Kristjansdottir, H. (2018). The influence of anxiety and depression symptoms on help-seeking intentions in individual sport athletes and nonathletes: The role of gender and athlete status. *Journal of Clinical Sport Psychology*, *13*(1), 134–151.

Turner, M. (2016). Rational emotive behavior therapy (REBT), irrational and rational beliefs, and the mental health of athletes. *Frontiers in Psychology*, *7*, 1423. doi:10.3389/fpsyg.2016.01423

Walker, N., Thatcher, J., & Lavallee, D. (2010). A preliminary development of the Re-Injury Anxiety Inventory (RIAI). *Physical Therapy in Sport*, *11*, 23–29.

Wood, S., Harrison, L. K., & Kucharska, J. (2017) Male professional footballers' experiences of mental health difficulties and help-seeking. *The Physician and Sportsmedicine*, *45*(2), 120–128.

Wylleman, P., Alfermann, D., & Lavallee, D. (2004). Career transitions in sport: European perspectives. *Psychology of Sport and Exercise*, *5*, 7–20.

Yang, J., Schaefer, J. T., Zhang, N., Covassin, T., Ding, K., & Heiden, E. (2014). Social support from the athletic trainer and symptoms of depression and anxiety at return to play. *Journal of Athletic Training*, *49*(6), 773–779. doi:10.4085/1062-6050-49.3.65

Part II

Supporting Athletes Transitioning Into Retirement

8 Delisted Footballers

Supporting Well-Being Through Continued Participation in State-Based Levels

Deborah Agnew and Elizabeth Abery

Australian football is a sport that is uniquely Australian. The national elite-level Australian Football League (AFL) competition offers full-time paid employment for male footballers. At an individual state level, second-tier league or sub-elite competitions include the South Australian National Football League (SANFL), the West Australian Football League (WAFL) and Victorian Football League (VFL). In the case of Australian football, the state leagues are independent systems and, whilst players are paid, the remuneration is considerably less than at the elite level; it is not considered full-time employment, and the players tend to have vocations in other industries in addition to playing in these competitions. Upon being drafted (contracted) to an AFL club, most young men have a firm belief that they will make a successful career from football and do not contemplate life after football and its consequences as their focus is on what is required to maintain their performance and stature as an elite player (Hickey & Kelly, 2008). The reality is that very few players develop long and sustainable careers in the elite national competition (Johnson, 2014) and "in the world of AFL football, retirement is rarely at the discretion of the player" (Hickey & Kelly, 2008, p. 501).

From the moment a player is drafted to an AFL club, he is constantly being told to prepare for life after sport; however, while the AFL implements player development and well-being programmes, there is an expectation that a player can juggle both domains, that of an elite athlete and also someone undertaking educational or career development (Stambulova, Ryba, & Henriksen, 2020) for an unknown future (Hickey & Kelly, 2008). These men have worked hard from a young age to achieve selection in the AFL, with their ongoing commitment to football outweighing their exploration of opportunities for educational or career development (Hickey & Kelly, 2008). Without adequate and appropriate support (Agnew, Marks, Henderson, & Woods, 2018), the player may not identify the perceived need or urgency in preparing for their post sporting career lives; the transition outcome is then unpredictable when retirement is unplanned and subsequently unprepared for (Agnew et al., 2018; Brown, Webb, Robinson, & Cotgreave, 2018; Hickey & Kelly, 2008).

102 *Deborah Agnew and Elizabeth Abery*

It cannot be disputed that retirement from sport is inevitable; however, player experiences are dependent on how the athlete perceives the circumstances surrounding their retirement, what their future holds and the support provided by the club or sporting association (Knights, Sherry, Ruddock-Hudson, & O'Halloran, 2019; Stambulova et al., 2020). Retirement from AFL may be voluntary, due to injury, as a result of deselection, or what is referred to within AFL as delisting. The retirement circumstances facing the athlete may influence their decisions around what life after football might look like.

No matter what the circumstances, retirement from elite sport is difficult and can cause many levels of distress and test a person's coping strategies (Agnew et al., 2018; Blakelock, Chen, & Prescott, 2019). As part of the AFL structure and direction, while players are contracted to a club, their well-being is a priority as it benefits not only the player but also the club. However, once a player is no longer contracted to that club, the club's responsibility and obligation for a player's well-being is no longer paramount, and the question of who is responsible to support athletes through the challenges of impending retirement is unclear (Agnew et al., 2018; Knights et al., 2019).

Delisting from an AFL club leaves a player with no control over the timing of retirement from the elite level of their chosen sport. Athletes may have enjoyed a successful playing career; however, where retirement is due to delisting the transition out of elite sport may be difficult. Lack of control over the timing of retirement may lead to vulnerability, feelings of failure, humiliation and identity loss (Agnew et al., 2018; Butt & Molnar, 2009; Alfermann & Stambulova, 2007). In addition, lack of planning and preparedness for the end of their professional career may lead to anger, frustration, disappointment and loss of direction, certainty and purpose in their life (Brown et al., 2018; Knights et al., 2019). Social and structural support is imperative to the transition process as players contemplate the challenges arising from their unplanned retirement (Agnew et al., 2018; Brown et al., 2018; Knights et al., 2019). Recent research has shown that despite player development and well-being programmes being in place, players perceive a lack of support in negotiating this phase of their professional career (Agnew et al., 2018; Brown et al., 2018; Knights et al., 2019).

Being delisted and the subsequent unplanned retirement from the elite level may entice some footballers to seek out a continuation of their athletic career through participation in lower levels of the sport such as the state second-tier league (Agnew et al., 2018), but this may also present as a challenging transition process, which we discuss later. Despite the potential for a perceived sense of downward social mobility through a loss of social status and prestige that playing at lower level portrays (Alfermann & Stambulova, 2007), delisted players often still believe they are capable of playing at a high standard and can contribute to the sport and their peers through their experience and leadership skills (Agnew et al., 2018) that can be passed on to younger players. Through involvement at the sub-elite level, other opportunities may evolve for future or concurrent employment with the club in coaching or leadership roles, or they may see playing at the lower level as an opportunity to re-enter the elite forum through reselection at a different AFL club.

Transition from an elite level of sport to a lower level may have positive and negative outcomes for players. Where a player is delisted, there is no control over the timing of retirement; hence, players may be unprepared and feel a sense of loss and change in identity. However, where there is an opportunity to transition into retirement by continuing to play the game, the opportunity for a new sense of purpose evolves in which players can undertake the role of mentor for younger, less experienced players, and there may be opportunity for protective factors in supporting their well-being through new friendships, ongoing structure and continued financial gain (Agnew et al., 2018). No matter how the outcome of retirement from elite sport unfolds, the athlete's well-being through this transition must be adequately considered. Responsibility for providing that care crosses a trajectory of time and events from the lifespan of a player's career and beyond. Outside the research study discussed in this chapter, there has been no known research that explores the process and outcomes where Australian footballers transition out of elite sport to retirement through playing their chosen sport at a lower level and the impacts this has on the transition process.

This chapter focuses on the experiences of male athletes[1] who are delisted from the AFL and choose to return to sub-elite competition rather than cease competing entirely. Using narrative inquiry through a life history approach, the qualitative study explored the transition experiences of Australian footballers who returned to the SANFL following deselection. The narratives are based on the experiences of ten footballers who took part in the study, which used semi-structured interviews to explore topics including their experiences in the national AFL competition, difficulties faced during the transition process, the support needed during this period and determining responsibility for player well-being during this time.

Methods

This study utilised a narrative inquiry to explore the transition experiences of Australian footballers who chose to return to state-based leagues following deselection from the national competition. Specifically, a stage-in-a-lifecycle approach (which can be captured through narrative life histories) was used because it has been identified that retirement from sport is a process rather than a single moment (Agnew, 2011; Kelly & Hickey, 2008). The footballers in this study had returned to state-based leagues and, as such,

104 *Deborah Agnew and Elizabeth Abery*

had not yet fully transitioned into life after sport, which also made a stage-in-a-lifecycle approach an appropriate method to capture these footballers' experiences.

Ten footballers who had been deselected from the national AFL competition and returned to state-based leagues took part in this research. Participants were between 20 and 32 years of age and had played in the national AFL competition for between 1 and 8 years. Following ethical approval from the Flinders University Human Research Ethics Committee, the footballers were purposefully recruited (Patton, 2002) through the football managers in state-based clubs who invited participation by sending out information about the study to eligible footballers via email. Participants took part in a semi-structured interview, which lasted between 28 minutes and 1 hour. The interviews explored the difficulties footballers faced during the retirement transition process and the support needed by footballers during this time to facilitate a positive transition. Interviews were digitally recorded and transcribed verbatim.

Data was analysed through a general narrative approach (Riessman, 2008), which allowed the focus to remain on thematic meaning of the responses. This method of analysis is particularly useful where participants have had similar experiences and the researchers are seeking to identify the common aspects amongst participant responses (Riessman, 2008; Bold, 2012). Thomas and Harden's (2008) three-step thematic analysis process was followed; line-by-line coding of the transcripts were then arranged into themes and analysed in accordance with the research questions. The research questions for this project were as follows:

1. What are the retirement transition experiences of footballers who return to state-based competition following a career in elite Australian football?
2. Who is responsible for the welfare of retired and transitioning Australian footballers?
3. How does the culture of Australian football contribute to difficult transition or retirement experience?

Through the analysis and synthesis process, initial themes may be merged or separated to provide a complete overview of the concepts (Thomas & Harden, 2008). In this project, it was not necessary to merge or separate themes once the analysis process was complete.

Creswell and Miller (2000) and Creswell (2012) state that at least two of eight strategies should be utilised to establish trustworthiness in a study. This study used member checking, peer debriefing and an audit trail to ensure validity. Despite recent critique over the use of member checks to establish trustworthiness (Smith & McGannon, 2017), the National Health and Medical Research Council (2015) and Harper and Cole (2012) argue that allowing participants to verify their statements is respectful and can lead to the perception that their feelings are validated. Therefore, participants in this study were given 2 weeks to review and edit their transcripts and invited to contact the researcher if they wished to make changes. No changes were requested: the transcripts were thus considered accurate and content trustworthy.

Throughout this study, the researcher utilised a critical friend who was an expert in player welfare in Australian football to discuss the process and findings. This allowed for regular dialogue through the reflective process rather than relying on inter-relater reliability (Smith & McGannon, 2017).

Trustworthiness and dependability in qualitative research can be established through establishing an audit trail (Ary, Jacobs, & Sorensen, 2010). In this study, detailed records including written accounts of meetings with the critical friend and the decisions made about the project and the process of analysis were kept in a well-organised and retrievable format to establish the audit trail.

Results and Discussion

The data presented in this chapter is part of a larger project on retirement from Australian football through continuing to play in state-based leagues. The focus of this chapter is specifically on player well-being; therefore, the themes derived from the larger project relating to well-being are discussed. Three themes related to well-being were developed from the analysis of the data; negotiating the delisting process, utilising the state-based club's resources and life after elite football. These themes are discussed in more detail later. Given delisted footballers have no control over the timing of their retirement, well-being can be negatively affected (Agnew et al., 2018; Butt & Molnar, 2009; Alfermann & Stambulova, 2007). However, state-based clubs may offer assistance with housing and employment as well as emotional support that can provide protective factors for well-being, which is significant for footballers returning from interstate in particular. In addition, returning to state-based leagues is a choice and can, therefore, offer footballers some control over the direction of their career. These themes are discussed in more detail in the subsequent section.

Negotiating the Delisting Process

All of the footballers talked about their delisting happening in an end of season meeting with the club but indicated that much more than a single meeting is required for a satisfactory process. Some footballers had subsequent exit meetings following their delisting, whilst others left the club on the same day and had no further contact. Regardless of the number of meetings concerning the delisting, retirement was described as a process that needs to be worked through over several months or years. Agnew (2011) and Kelly and Hickey (2008) support the notion that retirement is not a single moment. Some of the footballers in the current study admitted that they could see the delisting coming because they had been injured or knew that their form had dropped:

> Well the welfare manager rang me and said you have a meeting and you kind of know already and then it's legit two minutes and they just say you're not required, and then a week later you have like a meeting to explain why.

However, even if the footballers had a suspicion they would be delisted, the end of season review meeting was still described as being tough. For some, the exit meeting was the last contact they had with the club, and they were given a cardboard box to clean out their lockers; others had subsequent meetings with the player welfare managers from a week to up to 2 months after the initial meeting. Many participants described their delisting as horrible:

> Pretty much a pretty horrible job. They pretty much got me in the office, just said "look sorry [name] we don't see you as a long term player at our football club. Thanks for your services. See you later. Here's a cardboard box." Literally "here's a cardboard box, put your stuff in it."

The delisting process was described as being a dangerous time for players in terms of mental health and well-being, because being delisted could be perceived as being a failure and having let themselves down. Not only can athletes perceive the delisting as a failure, there are unrealised career expectations that can compound the issues faced (Butt & Molnar, 2009). However, for some athletes who return to lower levels of competition, the unrealised expectations can be a motivating factor to try and revive their careers at the elite level through reselection (Agnew et al., 2018). For the footballers in the current study, deselection caused the men to question their worth as a footballer, and also as a person. The following comment encapsulates the thought process footballers go through when they are told they are no longer required:

> Am I good enough? Was I good enough? Will that be the only—will this be the thing that defines me as a person?

When an athlete's contract with a sports club is not renewed, they are particularly vulnerable to experiencing poor well-being. Ongoing support from the club has been identified as being significantly beneficial for athletes as they transition out of the sport (Surujlal & van Zyl, 2014). However, because the contractual responsibilities for the club have been terminated, and therefore the club is no longer required to provide the same level of care, the athlete can often be left on their own to ask for assistance (Ellis, 2015).

Participants in the current study argued that the period following deselection is when the footballers need guidance more than ever; however in their experience, for most of the players, the guidance and support from their AFL clubs was not there. The consequences for the footballers not receiving guidance and support from their AFL clubs means that they are required to seek assistance during a difficult period, of their own volition, which they are often not prepared to do (Agnew et al., 2018). A further barrier for delisted footballers is that they may experience feelings of bitterness towards the club that deselected them, which can discourage them asking for help (Petitpas, 2009). The current study, however, indicates footballers want guidance and support from their AFL clubs. Therefore, if clubs were to offer assistance during the transition period rather than the footballers having to ask for it, well-being could be better supported through the retirement transition process.

Utilising the State-Based Clubs' Resources

Not-for-profit sports clubs, such as state-based sports organisations, face a shortage of resources, which can impact on their ability to cope with the associated challenges of delisted elite players (Wicker & Breuer, 2011). All participants in the current study recognised that the resources in elite football clubs are superior to those at a state-based level. Whilst one participant stated he did not believe footballers returning to the state-based club needed much, others were able to benefit from the networks the clubs had to assist them with finding both housing and employment, particularly if they had moved back from interstate to play in the SANFL. Although they recognised it is not the SANFL club's main responsibility to find them employment outside football, participants were conflicted, exhibiting an expectation that the club *could* help:

> No. I don't think it's probably a fair expectation but I think they probably should help especially for guys that are coming back from interstate because you don't have any contacts so you don't know anyone here where the guys that are already here and most have contacts, but also with the SANFL cubs they would have a big supporter base and a hell of a lot more contacts than any player would have. So I think say the majority of clubs would send out feelers saying is there any work going or what's the go with that? But I reckon they probably should try to help out.

The footballers admitted that whilst they were playing AFL at the elite level, the clubs did everything for them. This led to an expectation when coming back to the SANFL that their state-based clubs would be able to assist with finding them a job outside football and accommodation if they were moving from interstate. It was a learning curve for the footballers to

108 _Deborah Agnew and Elizabeth Abery_

take responsibility for themselves, and whilst the state-based clubs would assist where they could, they do not have the same resources as AFL clubs. Despite this, the footballers expressed gratitude for the assistance provided to them by the SANFL club and recognised this assistance was helpful in the transition out of elite football:

> Yeah a job, that took me 4 months before I found a job coming back, just because it's to the end of the year, start of the year, it's a tough time, but yeah the club was very helpful. So they did all they could in terms of putting my name out there and sort of making calls and stuff like that to try and get me employment. So they have—yeah I don't think they could have done much more.

Coming back to SANFL meant that whilst the resources were not the same, they never-the-less were coming back to supportive environments with club staff who would try and help them adjust. In this way, coming back to the SANFL provided some protective factors for the footballers in terms of well-being because they received some assistance. Comments were positive regarding such assistance:

> Yeah look pretty good. As I said clubs at this level don't have all the resources in the world but a few people around the club have been real good to me. And that's what I like about it as well. You've got people around the social club, and that sort of thing in the SANFL, probably as opposed the VFL club that will try and get the foot in the door for somewhere for a job and things like that. So they've been quite helpful in finding me houses, and people to move in with, and that sort of stuff. But there is definitely—obviously a little bit of a drop in terms of you do have to organise a bit more for yourself, and stand up for yourself a bit more, and make sure you get things done, otherwise it won't get done sometimes, yeah.

Life After Elite Football

Despite the challenges faced during the transition period, all participants were positive about their post elite football lives. This research confirms that transitioning out of elite sport is a process (Agnew, 2011; Kelly & Hickey, 2008), and given time most footballers are able to make the transition successfully. The transition out of elite sport for the footballers in this research was difficult because the timing of the end of their elite careers was decided for them and all felt they still had more to give at the national level. This finding is consistent with previous research findings that non-normative transitions such as being deselected from the team are the most difficult because the timing is somewhat unpredictable and uncontrollable for athletes (Petitpas, 2009; Stambulova, 2010). All of the men were still playing football at a lower grade because they still wanted to be involved and were still driven to play football. Coming back to the SANFL means that the footballers could continue to play at the highest level possible.

> Yeah just normal I think. Yeah just the same as everyone else, sort of working and playing footy and just yeah, just trying to do what you've got to do to put food on the table and yeah, just living life.

Continuing to play SANFL football can provide support and protective factors for well-being because the footballers are surrounded by teammates and have a purpose. A new club can motivate footballers because they want to make an impression at the new club. As indicated by the following quote, the footballers felt that continuing to play football was the right decision for them:

> [I]t just felt like it came at the right time, and I felt like I needed a bit of a change. I think when you're at a club for a little bit of time you can definitely get a bit stale, and change of things up really makes you want to- you're around a new bunch of guys, a new club, you want to impress, and all that scene. And it just felt like- it just felt right, and it felt like the right time. So- yeah we kept in touch and- yeah I ended up making the move, and enjoying it.

Despite the difficult transition period experienced by the footballers in this research, all described their lives after elite Australian football positively. Consistent with previous research, successfully negotiating the transition process is possible (Agnew, 2011):

> I would say I'm pretty positive now a days. And everything back in my footy career good or bad, I don't blame anyone for. I think it takes- when you start taking responsibility for the things that have happened good or bad in the past, that's when you can truly move on with your life and be happy, and be the person you want to be. So that's the big thing for me- yeah that's come out of it.

Conclusion

A relatively high proportion of delisted footballers transition out of elite football by continuing to compete in lower levels of the sport such as in the SANFL. This research concludes that delisted footballers are particularly vulnerable to experiencing poor well-being due to the lack of control over the timing of the end of their AFL career and often feel underprepared for this transition. Returning to a state-based club can offer some protective factors to promote well-being through the support offered by the SANFL club, including helping to find accommodation and subsequent employment.

110   *Deborah Agnew and Elizabeth Abery*

The support offered by the SANFL clubs is particularly important for footballers who move interstate to compete in the state-based leagues because they have multiple and immediate needs. Further protective factors offered by participation in state-based competitions include friendship, structure, and financial support, and providing the footballers with an avenue to control some of the circumstances during this difficult time; these factors can all facilitate positive well-being. In addition, this research found that the general supportive environment of SANFL clubs can assist a player to positively negotiate the retirement transition process. For the footballers in this research returning to the SANFL, these factors appeared to play an important role in the successful transitioning out of elite sport process.

The footballers in this research recognised that once they were no longer contracted to the AFL club, that club needed to focus on the current players and not the ones who have left. However, they still believed that the AFL club has a level of responsibility in caring for footballers who have been delisted. Simple gestures such as regular follow-up conversations to check in on the delisted footballers' well-being were argued as being a necessity during the transition process. State-based clubs such as SANFL do not have the same resources as AFL clubs and subsequently are often ill-equipped to support delisted footballers in the transition out of elite sport, particularly those who are experiencing poor mental health and well-being. It was evident through this research that AFL clubs have different methods in how they delist footballers. For some clubs, there was one meeting, others had several meetings at the end of the season, which when implemented would provide further opportunities to assess the well-being of the delisted footballer. Regardless of whether there was one or more meetings for the delisting, we know that transitioning out of elite sport is a process, and it is, therefore, arguable that an exit programme rather than only one exit meeting may provide opportunities to provide the guidance that footballers require during this difficult time.

Implications for Practice

It is recognised that retirement from elite sport is inevitable and that elite-level clubs are a business, therefore having no obligation to footballers they no longer employ. However, the experiences of elite Australian footballers who, once no longer contracted to a club, are discarded without regular follow-up on their well-being highlight the unanswered question of responsibility of elite clubs with regard to duty of care. It is known that the retirement transition is a difficult period for athletes and that those who are unable to choose the timing of their retirement, such as delisted athletes, experience more difficult transitions. Therefore, it is important for elite-level clubs to continue to support footballers during the transition period to facilitate a positive and successful life after elite sport. Whilst state-based clubs offer assistance to footballers under their care, they are

Delisted Footballers 111

under-resourced, which limits the assistance they are able to give. More resources from the national competition need to be directed to state-based leagues to help support footballers who require assistance during the transition period. In addition, the development of a structured exit programme is recommended as this would treat retirement as a process rather than a single moment, which this research demonstrates may more effectively facilitate healthy adjustment to life after elite football.

Note

1. The Australian Football League does have an elite female competition; however, it is not a full-time occupation for the women involved, therefore this chapter is specifically focused on the elite men's competition.

References

Agnew, D. (2011). *Life after football: The construction of masculinity following a career in elite Australian rules football* (Thesis PhD). Adelaide: Flinders University.

Agnew, D., Marks, A., Henderson, P., & Woods, C. (2018). Deselection from elite Australian football as the catalyst for a return to sub-elite competitions: When elite players feel there is 'still more to give.' *Qualitative Research in Sport, Exercise and Health, 10*(1), 117–136.

Alfermann, D., & Stambulova, N. (2007). Career transitions and career termination. In G. Tenenbaum & R. C. Eklund (Eds.), *Handbook of sport psychology* (pp. 712–736). New York: Wiley.

Ary, D., Jacobs, L., & Sorensen, C. (2010). *Introduction to research in education* (8th ed.). Wadsworth: Belmont.

Blakelock, D., Chen, M., & Prescott, T. (2019). Coping and psychological distress in elite adolescent soccer players following professional academy deselection. *Journal of Sport Behavior, 42*(1), 3–28.

Bold, C. (2012). *Using narrative in research.* London: Sage.

Brown, C. J., Webb, T. L., Robinson, M. A., & Cotgreave, R. (2018). Athletes' experiences of social support during their transition out of elite sport: An interpretive phenomenological analysis. *Psychology of Sport & Exercise, 36*, 71–80.

Butt, J., & Molnar, G. (2009). Involuntary career termination in sport: A case study of the process of structurally induced failure. *Sport in Society, 12*(2), 240–257.

Creswell, J. W. (2012). *Educational research: Planning, conducting, and evaluating quantitative and qualitative research* (4th ed.). Boston: Pearson Education.

Creswell, J. W., & Miller, D. L. (2000). Determining validity in qualitative inquiry. *Theory into practice, 39*(3), 124–130.

Ellis, L. (2015, February 6). Clarke Carlisle has spelt it out: Retiring from sport can be a traumatic loss. *The Guardian.* Retrieved from www.theguardian.com/commentisfree/2015/feb/05/clarke-carlisle-retiring-sport-professional-athletesdepression

Harper, M., & Cole, P. (2012). Member checking: Can benefits be gained similar to group therapy? *The Qualitative Report, 17*(2), 510–517.

Hickey, C., & Kelly, P. (2008). Preparing to not to be a footballer: Higher education and professional sport. *Sport, Education and Society, 13*(40), 477–494.

112 *Deborah Agnew and Elizabeth Abery*

Johnson, B. (2014, May 27). *Off-field focus a key to success.* Retrieved from www.aflplayers.com.au/article/off-field-focus-a-key-to-success/

Kelly, P., & Hickey, C. (2008). *The struggle for the body, mind and soul of AFL footballers.* North Melbourne: Australian Scholarly.

Knights, S., Sherry, E., Ruddock-Hudson, M., & O'Halloran, P. (2019). The end of a professional sport career: Ensuring a positive transition. *Journal of Sport Management, 33,* 518–529.

National Health and Medical Research Council. (2015). *The national statement on ethical conduct in human research, 2007.* Canberra: The National Health and Medical Research Council, the Australian Research Council and the Australian Vice Chancellors' Committee.

Patton, M. (2002). *Qualitative evaluation and research methods.* Beverly Hills, CA: Sage.

Petitpas, A. (2009). Sport career transition. In B. Brewer (Ed.), *Handbook of sports medicine and science: Sport psychology* (pp. 113–120). West Sussex, UK: Wiley-Blackwell Publishing. doi:10.1002/9781444303650.ch11.

Riessman, C. K. (2008). *Narrative methods for the human sciences.* London: Sage.

Smith, B., & McGannon, K. R. (2017). Developing rigor in qualitative research: Problems and opportunities within sport and exercise psychology. *International Review of Sport and Exercise Psychology, 11*(1), 1–21.

Stambulova, N. B. (2010). Counseling athletes in career transitions: The five-step career planning strategy. *Journal of Sport Psychology in Action, 1*(2), 95–105.

Stambulova, N. B., Ryba, T. V., & Henriksen, K. (2020). Career development and transitions of athletes: The international society of sports psychology position stand revisited. *International Journal of Sport and Exercise Psychology.* doi:10.1080/161219X.2020.1737836

Surujlal, J., & van Zyl, Y. (2014). Understanding the dynamics of sport-career transition of Olympic athletes. *Mediterranean Journal of Social Sciences, 5*(20), 477–484.

Thomas, J., & Harden, A. (2008). Methods for the thematic synthesis of qualitative research in systematic reviews. *BMC Medical Research Methodology, 8,* 45–55.

Wicker, P., & Breuer, C. (2011). Scarcity of resources in German non-profit sport clubs. *Sport Management Review, 14*(2), 188–201.

9 Understanding Parents' Experiences With Athlete Retirement

Patricia Lally and Richard Lally

Introduction

A significant amount of research has examined the experiences of parents in their children's initial and subsequent athletic careers. Parents are typically responsible for introducing their children to sport and encouraging an interest in exploring athletic opportunities (Côté, 1999; Fredricks & Eccles, 2005). Should their children choose to pursue competitive athletic careers, parents often dedicate considerable emotional and material support to their children's athletic goals (Wylleman & Lavallee, 2004; Wolfenden & Holt, 2005). Evidence suggests parents can become strongly involved in their children's athletic careers and experience emotions ranging from tremendous joy and pride to frustration, disappointment and anger, sometimes impacting their marital, familial, social and financial relationships (Côté, 1999; Dorsch, Smith, & McDonough, 2015; Kerr & Stirling, 2012).

An equally substantial body of research has examined the retirement experiences of athletes, particularly high-level competitors from collegiate, national, Olympic and World Championship levels who commit years to their athletic pursuits (Allison & Meyer, 1988; Blinde & Greendorfer, 1985; Svoboda & Vanek, 1982; Werthner & Orlick, 1982). Early theories adapted from thanatology, the study of death and dying (Rosenberg, 1982), and social gerontology, the study of ageing (Blinde & Greendorfer, 1985; Schlossberg, 1981), were discarded in favour of transition models (Taylor & Ogilvie, 1994; Wylleman, Reints, & DeKnop, 2013) that define athletic retirement as a process that takes place over time starting as early as years prior to athletes' actual withdrawal from sport. Many researchers have since examined athletic retirement through the components of Taylor and Ogilvie's framework (Carapinheira, Mendes, Carvalho, Torregrossa, & Travassos, 2018).

In summary, considerable research has documented parents' experiences from the start through the height of their children's athletic careers and athletes' retirement experiences. Comparatively much less is known about the intersection of these two, that is, the experience of parents as their children withdraw from sport. With only a handful of exceptions, the

114 *Patricia Lally and Richard Lally*

literature has overlooked the experiences of parents as they and their children adjust to life without competition. The purpose of this chapter is to synthesise the available literature on three related but distinct topics: parents' perceptions of their children's transition out of competition, parents' role in their children's withdrawal from sport and parents' own experiences with athletic retirement.

Parents' Perceptions of Their Children's Athletic Retirement Experiences

The majority of the athletic retirement literature has examined the athlete's own perspective (Carapinheira et al., 2018; Lally, 2007; Roberts, Mullen, Evans, & Hall, 2015). In fact, much of this literature has been based on first-hand accounts from athletes primarily retrospectively, although several prospective accounts are available. Carapinheira and his colleagues (2018), for example, conducted retrospective, semi-structured interviews with 90 male Portuguese former elite football players, Warriner and Lavallee (2008) seven international female gymnasts and Roberts and his co-authors (2015) nine male professional cricketers, while Lally (2007) conducted prospective interviews with seven high-level athletes from various sports as they approached and progressed through athletic retirement. This literature has provided incredible insight into the lived experiences of athletes as they navigate the athletic retirement process.

Several studies have extended this line of inquiry to consider an alternative view of athletes' retirement experiences, that of their parents. As central figures in their children's athletic careers including its final stages and because many athletes retire at relatively young ages before they establish permanent residences of their own, parents often witness their children's withdrawal and can provide valuable depth to our understanding of the withdrawal transition.

An important objective of the athletic retirement literature has been to examine the quality of the retirement transition. First-hand accounts from athletes suggest withdrawal can be difficult (Brewer, Van Raalte, & Linder, 1993; Stambulova, 2003; Taylor & Ogilvie, 1994) and parents agree (Brown, Webb, Robinson, & Cotgreave, 2019). When asked to describe their children's emotions following their retirement, many parents observed their children struggle with feelings of void, loss, frustration and anger (Brown et al., 2019; Lally & Kerr, 2008). Parents of elite gymnasts indicated their daughters struggled with several post transition physical challenges such as chronic pain, weight gain, as well as psychological challenges including loss of identity and lack of purpose (Lally & Kerr, 2008).

A prominent theme in the career termination research has been the impact of withdrawal on athletes' self-identities in particular. Researchers have documented both significant disruption to athletes' sense of self and prolonged periods of redefinition (Adler & Adler, 1991; Brewer et al., 1993;

Cavallerio, Wadey, & Wagstaff, 2017; Cecić Erpič, Wylleman, & Zupančič, 2004; Cosh, LeCouteur, Crabb, & Kettler, 2012; Kerr & Dacyshyn, 2000; Sparkes, 1998). Lavallee and Robinson (2007), for example, reported the gymnasts in their study prematurely committed to the athlete identity and felt helpless and lost when they retired. Parents concur that their children suffer significant disruption to their self-identities (Brown, Webb, Robinson, & Cotgreave, 2018; Brown et al., 2019). Parents have described watching as their children wrestle with reshaping their identities—letting go of their athlete selves, redefining their relationship with their physical selves and connections to their sports, and searching for new purpose (Lally & Kerr, 2008).

Athletes likewise experience significant disruption to their social identities. For many athletes, their peers are almost exclusively teammates and other athletes, and they are typically perceived by others primarily through their athlete roles (Brewer et al., 1993; Danish, Petitpas, & Hale, 1993; Lally, 2007). This changes dramatically when they retire. Athletes report feeling they no longer belong in their former athletic circles, yet as they try to develop new social connections, they continue to be defined by others through their athlete personas (Lally, 2007). Parents disclosed seeing their children in this social limbo—no longer belonging to their sport circles but unable to shed the public persona of athlete (Brown et al., 2019). Parents felt this exacerbated their children's transition out of sport and development of ties with groups that could reinforce emerging non-athlete regular person or "NARP" identities.

Parents' assessment of their children's readiness for transition from competitive sport is noteworthy. Parents have remarked their children did not seem to be prepared for the process of retiring (Brown et al., 2018). They observed few had done any meaningful pre-retirement planning (Brown et al., 2018) and, in some cases, felt they had either intentionally chosen not to do so or been actively discouraged by coaches and their clubs from doing so on the basis it would distract from their athletic goals. This is consistent with research with athletes and coaches (Lavallee & Robinson, 2007; Park, Lavallee, & Tod, 2012).

Some parents felt the difficult nature of athletic retirement combined with the intentional deferral of pre-retirement planning on the part of the athlete themselves and/or their coaches and clubs left athletes unprepared to cope effectively with such momentous life changes. Further, parents criticised the lack of any formal or informal assistance for athletes. Whilst some athletes were satisfied with the level of contact with former coaches or happy they no longer controlled their lives, some felt cut off. And, both athletes and parents criticised the lack of formal programming from coaches, clubs, organisations and governing bodies (Brown et al., 2018; Clowes, Lindsay, Fawcett, & Knowles, 2015; D'Angelo, Reverberi, Gazzaroli, & Gozzoli, 2017). This angered parents who felt their children, seemingly overnight, no longer mattered to the sport community to which they had given

116 *Patricia Lally and Richard Lally*

so much of themselves. These findings parallel athletes' accounts of being abandoned, isolated and forgotten by their coaches and clubs (Brown & Potrac, 2009; Clowes et al., 2015).

Parents' Role in Their Children's Withdrawal From Competitive Sport

As noted earlier, many athletes characterise their withdrawal from sport as a difficult process that takes place over months, even years, often marked by feelings of loss, void, anger and confusion (Brewer et al., 1993; Sparkes, 1998; Taylor & Ogilvie, 1994). During this time, parents provide various forms of support (Kadlcik & Flemr, 2008; Sinclair & Orlick, 1993). Parents gave emotional comfort and empathy, often times just being someone to talk to or a shoulder to cry on (Clowes et al., 2015). In fact, Brown and colleagues (2019) noted emotional and psychological support was the most common form of support parents provided following athletic retirement. Brown and colleagues (2019) also noted parents sometimes helped athletes interpret the meaning of the strong, sometimes unfamiliar feelings that surfaced during their transition.

In addition to providing significant emotional guidance, parents often also provided much-needed material support, including financial resources, living accommodations and employment (Kadlcik & Flemr, 2008). Research indicates parents also often provided educational and career guidance. A small number of studies have found pre-retirement career planning amongst athletes (Brown et al., 2018; Clowes et al., 2015; Lally & Kerr, 2005), but the majority of competitive athletes do not actively explore educational or vocational options prior to withdrawing from high-level sport (Alfermann, Stambulova, & Zemaityte, 2004; Lavallee, 2007). This means it is often one of the first challenges athletes encounter in their post-retirement lives. Parents were one of the primary sources of career exploration and advice. Some parents described assisting with routine employment tasks such as writing cover letters and resumes and checking job posting sites (Brown et al., 2019). More importantly, however, was helping their retired children identify educational and career interests that could replace their athletic ones.

This task of helping retired athletes explore their educational and career interests was part of a larger role parents played in helping athletes establish new lives beyond sport. This included helping the former athletes identify short- and long-term goals, develop new relationships as access to their sport-related social networks and friendships faded (Clowes et al., 2015) and negotiate new connections with their physical selves, their sports and their sport networks. Parents' involvement in their children's retirement transitions was particularly important, given the lack of formal transition programmes for retiring athletes noted earlier (Carapinheira et al., 2018; Roberts et al., 2015).

Although parents were often one of the primary sources of social support for athletes as they withdrew from sport, this support was not always ideal or infinite. Some athletes have reported not receiving the support they needed from their parents (Fortunato & Marchant, 1999; Lagimodiere & Strachan, 2015). Likewise, some parents described feeling ill-prepared for this particular role, not knowing what to say or do to help their children. Unlike one father who had been a competitive athlete and had an experienced firsthand a retirement of his own, some parents acknowledged they did not completely understand what their children were going through and did not know how to communicate with them as they tried to navigate their withdrawal from sport and the transition that followed (Brown et al., 2019). Parents described sadness, disappointment and guilt about the manner in which they helped their children during this period (Brown et al., 2019). Others characterised having to help their children through this period as a burden from which they sometimes expressed a need to escape. In a study by Brown and his colleagues (2019), a parent, for example, disclosed starting a new sport of her own in order to get some time away from the stress and pressure of being her retired child athlete's primary source of support. Brown and his colleagues suggested parents may have found it difficult to constantly support athletes navigating the athletic retirement process while undergoing a transition of their own.

Parents' Personal Experiences With Transition

It is reasonable to anticipate parents, particularly those who had invested heavily in their children's athletic careers, would also face changes as their children withdrew from sport. Indeed, we know from Lally and Kerr (2008) that parents served not only as witnesses of their children's athletic retirement, but underwent their own transitions. Parents of retired elite athletes interviewed by Brown and his colleagues (2019) described going through a retirement transition distinct from their child's and acceded that their child's never-ending transition sometimes meant a never-ending transition of their own marked by intense emotional reactions including anger, sadness and worry.

One of the most prevalent retirement transition models in the athlete retirement literature is Taylor and Ogilvie's Conceptual Model of Adaptation to Retirement (1994). Although there is comparatively less literature that examines the transition experiences of parents as their child athletes exit competitive sport, that which is available can be examined within the framework of Taylor and Ogilvie's model.

Causes of Athletic Retirement

The model begins with the causes of career termination where a distinction is made between voluntary and involuntary forms of athletic retirement.

118   *Patricia Lally and Richard Lally*

Research with athlete populations has consistently found withdrawal from sport was more difficult when it was unpredictable or uncontrollable due to, for example, injury or non-selection (Clowes et al., 2015; Martin, Fogarty, & Albion, 2014). Research with parents has not been consistent. Lally and Kerr (2008) determined parents did not seem to be affected by the cause of their daughters' exit from elite-level gymnastics. Their reactions did not meaningfully differ whether their child made the decision to retire after attaining their goal of competing in the Olympic Games or retired involuntarily after not being selected for an Olympic team. Lally and Kerr suggested the predictability or controllability of retirement, although a significant factor for athletes, may not be relevant to parents and recommended additional research. Brown and his colleagues (2019) subsequently examined parents' experiences with their children's athletic retirement and found parents were more distressed when their children's withdrawal was unforeseen or uncontrollable. This was particularly the case when their children were given no forewarning or input in the decision of coaches and/or clubs/organisations to "cut" the athlete or go in a different direction. Given the varied findings, additional research exploring the impact of the causes of athletic retirement on parents' experiences should be pursued.

Factors Related to Adaption to Retirement

Developmental Experiences

Taylor and Ogilvie (1994) suggested one's developmental experiences could help mitigate the effects of athletic retirement. Having to manage or cope with former life events could provide individuals the resilience necessary to successfully navigate subsequent changes such as disengagement from athletic competition. Ample research supports Taylor and Ogilvie's assertion with athlete populations (for review, see Knights, Sherry, & Ruddock-Hudson, 2016).

While this question has not been posed specifically with regard to parents and coping with their child's athletic retirement, it does seem warranted to assert previous life experiences, including education, employment, marriage and childrearing, would play a role in parents' adaptation to athletic retirement as a life change. It is likely parents who have experienced a retirement of their own—athletic, career—would be prepared to manage the transition associated with their child's disengagement from competitive sport. It also stands to reason that parents of high-level athletes in particular, having faced the many challenges that accompany assimilation into the culture of elite sport such as extensive training and travel requirements, significant emotional, financial and time commitments, and incredibly demanding coaches and clubs/organisations (Kerr & Stirling, 2012), would be equipped to cope with their later departure from it. Research examining the impact of developmental experiences of parents on the quality of their adaptation to both their children's and their own withdrawal from sport is recommended.

Self-Identity

Like their children, one of the transition challenges parents face is having to establish new identities (Brown et al., 2019; Lally & Kerr, 2008). For many years, parents had been closely involved in the athletic careers of their children and had developed identities as parents of successful competitive athletes (Baillie & Danish, 1992; Brewer et al., 1993; Cecić Erpič et al., 2004). Much of the research on athletic retirement has referred to either the loss of the athlete role or the loss of the athlete identity or both interchangeably (Brewer, 1993; Brewer et al., 1993; Cosh et al., 2012; Kerr & Dacyshyn, 2000; Sparkes, 1998). This is problematic as the athlete role and athlete identify are not the same construct. It is the persistence of the athlete identity but loss of the athlete role through which it is actualised that precipitates the identity crisis that can mark the retirement process. The retired competitor still sees themselves as an athlete but no longer has the same role through which to express it. In parallel terms, parents lose the role of being the parent of an elite athlete—no more practices or competitions, interaction with coaches, affiliated recognition or engagement with the sport community—yet still see themselves as the parents of elite athletes. Much like their child athletes, parents have to adjust their self-identities. The limited research suggests parents initially struggle but navigate redefining their identities more easily than their athlete children over the long term (Lally & Kerr, 2008). It may be, for example, that parents had made comparable adjustments to their identities across their lifespan—from high school student to college student, for example, or from single to married to married with children—and were, therefore, developmentally more prepared for another identity shift. Additional research comparing the identity redefinition of athletes and their parents following athletic career termination is warranted.

Control

The three primary causes of withdrawal—ageing, injury and deselection—highlight the often-involuntary nature of one's exit from competitive sport. The athletic retirement literature has consistently illustrated athletes fare worse when they exit from competitive sport is out of their control (see Park et al., 2013, for a review). We have already seen parents' responses based on the cause of their child's withdrawal from sport are mixed. Yet, we know of no research that has examined parents' perceptions of their personal control in the retirement phase of their child's athletic career. Parents in Lally and Kerr's (2008) study discussed losing control of their daughters to

120 *Patricia Lally and Richard Lally*

coaches during their gymnastic careers but did not assess parents' degree of control in their career termination. Likewise, parents studied by Brown and colleagues (2019) discussed a lack of control with regard to the post-withdrawal transition, but not necessarily specifically with regard to the cessation of their children's athletic careers. It is possible parents of high-level athletes who have already largely relinquished control to coaches across their child's engagement with the sport world do not experience a sense of lack of control during the child's removal from it. More work is needed here.

Available Resources

Social Support

Social support has been identified as any important factor in the quality of an athlete's withdrawal from competitive sport (Brown et al., 2018). Researchers have documented the role of social support from coaches, both the abundance and lack thereof, as well as social support from teammates, trainers and others including, of course, parents (see Park et al., 2013, for a review).

Research has not specifically assessed the role of social support in parents' adjustment to their child athletes' disengagement from sport. Evidence does indicate parents experience a change in their social networks, which may provide some insight into their social support during this transition period. With no reason to be at practices or games/events, parents found themselves disconnected from their immediate peer group. Lally and Kerr (2008) noted parents of former gymnasts talked about missing their friends at the gym, what one gymnastics' mom described as "one big family." Another mom from the same study who also described her gymnastics social network as a "close-knit" group said she had understood these relationships were connected to their kids and would fade when they retired.

Parents had developed strong personal relationships with other sport parents and sport figures and, by extension, may not have developed equally strong or extensive social networks outside sport. Parents adjusting to their child's athletic retirement do seem to seek social support from their spouses. The parents of former elite gymnasts described reconnecting with their spouse and exploring new shared interests after an initial period of awkwardness (Lally & Kerr, 2008).

Tertiary Contributions

Taylor and Ogilvie (1994) presumed that personal, social and environmental factors including socioeconomic status, ethnicity and gender may also contribute to the quality of an athlete's adaptation to athletic retirement. It is likely the same applies to parents. Factors such as employment status and

Understanding Parents' Experiences With Athlete Retirement 121

familial dynamic may impact parents' responses to the changes their child's athletic retirement initiate. It may be, for example, that working parents had less time to become fully immersed in their child's athletic pursuits and navigated the athletic retirement transition more easily than those who did. It is also possible, for example, that family structure plays a role in that parents who have younger children actively engaged in competitive sport or other interests may not see their older child's exit as their own retirement from sport yet. Future research should consider the role of relevant tertiary factors in parents' athletic retirement experiences.

Quality of Retirement

The athlete retirement literature indicates many athletes navigate the athlete retirement process well and transition to new roles and interests without hugely disruptive emotional and psychological distress (Allison & Meyer, 1988; Baillie & Danish, 1992; Perna, Ahlgren, & Zaichkowsky, 1999; Perna, Zaichkowsky, & Bocknek, 1996). But this is not true of all athletes. Researchers estimate between 20% and 60% of athletes experience significant distress during their withdrawal from sport (Taylor & Ogilvie, 1994; Werthner & Orlick, 1982).

There is too little research on the retirement experiences of parents to provide an estimate of how many cope well with the change and how many struggle. The limited research with parents confirms they do experience a retirement transition of their own and that there are some beneficial outcomes, such as more time to themselves and closer relationships with their spouses and other children. Spouses enjoyed the opportunity to reconnect with one another and identify new shared interests, although they initially grappled with changes to schedules and finding new topics of conversation. Likewise, parents found themselves with more time to spend with their other children and their athletic and other pursuits.

Two different patterns with regard to the relationships between parents and the retired child athlete appeared in the literature. Some parents found they actually grew much closer to their children as they became their child's primary source of social support during the child's athletic retirement process (Brown et al., 2018; Clowes et al., 2015). As the parents helped their children make sense of the changes happening in their lives, they engaged in lengthy, personal and often very difficult discussions. Some parents described their relationships were "closer and stronger" (Brown et al., 2019) as a result of going through the withdrawal process together.

Conversely, the parents in Lally and Kerr's (2008) study anticipated they would get to spend more quality versus perfunctory (observing in stands, waiting during practice, mandatory volunteer hours) time with their daughters, yet found they had less time with them. As their daughters explored new interests including attending college and connecting/reconnecting with NARP peers, parents found they did not see their daughters as much

122 *Patricia Lally and Richard Lally*

as they had hoped. These parents found they had to adjust to life without both their daughters and the gymnastics community.

The other major factor that influenced the quality of the parents' transition was the regret over some of their parenting decisions throughout their child's athletic careers. The bulk of research to date has involved parents of elite athletes—national, Olympic and World Championship levels. By nature, careers that reach these levels are replete with sacrifices by athletes, their parents and their families (Côté, 1999). Upon reflection in the months and years following their children's withdrawal from sport, parents expressed some concern about these sacrifices and the role they played in facilitating them as their children progressed through increasingly competitive levels (Kerr & Stirling, 2012; Lally & Kerr, 2008). Lally and Kerr (2008) found parents of elite female gymnasts had lingering doubts about the long-term physical costs of chronic pain and injuries and the impact of their daughters' prolonged singular focus on gymnastics on their lives including their peer socialisation and their educational and vocational maturation.

Parents also expressed concern over their daughters' treatment by coaches across their athletic careers and their failure to intervene. Looking back, some parents reported worry and regret over their failure to question verbally and physically abusive coaching practices (Lally & Kerr, 2008). In their study of parents' experiences with abusive coaches, Kerr and Stirling (2012) categorised participants' experiences into five phases of socialisation across their children's athletic careers beginning with talent identification. In the second phase, relinquishing control, some parents were troubled with the degree of control assumed by coaches. This is intensified in the next phase as their children grappled with coaches' high demands and sometimes severe coaching practices. Parents described feeling trapped between protecting their children and risking their children's dreams of competing at the highest levels by questioning their coaches. In the final phase that followed their children's retirement, parents' appraisal of coaches' behaviour was much more negative. In hindsight, parents recognised they gave up too much control to coaches who were often physically and mentally abusive to their daughters. Their guilt, remorse and self-doubt were extremely distressing. It is possible parents processing feelings of guilt and regret have more difficult or prolonged retirement transition experiences than parents without these recriminations. Comparative work in this area is needed.

Implications for Practice

The emotional and psychological distress that marks the athletic retirement experiences of some athletes and the related maladaptive coping responses including substance abuse and risk behaviour seen amongst athletes prompted some researchers and practitioners to develop interventions for athletes (Taylor & Ogilvie, 1994). These included programmes designed to help athletes examine their educational and vocational interests both within (i.e. coaching) and beyond sport, and develop long-term financial plans. Programmes have expanded and can be found in many clubs and organisations at the high school, college, national, professional and international levels (Hattersley et al., 2019), although the degree to which these are used by athletes has been questioned (Brown et al., 2018; Clowes et al., 2015).

There is no evidence of formal interventions for parents. In fact, the paucity of data on the experiences of parents and notably partners suggests little attention is paid to the retirement experiences of parents and other sport figures from a research or applied perspective. That is, there does not appear to be any pre- or post-retirement interventions for parents struggling to adapt to their own transition following their child's disengagement from sport. And, as noted earlier, parents often leave the sport setting and their sport social support network as soon as their children retire, precluding an exchange of ideas regarding how to manage withdrawal from sport between parents who have gone through it and those about to. This highlights the need for both additional research on the athletic retirement experiences of parents and other sport figures, as well as the need to introduce pre- and post-retirement support initiatives for parents and important others.

Conclusions

The purpose of this chapter was to synthesise the limited literature specifically examining the impact of athletic retirement on parents with the related but more robust transition literature and athlete development literature to cultivate a better understanding of parents' experiences with the last phase of their children's athletic careers, their transition out of competitive sport. Emphasis was placed on parents as the central figures in the athletic retirement process rather than as secondary ones. While parents' perceptions of athletes' experiences with disengagement from sport parallel the athletic retirement literature, much less is known about parents' personal transitions with athletic retirement. This chapter highlighted several key areas that warrant additional research, as well as the need for both pre- and post-retirement interventions for parents, particularly of high-level competitive athletes.

References

Adler, P., & Adler, P. (1991). *Backboards and blackboards: College athletes and role engulfment.* New York: Columbia University Press.

Alfermann, D., Stambulova, N., & Zemaityte, A. (2004). Reactions to sport career termination: A cross-national comparison of German, Lithuanian, and Russian athletes. *Psychology of Sport and Exercise, 5,* 61–75.

124 Patricia Lally and Richard Lally

Allison, M., & Meyer, C. (1988). Career problems and retirement among elite athletes: The female tennis professional. *Sociology of Sport Journal, 5,* 212–222.

Baillie, P. H., & Danish, S. J. (1992). Understanding the career transition of athletes. *The Sport Psychologist, 6*(1), 77–98.

Blinde, E., & Greendorfer, S. (1985). A reconceptualization of the process of leaving the role of competitive athlete. *International Review for Sociology of Sport, 20,* 87–93. https://doi.org/10.1177/101269028502000108.

Brewer, B. W. (1993). Self-identity and specific vulnerability to depressed mood. *Journal of Personality, 61,* 343–364.

Brewer, B. W., Van Raalte, J. L., & Linder, D. E. (1993). Athletic identity: Hercules' muscles or Achilles heel? *International Journal of Sport Psychology, 24,* 237–254.

Brown, C. J., Webb, T. L., Robinson, M. A., & Cotgreave, R. (2018). Athletes' experiences of social support during their transition out of elite sport: An interpretive phenomenological analysis. *Psychology of Sport and Exercise, 36,* 71–80. https://doi.org/10.1016/j.psychsport.2018.01.003

Brown, C. J., Webb, T. L., Robinson, M. A., & Cotgreave, R. (2019). Athletes' retirement from elite sport: A qualitative study of parents and partners' experiences. *Psychology of Sport and Exercise, 40,* 51–60. https://doi.org/10.1016/j.psychsport.2018.09.005

Brown, G., & Potrac, P. (2009). 'You've not made the grade, son': Deselection and identity disruption in elite level youth football. *Soccer and Society, 10,* 143–159. http://dx.doi.org/10.1080/14660970802601613

Carapinheira, A., Mendes, P., Guedes Carvalho, P., Torregrossa, M., & Travassos, B. (2018). Career termination of Portuguese elite football players: Comparison between the last three decades. *Sports, 6,* 155. https://doi:org/10.3390/sports6040155

Cavallerio, F., Wadey, R., & Wagstaff, C. (2017). Adjusting to retirement from sport: Narratives of former competitive rhythmic gymnasts. *Qualitative Research in Sport, Exercise and Health,* 1–13. doi:10.1080/2159676X.2017.1335651

Cecić Erpič, S. C., Wylleman, P., & Zupančič, M. (2004). The effect of athletic and nonathletic factors on the sports career termination process. *Psychology of Sport and Exercise, 5,* 45–59. https://doi.org/10.1016/S1469-0292(02)00046-8

Clowes, H., Lindsay, P., Fawcett, L., & Knowles, Z. (2015). Experiences of the pre- and postretirement period of female elite artistic gymnasts: An exploratory study. *Sport and Exercise Psychology Review, 11,* 4–21.

Cosh, S., LeCouteur, A., Crabb, S., & Kettler, L. (2012). Career transitions and identity: A discursive psychological approach to exploring athlete identity in retirement and the transition back into elite sport. *Qualitative Research in Sport, Exercise and Health, 5,* 1–22. https://doi.org/10.1080/2159676X.2012.712987

Côté, J. (1999). The influence of the family in the development of talent in sport. *The Sport Psychologist, 13,* 395–417. doi:10.1123/tsp.13.4.395

D'Angelo, C., Reverberi, E., Gazzaroli, D., & Gozzoli, C. (2017). At the end of the match: Exploring retirement of Italian football players. *Journal of Sport Psychology, 26,* 130–134.

Danish, S., Petitpas, A., & Hale, B. (1993). Life development intervention for athletes: Life skills through sports. *Counseling Psychologist, 21,* 352–385. doi:10.1177/0011000093213002

Dorsch, T. E., Smith, A. L., & McDonough, M. H. (2015). Early socialization of parents through organized youth sport. *Sport, Exercise, and Performance Psychology, 4*(1), 3–18. https://doi.org/10.1037/spy0000021

Understanding Parents' Experiences With Athlete Retirement   125

Fortunato, V., & Marchant, D. (1999). Forced retirement from elite football in Australia. *Journal of Personal and Interpersonal Loss*, *4*, 269–280. https://doi.org/10.1080/1081144990840

Fredricks, J., & Eccles, J. (2005). Family socialization, gender, and sport motivation and involvement. *Journal of Sport & Exercise Psychology*, *27*, 3–31. doi:10.1123/jsep.27.1.3

Hattersley, C., Hembrough, D., Kaseem, K., Picken, A., Maden-Wilkinson, T., & Rumbold, J. (2019). Managing the transition into retirement from sport for elite athletes. *Professional Strength & Conditioning*, *53*, 11–16.

Kadlcik, J., & Flemr, L. (2008). Athletic career termination model in the Czech republic: A qualitative exploration. *International Review for the Sociology of Sport*, *43*, 251–269. http://dx.doi.org/10.1177/1012690208098544

Kerr, G., & Dacyshyn, A. (2000). The retirement experience of elite, female gymnasts. *Journal of Applied Sport Psychology*, *12*, 115–133. https://doi.org/10.1080/10413200008404218

Kerr, G., & Stirling, A. (2012). Parents' reflections on their child's experiences of emotionally abusive coaching practices. *Journal of Applied Sport Psychology*, *24*, 191–206. https://doi.org/10.108/10413200.2011.608413

Knights, S., Sherry, E., & Ruddock-Hudson, M. (2016). Investigating elite end-of-athletic-career transition: A systematic review, *Journal of Applied Sport Psychology*, *28*, 291–308. doi:10.1080/10413200.2015.1128992

Lagimodiere, C., & Strachan, L. (2015). Exploring the role of sport type and popularity in male sport retirement experiences. *Athletic Insight*, *7*, 1–18.

Lally, P. (2007). Identity and athletic retirement: A prospective study. *Psychology in Sport and Exercise*, *8*, 85–99. http://dx.doi.org/10.1016/j.psychsport.2006.03.003

Lally, P., & Kerr, G. (2008). The effects of athlete retirement on parents. *Journal of Applied Sport Psychology*, *20*, 42–56. doi:10.1080/10413200701788172

Lally, P. S., & Kerr, G. (2005). The career planning, athletic identity and student role identity of intercollegiate student-athletes. *Research Quarterly for Exercise and Sport*, *76*, 275–285.

Lavallee, D. (2007). Theoretical perspectives on career transitions in sport. In D. Lavallee & P. Wylleman (Eds.), *Career transitions in sport: International perspectives* (pp. 1–27). Morgantown, WV: Fitness Information Technology.

Lavallee, D., & Robinson, H. K. (2007). In pursuit of an identity: A qualitative exploration of retirement from women's artistic gymnastics. *Psychology of Sport and Exercise*, *8*, 119–141. https://doi.org/10.1016/j.psychsport.2006.05.003

Martin, L. A., Fogarty, G. J., & Albion, M. J. (2014). Changes in athletic identity and life satisfaction of elite athletes as a function of retirement status. *Journal of Applied Sport Psychology*, *26*, 96–110. https://doi.org/10.1080/10413200.2013.798371

Park, S., Lavallee, D., & Tod, D. (2013). Athletes' career transition out of sport: A systematic review. *International Review of Sport and Exercise Psychology*, *6*, 22–53. https://doi.org/10.1080/1750984X.2012.687053

Perna, F. M., Ahlgren, R. L., & Zaichkowsky, L. (1999). The influence of career planning, race, and athletic injury on life satisfaction among recently retired collegiate male athletes. *The Sport Psychologist*, *13*, 144–156.

Perna, F. M., Zaichkowsky, L., & Bocknek, G. (1996). The association of mentoring with psychosocial development among male athletes at termination of college career. *Journal of Applied Sport Psychology*, *8*, 76–88.

126 *Patricia Lally and Richard Lally*

Roberts, C. M., Mullen, R., Evans, L., & Hall, R. (2015). An in-depth appraisal of career termination experiences in professional cricket. *Journal of Sports Science, 33,* 935–944. doi:10.1080/02640414.2014.977936

Rosenberg, E. (1982). Athletic retirement as social death: Concepts and perspectives. In N. Theberge & P. Donnelly (Eds.), *Sport and the sociological imagination* (pp. 245–258). Texas: Texas Christian University Press.

Schlossberg, N. K. (1981). A model for analyzing human adaptation to transition. *The Counseling Psychologist, 9,* 2–18. https://doi.org/10.1177/001100008100900202

Sinclair, D. A., & Orlick, T. (1993). Positive transitions from high performance sport. *The Sport Psychologist, 7,* 138–150.

Sparkes, A. C. (1998). Athletic identity: An Achilles' heel to the survival of self. *Qualitative Health Research, 8,* 644–664.

Stambulova, N. (2003). Symptoms of a crisis-transition: A grounded theory study. In N. Hassmén (Ed.), *SIPF Yearbook* (pp. 97–109). Örebro: Örebro University Press.

Svoboda, B., & Vanek, M. (1982). Retirement from high level competition. In T. Orlick, J. Partington, & J. Salmela (Eds.), *Mental training for coaches and athletes* (pp. 166–175). Ottawa: Coaching Association of Canada.

Taylor, J., & Ogilvie, B. (1994). A conceptual model of adaptation to retirement among athletes. *Journal of Applied Sport Psychology, 6,* 1–20. doi:10.1080/10413209408406462

Warriner, K., & Lavallee, D. (2008). The retirement experiences of elite female gymnasts: Self-identity and the physical self. *Journal of Applied Sport Psychology, 20,* 301–317. doi:10.1080/10413200801998564

Werthner, P., & Orlick, T. (1982). Retirement experiences of successful Olympic athletes. *International Journal of Sport Psychology, 17,* 337–363.

Wolfenden, L., & Holt, N. (2005). Talent development in elite junior tennis: Perceptions of players, parents, and coaches. *Journal of Applied Sport Psychology, 17,* 108–126. doi:10.1080/10413200590932416

Wylleman, P., & Lavallee, D. (2004). A developmental perspective on transitions faced by athletes. In M. Weiss (Ed), *Developmental sport and exercise psychology: A lifespan perspective* (pp. 503–524). Morgantown, WV: Fitness Information Technology.

Wylleman, P., Reints, A., & Knop, P. (2013). A developmental and holistic perspective on athlete career development. *Managing High Performance Sport,* 159–182. https://doi.org/10.4324/9780203132388

Part III

Contextual Insights From Global Sports

10 The Next Logical Step? An Examination of Elite Athletes' Transitions Into Post-Athletic High-Performance Coaching Roles

Alexander D. Blackett, Adam B. Evans, and David Piggott

Introduction

The trend of elite athletes retiring from competitive sport and moving into high-performance coaching roles is now widespread across many sports (Mielke, 2007). When reviewing the background credentials of most elite and successful coaches across men's or women's sport, experience as a former competitive athlete can quite easily be identified as a regular and seemingly important theme (Barker-Ruchti, Lindgren, Hofmann, Sinning, & Shelton, 2014). Indeed, a high-performance coach not possessing a prior competitive-athletic career is rare (Kelly, 2008). Subsequently, for athletes considering a post-athletic career when approaching retirement, the historical and cultural acceptance of this pathway has resulted in the transition into a coaching position to be regarded as the 'next logical' step to follow. As highlighted later in this chapter, the career trajectory between athlete and coach has been regarded by the athletes themselves, fellow coaches and senior sports club directors to not only be a logical progression but one that is seamless. These perspectives have been mirrored by empirical research that has analysed coach development pathways. The coach pathway models that have been created have thus represented the transition between athlete and coach in what can be best described as a functionalist attitude on account that such transitions are unproblematic (Christensen, 2013).

Perceptions of a logical and seamless transition from athlete to coach have even been made by national governing bodies (NGBs) of sport and their respective coach education programmes. Increasingly, many NGBs now offer bespoke coach education programmes for current and former high-performance athletes. Within the UK's elite sporting circles, these are regularly referred to as 'senior pros' courses (see Blackett, Evans & Piggott, 2018, 2020). These courses accelerate the athlete to coach transition further through affording current and former senior professional athletes with concessions to register onto higher level coaching qualifications without

130   *Alexander D. Blackett, Adam B. Evans, and David Piggott*

having acquired the lower entry-level qualifications. Such accreditation is necessary for entry into a high-performance environment and has led to the perception that elite athletes are 'fast-tracked' into high-performance coaching roles (McMahon, Zehntner, McGannon, & Lang, 2020), a luxury not afforded to aspirant high-performance coaches without a competitive-athletic tenure (Rynne, 2014).

Yet, counter to this assumption, both current affairs news stories and scholarly research have recently begun to report how the onset of retirement from an elite competitive-athletic career is a difficult transition for individuals to negotiate (Crocket, 2014; Jones & Denison, 2017). Although much of this research has approached the subject of athletes' retirement from a psychological discipline, recent studies have also now increasingly used a sociological lens to analyse this issue to explore notions of identity (re)creation. These studies have shed light on the power dynamics attached to the socio-cultural environment, which athletes leaving sport are susceptible to. Theoretical appraisal of these lived experiences has been beneficial for a range of stakeholders in helping to provide more support that contributes to improved experiences for such athletes when transitioning out of sport. Importantly, however, these studies have been significant in helping signpost athletes themselves to a range of cultural issues that they can become ever more attuned to when preparing for life after sport.

This chapter offers an account of a group of men's rugby union and football players based in the United Kingdom who negotiated a 'fast-tracked' career trajectory into a post-athletic high-performance coaching role. This chapter principally draws upon the work of Blackett's (2017) doctoral research whilst referring to published work emanating from this project (e.g. Blackett, Evans, & Piggott, 2017; Blackett et al., 2018; Blackett, Evans, & Piggott, 2019; Blackett et al., 2020). The objective of Blackett and colleagues' analysis was to investigate the lived experiences of the 'fast-tracked' coach pathway phenomenon through a socio-cultural lens. Their research principally sought to identify the social processes, which supported this pathway and how individuals as active social agents negotiated it. Before reporting on the results of their final study, which followed a cohort of current and former elite athletes enrolled on a 'fast-tracked' coach accreditation course in football and rugby union, an overview of Blackett and colleagues' proceeding iterative works offers important contextual background information so that a more complete picture of the group's experiences can be provided.

Based on scant empirical analyses having been conducted on this phenomenon, a Straussian grounded theory methodology was selected for the project to follow. The outcome was to develop a middle-range theory that explained and theorised the career trajectory across the two sports (Corbin & Strauss, 2015). A proceeding theoretical sensitivity phase overviewed coach development studies and the sociological theories that had been utilised in them. Post-positivist theoretical frameworks devised by Erving

Elite Athletes' Transitions Into Coaching Roles 131

Goffman, Pierre Bourdieu and Michel Foucault were found to have been frequently drawn upon to theorise and conceptualise a range of social mechanisms affecting coach efficacy, behaviour and learning for coaches situated across participatory, development and performance contexts. Consequently, these frameworks and their associated concepts acted as 'sensitising concepts' (Bowen, 2006) that guided the framing of data collection and analysis. An abductive research methodology was, therefore, applied to the project, whereby an interplay through constant comparisons with existing theory and new theory grounded amongst the data could be made (Hallberg, 2006).

The theoretical sensitivity phase also critiqued the samples of extant literature in the area of coach learning and development. This identified how published work had largely conducted coach-centric designs for their studies by primarily having sampled coaches on several topics such as their general athletic and coaching experiences and perceptions of coaching efficacy along with coaching knowledge acquisition. Analysis on the wider structural mechanisms associated with coaches' social environments was lacking. For example, key stakeholders like senior club directors and youth academy directors who indirectly and directly supported the fast-track pathway by acting as mentors, facilitators and, ultimately, employers of these coaches had not been analysed. Therein, senior boardroom directors and youth-performance academy directors of elite UK rugby union and football clubs were identified as original theoretical samples to address two overarching questions of (a) why they supported the fast-track pathway by appointing former elite athletes with limited or no coaching experience as head coaches for their respective clubs? and (b) when identifying future coaching talent, how did they facilitate athletes' transitions into coaching within either their respective club's senior team and youth academy environments?

Coach Talent Identification: Key Stakeholder Perspectives

After receiving ethical approval from a University ethics board, a total of 20 white male directors participated in the research and were each interviewed on one occasion. Eight participants resided on the senior boardrooms and thus had central involvement in the selection and recruitment process of appointing head coaches for their club's senior teams (football = three and rugby union = five). Twelve participants were central to the coach recruitment processes for their respective club's youth academy (football = seven and rugby union = eight). Eight participants were themselves former professional athletes in their sports (football = three and rugby union = five).

The results indicated how both sets of directors preferred to appoint former elite athletes as coaches of the senior team or as academy coaches in comparison to appointing external candidates without a competitive-athletic tenure because of two main points: (a) trust and (b) respect. During a

132 *Alexander D. Blackett, Adam B. Evans, and David Piggott*

competitive-athletic career, athletes were subjectively profiled through coach talent identification processes and judged on how *trustworthy* they were to continue upholding each club's principles and values in any future coaching practice. Former elite athletes were judged to be better served in attaining athlete to coach *respect*. The ability to acquire respect was seen to enable a newly appointed coach to quickly, if not immediately, legitimise their positions of authority. For the senior club directors, coaches legitimising their authority and establishing athlete respect were foreseen to best achieve successful on-field team performances and results (Blackett et al., 2017). Academy directors' priority, however, was for coaches to help develop youth players over a longer period in order to progress them into the senior teams, rather than winning matches in the immediate future (Blackett et al., 2019).

For both senior and academy directors, there was a heightened level of cynicism and scepticism on the value NGB coach education courses had in developing their interpretations of necessary skills and knowledge for coach efficacy. This is because the priority of reproducing a club's culture and values through coaching practice was not seen to be something that was imparted within these contexts and was the central reason as to why they held less value in the minds of these key stakeholders. Such sentiments signified how the senior club directors, therefore, acted as cultural intermediaries and "arbiters of taste" in valorising skills and knowledge attached to their club's cultural fields (Blackett et al., 2017, p. 755). Hence, Bourdieusian concepts of capital, habitus, field and practice were applied to theorise these interpretations and illuminate the socio-cultural issues for such coaching appointments.

To promote the acquisition of field-specific coaching skills and knowledge valued by clubs, current senior players were actively encouraged and mandated as part of their contractual obligations to fulfil coaching roles within their club's community programmes and youth academy settings. Experience in these environments offered athletes an initial coaching apprenticeship, an important setting that has been frequently reported to be part of elite coaches' pathways (Watts & Cushion, 2017). These apprenticeships acted as important socialisation processes as they were laden with cultural messages so prospective coaches would begin to embody the club's values to then be practiced in future coaching roles. The remit of the academy directors was to proactively facilitate these forms of learning through covert socialisation practices. Blackett et al. (2019, p. 91) defined the role of an academy directors as one that reprised a "cultural governor," as they discursively imparted coaching knowledge aligned to the club's values and culture onto novice coaches.

Theorisation of the social processes enacted by academy directors in this instance aligned more to Foucauldian disciplinary concepts of control, surveillance, normativity and docility. That is, academy directors acted as significant figures in disciplining athletes' developing coaching knowledge

Elite Athletes' Transitions Into Coaching Roles   133

and practice to correspond with their respective academy's, and importantly, their club's overarching 'club culture.' The mechanisms enacted here by the academy directors promoted subjected knowledge by tightly controlling what coaching knowledge and practices these prospective coaches acquired. By recruiting coaches internally in this way was viewed to minimise any potential disruption so the status quo of the club's culture of coaching and playing philosophies would remain. The advantage of recruiting academy coaches who had an existing affiliation with the club through a playing career was, therefore, founded on perceived greater levels of conformity. This was because these individuals were judged to have already previously been socialised and thus more willing to accept the club's culture towards coaching and playing styles that reflected each club's collective identity.

By ascertaining some of the broader structural aspects that contribute to supporting the 'fast-track' pathway in rugby union and football, Blackett et al. (2017, 2019) identified some significant social processes and mechanisms that support athletes' transitions out of sport and into post-athletic coaching roles. Yet after investigating the thoughts from key stakeholders, the criticism that these perceptions were overtly deterministic and reductive was applicable. Therefore, the requirement to ascertain whether those experiencing this pathway conformed or resisted these normative club values when negotiating the transition out of sport and into a coaching role was important.

Following Athletes' Transitions Into Post-Athletic Coaching Roles

The project's following iteration purposefully sampled fifteen current and former elite male athletes in the sports of rugby union (n = 10) and football (n = 5). Following ethical approval, each participant was interviewed on two separate occasions over a 12-month period (Blackett, 2017; Blackett et al., 2018, 2020). The objective here was to progressively follow the cohort (a) who was still actively competing in sport but planning for a future high-performance coaching role or (b) who had just retired from a competitive-athletic career and who was in the process of becoming high-performance coaches. All participants were recruited on account that they were at the time of invitation beginning their enrolment on a level three coach qualification in rugby union or football. Only current or former elite athletes were eligible to enrol onto these courses. Eligibility criteria onto these courses did not require the candidates to possess any prior entry-level qualifications such as level one and two coach accreditations. Interviews were conducted at the start and end of the courses. Table 10.1 outlines the participants' characteristics in further detail.

As Table 10.1 indicates, Calvin was the only participant who remained as a full-time competitive athlete at the point of the second interview, with all

Table 10.1 Competitive-athletic career characteristics and coaching roles of participants at each interview (adapted from Blackett, 2017)

Sport	Pseudonym	Highest athletic level (international/domestic club representation)	Length of competitive athletic career (years)	Employment status at interview one (part time or full time)	Employment status at interview two (part time or full time)
Rugby	Sonny	Full International/ Premiership	12	Premiership athlete (FT)	PT voluntary school assistant coach
	Henry	U20 International/ Championship	4	Championship athlete (FT)	Championship athlete (PT) but also FT college team coach
	Casper	Full International/ Premiership	18	Adult semi-professional head coach (PT)	Adult semi-professional head coach (PT—same club as interview one)
	Rory	Full International/ Premiership	8	Adult semi-professional joint head coach (PT)	Unemployed/unattached coach
	Conrad	Full International/ Premiership	13	Professional coach (FT)	Professional coach (FT—same club as interview one)
	Calvin	Full International/ Premiership	8	Championship athlete (FT)	Premiership athlete (FT)
	Mark	Premiership	15	Adult semi-professional coach (PT)	Adult semi-professional coach (PT—same club as interview one)
	Greg	Championship	11	Semi-professional player-coach (PT)	Coach (FT—different club as interview one)
	Billy	Full International/ Premiership	15	Professional coach (FT)	Professional coach (PT—same club as interview one)
	Connall	Premiership	14	Director of rugby at semi-professional level (PT) and coach at Premiership club (PT)	Coach at Premiership club (PT—same club as interview one)

Football	Kieran	Premier League	16	Youth academy coach (FT)	Youth academy coach (FT—different club to interview one)
	Eamon	Championship	18	Youth academy coach (PT)	Youth academy coach (PT—same club as interview one)
	Tim	U20 International/ Premier League	14	Youth academy coach (FT)	Youth academy coach (FT—same club as interview one)
	Owen	U21 International/ Championship	18	Professional athlete and youth academy coach (PT)	Non-league adult assistant coach (FT—same club as interview one)
	Stuart	Full International/ Premier League	15	Under 21 &18 assistant coach at Premiership club	Premiership U21 head coach (FT—different club as interview one)

136 *Alexander D. Blackett, Adam B. Evans, and David Piggott*

other participants having transitioned into a post-athletic coaching career, albeit with varying degrees of success.

Results

In contrast to previous coach pathway models, this chapter identified multiple trajectories when transitioning into post-athletic coaching roles. Importantly, not all participants felt that they had successfully navigated entry into a high-performance coaching role either, but instead were still partway on this pathway. Some participants encountered what can be considered as fluent and seamless transitions, whereas others had faced difficulties that had somewhat disrupted their transitions in either acquiring or retaining a post-athletic coaching role. Although there were some similar themes across the sample that can contribute to the development of a middle-range theory, there were differences between sports but also within sports. Shared characteristics and themes for the transition are first reported. The discussion then culminates by being framed around the theme of identity (re)creation as this was a significant theme grounded in the data.

Active and Passive Coach Pathways

During their competitive playing careers, all participants were encouraged to fulfil minor coaching roles within either their club's youth academy settings or community departments. These were informal, ad hoc in nature and did not have any significant responsibilities attached to them (Blackett et al., 2018). These opportunities were created by the club hierarchy, serving to provide the athletes with an introduction to coaching whilst offering the hierarchy an opportunity to profile prospective coaching talent. Hence, these initial coaching roles were categorised as 'introductory coaching roles' and, for some of the participants, acted as a catalyst to pursue further, more formalised coaching roles.

From this point, two categories of coaching pathways were identified in the form of 'active' and 'passive' pathways (Blackett et al., 2018). Active pathways represented individuals who throughout their competitive-athletic careers had intentionally, and by their own accord, accumulated both entry-level coaching qualifications and direct coaching experience to help them prepare for their retirement and transition into a coaching post. These coaching experiences were classified as 'first formalised coaching roles.' They were intentional commitments alongside their athletic careers rather than a continuation of the ad hoc forays working with academy teams or contractual obligations to work within the clubs' community programmes imposed by their club's key stakeholders (e.g. senior and academy directors). Out of the ten rugby union participants interviewed, seven were classified as having undertaken an active pathway along with two of the five football participants. Those classified as having undertaken

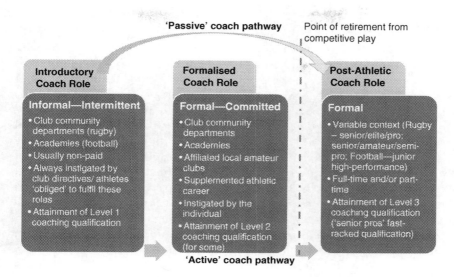

Figure 10.1 Distinction between 'active' and 'passive' coach pathways (Blackett et al., 2018)

a passive pathway had neither their own self-initiative sought additional coaching experiences nor any entry-level coaching qualifications. Consequently, only those coaches who were recorded to have followed a passive coach pathway were considered to have undertaken a 'fast-tracked' career trajectory like that as described by Rynne (2014). Figure 10.1 illustrates the two pathways.

The reason why more rugby union participants followed an active coach pathway was because of financial constraints compared to their footballing counterparts. The lower salaries as a rugby union player compared to those available in football meant that many of the rugby union participants felt they had to occupy dual careers where their coaching pay would supplement their athletic pay. Footballers, on the other hand, could afford to (a) not have to supplement their playing salaries with extra coaching work nor did they necessarily need to proactively prepare for life after being an athlete, or (b) if they were interested in coaching, then they could voluntarily work within their youth academies rather than seek out additional paid coaching roles (Blackett et al., 2018). Nevertheless, mirroring the results from the previous studies when interviewing the directors (Blackett et al., 2017, 2019), the locations of where the majority of participants' first formalised coaching roles were located whilst they were still playing, or when they had retired form a competitive-athletic career was an interesting theme. This highlighted the importance of establishing and maintaining social networks and is the theme that the following section outlines.

Club Attachment of Coaching Destinations: Significant Others Offering Roles

Apart from two rugby union participants (Henry and Casper), the remaining thirteen participants had been offered a first formalised coaching role by the same club they had once represented as a professional athlete. None of the participants had to formally apply or be interviewed for these positions. It was key stakeholders labelled as 'significant others' who offered these roles (Blackett et al., 2018). For eight of the participants (football = two and rugby union = eight), these roles were located within the *last* club they were contracted to as a player. This trajectory was categorised as a 'continuation' pathway whereby the internal transition from athlete to coach was followed within their last club. For the other five participants (football = three and rugby union = two), these roles were at the *first* club they had professionally been contracted to as a player. This was categorised as a 'boomerang' pathway, like a child returning to the parental home after graduating from university. Both pathways are illustrated in Figure 10.2. Two participants' pathways deviated, however, from these two categorisations. Henry began coaching a tertiary education team. This team was one Henry had previously represented as an athlete prior to obtaining a professional contract elsewhere. Thus, Henry's pathway shared similarities with the boomerang pathway, but unlike the others, Henry's first formalised coaching role was not attached to a professional club. Casper, therefore, was the anomaly, as he obtained a coaching position with a club that he had not previously represented, nor did he have any prior affiliation with.

None of the participants reported any awareness that these clubs had performed any subjective modes of coaching talent identification processes and were therein strategically recruiting current and former athletes in coaching posts as a result. From an agential perspective, underlying reasons why the first and last clubs were preferable destinations to begin the transition into coaching were pragmatic ones, like being close to their home locations. Yet additional factors such as familiarity with the club environment concerning the institutionalised social capital regarding relationships with

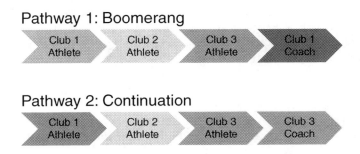

Figure 10.2 Categories for destination of first formalised coaching role

staff and players were important. Familiarity with the ephemeral features of coaching and playing philosophies associated with the overarching club cultures acted as more significant incentives though (Blackett et al., 2020). Prior socialisation in these settings meant that the participants had subconsciously embodied these external club values onto their own internal selves. As such, the alignment of these structural and agential values meant these clubs were deemed sanctuaries where the novice coaches could establish and then consolidate their developing coaching identities (Blackett, 2017). A preference was evident for returning to a previous club rather than going to a new environment to begin creating a new coaching identity. The following section conceptualises this theme further and reports the difficulties encountered by some of the participants in balancing these values with their strengthening coaching identities.

Creating a 'Coach Identity' From an 'Athlete Identity'

The successful transition into a post-athletic coaching role was principally based on the perception of (re)creating their identities from that of an 'athletic identity' into a 'coach identity.' Upon starting a new coaching role, either by returning to a previous club or by continuing with an existing club, the need to quickly consolidate a coaching identity through defining a 'coaching philosophy' was seen to be of central importance (Blackett et al., 2020). This process, however, was not a fluent and seamless process for many participants. Having an existing affiliation with the club, its players and fellow coaches meant that separating themselves and (re)creating an identity away from their previous athletic identities brought tensions. When beginning a new post-athletic coaching role, the common perception held by the cohort was that coaches should possess more authority (Potrac, Jones, & Armour, 2002). This subconsciously influenced their attitudes towards how they should act and behave as a coach differently to how they behaved as an athlete (Cushion & Jones, 2014). When attempting to present a new coach identity that exhibited more authority but was alternative to their athletic identities though, this resulted in feelings of dishonesty by way of them perceiving to have been presenting a coaching 'front' or façade. Unlike other studies on coaching expertise that has highlighted the benefit of employing multiple identities in the act of coaching (e.g. Consterdine, Newton, & Piggin, 2013), these novice coaches judged dishonesty to be the principal feature of coaches either quickly losing their athletes' respect or never gaining it.

Negotiating this problematic issue initiated deep and meaningful reflexive processes on how to overcome this in a mode corresponding to Foucault's (1997) askesis and ethic of self-care. Here the novice coaches reflected on their own values, but also began to reflect on how they had folded the external club values like coaching and playing philosophies. They had begun to turn subconscious knowledge into consciousness.

140 *Alexander D. Blackett, Adam B. Evans, and David Piggott*

In conjunction with everyday experiences of practicing within their club environments, the 'senior pros' courses instigated this level of reflexivity. It is on this point where some of the participants began to either contest or conform to their club's cultures and ideologies towards coaching and playing styles. The experiences of those that did contest the club culture were negative and resulted in them losing their coaching position and then having to depart the club. At the time of the second interview, Greg (rugby union) along with Stewart and Kieran (football) had gained new coaching roles at alternative clubs to those they had previously been with at the time of the first interview. Rory was unattached and continued to seek a club to coach (see Table 10.1). Irrespective of whether they had followed an active or passive coaching pathway, after being profiled and then supported into these post-athletic coaching roles, these four coaches by the time of the second interview had explicitly rejected and contested their clubs' coaching ideologies towards coaching and playing philosophies. By undertaking these conscious actions meant that they had not become docile in accepting the overarching club ideologies as the previous iterations had suggested. It is here where Bourdieu's habitus development can be critiqued in accordance with its overtly reductive and deterministic nature. Rather, in these four instances, Foucault's concepts of askesis and ethic of self-care offer a more relational conceptualisation of power by indicating the agential capabilities to employ their own reflexive strategies for creating their own 'coaching identity' (Blackett et al., 2020).

For the other eleven participants, there too was a conscious recognition that they complied with the club culture and its methods of playing and caching philosophies. This level of consciousness was not present at the first interview; however, these cultural tensions had been brought into consciousness and reflected upon 12 months later during the second interview, which coincided with the culmination of their level three 'senior pros' course. The justification for why coaches complied was because either they agreed with the overarching philosophy or they simply wanted to avoid jeopardising their career after recognising the micropolitical environment in which they practiced within. Many of those who had accepted their respective club cultures had come to regard their newly created coaching identity to be a fixed construct whereby they had already consolidated their perceptions, philosophy and identity towards coaching. Those who had contested the club cultures, however, were more likely to regard their coaching identity as a fluid entity: they considered the journey to coaching efficacy to be the destination, likely to change through further education, experience and reflection (Jacobs, Claringbould, & Knoppers, 2016).

Implications for Practice

The project sought to understand the processes and lived experiences of elite athletes supposedly being fast-tracked into high-performance coaching

Elite Athletes' Transitions Into Coaching Roles   141

roles within men's rugby union and football. Importantly, the pathways undertaken by the cohort were not one dimensional as has been previously reported. Some of the cohort followed a fast-tracked career trajectory into a post-athletic coaching role. Others meanwhile had invested significant time and effort in accumulating both formalised coaching experiences and qualifications when actively preparing for a post-athletic coaching career (see Figure 10.1). This pathway did not represent a fast-tracked route. Nonetheless, the limitations of this study are that there is no suggestion as to which pathway led to more coaching success. Recommendations for future research would benefit by employing further longitudinal research by continuing to follow such coaches over a greater duration of their careers to ascertain the outcomes of each pathway.

The project's findings have implications for both the individual athletes transitioning into post-athletic coaching roles along with the structural support mechanisms such as coach education systems and the coach talent identification processes. Firstly, for the individual athletes, the lessons learnt by the participants in this study signify that there were advantages and disadvantages for becoming consciously aware of the structural and cultural issues that covertly influenced and shaped their coach learning. Consciously reflecting on the club's cultures (i.e. their ideologies towards coaching and playing strategies) resulted in these four individuals losing their first post-athletic coaching jobs. The acquisition of this new knowledge, along with the understanding of how to critically appraise existing norms, was, therefore, disadvantageous to a degree because their actions resulted in job losses. Interestingly though, these four participants claimed that these decisions were beneficial as they viewed this as having made them better coaches in the long term. In their eyes, questioning their current club's coaching dogma, then departing for a new club and experiencing different coaching and playing styles made them more rounded coaches. These coaches all had a fluid attitude towards the development of their coaching identities. In so doing, they seemed to be open and eager to avoid reproducing and recycling existing coaching and playing styles. This itself can be a positive as it prevents toxic coaching practices from being recycled (McMahon et al., 2020) or for outdated styles of play to be unquestionably socially reproduced (Denison, Mills, & Konoval, 2017).

From a coach development perspective, if coaching knowledge and practices are to continually advance, then reliance of former athletes transitioning into high-performance coaching roles, fast-tracked or not, is dependent upon not uncritically reproducing the doctrine of club's coaching cultures and ideologies. Should the career transition between elite athlete and high-performance coach persist, however, then the benefits of current elite athletes acquiring experiences from other cultural fields (i.e. other clubs and sports) to broaden their horizons and assist their abilities to critique the status quo of their current club's ideologies is recommended. Even if this helps strengthen their acceptance of their club's approaches to coaching and playing, this can help these athletes more quickly consolidate their emerging coaching identities. Finally, recommendations can be made about the potential difficulties of transitioning into a coaching role with a club that individuals had previously represented, either through a boomerang or through continuation pathway. Balancing tensions between maintaining relationships with friends who continue to play, but who are now being coached by those beginning their coaching careers, was problematic. It was a strain exhibiting and sustaining authority whilst retaining these relationships, as was negotiating new relationships with fellow coaches and line managers such as academy directors and/or senior directors.

The research findings can also inform the structural support mechanisms such as how coach education and learning processes are designed to support these novice coaches along with the key stakeholders categorised as significant others such as senior directors and academy directors. For example, when most research on coach development and learning report coaches to not value formal coach education courses (e.g. Piggott, 2012; inter alia), after initially holding some resentment towards the 'senior pros' course at the beginning, the study's participants did come to value them by the end. Therefore, if it is important for elite athletes to extend their coaching experiences and learning away from their present clubs, then, in some instances, NGB coach education course is the only avenue for offering this. By shortening these courses, accelerating current and former elite athletes through these courses therein seems counter-intuitive if further critical appreciation of coaching is to be conducted. In so doing, then hopefully the consolidation of a coaching identity can be made, one that is continually developing rather than being a fixed entity.

References

Barker-Ruchti, N., Lindgren, E.-C., Hofmann, A., Sinning, S., & Shelton, C. (2014). Tracing the career paths of top-level women football coaches: Turning points to understand and develop sport coaching careers. *Sports Coaching Review, 3*(2), 117–131. doi:10.1080/21640629.2015.1035859

Blackett, A. D. (2017). *Understanding the 'fast-track' transition between elite athlete and high-performance coach in men's association football and rugby union: A grounded theory* (Doctoral dissertation). University of Lincoln, UK. Retrieved from http://eprints.lincoln.ac.uk/id/eprint/28658/

Blackett, A. D., Evans, A. B., & Piggott, D. (2017). Why 'the best way of learning to coach the game is playing the game': Conceptualising 'fast-tracked' high-performance coaching pathways. *Sport, Education and Society, 22*(6), 744–758. doi:10.1080/13573322.2015.1075494

Blackett, A. D., Evans, A. B., & Piggott, D. (2018). "Active" and "passive" coach pathways: Elite athletes' entry routes into high-performance coaching roles. *International Sports Coaching Journal, 5*(2), 213–226. doi:10.1123/iscj.2017-0053

Blackett, A. D., Evans, A. B., & Piggott, D. (2019). "They have to toe the line": A Foucauldian analysis of the socialisation of former elite athlete into academy coaching roles. *Sports Coaching Review, 8*(1), 83–102. doi:10.1080/21640629.2018.1436502

Elite Athletes' Transitions Into Coaching Roles   143

Blackett, A. D., Evans, A. B., & Piggott, D. (2020). Negotiating a coach identity: A theoretical critique of elite athletes" transitions into post-athletic high-perfor mance coaching roles. *Sport, Education and Society*. (Advance online publication). doi:10.1080/13573322.2020.1787371

Bowen, G. A. (2006). Grounded theory and sensitizing concepts. *International Journal of Qualitative Methods, 5*(3), 1–9. doi:10.1177/160940690600500304

Christensen, M. K. (2013). Outlining a typology of sports coaching careers: Paradigmatic trajectories and ideal career types among high-performance sports coaches. *Sports Coaching Review, 2*(2), 98–113. doi:10.1080/21640629.2014.898826

Consterdine, A., Newton, J., & Piggin, S. (2013). 'Time to take the stage': A contextual study of a high performance coach. *Sports Coaching Review, 2*(2), 124–135. doi :10.1080/21640629.2014.908626

Corbin, J., & Strauss, A. (2015). *Basics of qualitative research: Techniques and procedures for developing grounded theory* (4th ed.). Thousand Oaks, CA: Sage.

Crocket, H. (2014). I had no desire to be having this battle with this faceless man on the soccer field anymore: Exploring the ethics of sport retirement. *Sociology of Sport Journal, 31*(2), 185–201. doi:10.1123/ssj.2012-0109

Cushion, C. J., & Jones, R. L. (2014). A Bourdieusian analysis of cultural reproduction: Socialisation and the 'hidden curriculum' in professional football. *Sport, Education and Society, 19*(3), 276–298. doi:10.1080/13573322.2012.666966

Denison, J., Mills, J. P., & Konoval, T. (2017). Sports' disciplinary legacy and the challenge of 'coaching differently'. *Sport, Education and Society, 22*(6), 772–783. doi:10.1080/13573322.2015.1061986

Foucault, M. (1997). The ethics of the concern of the self as a practice of freedom. In P. Rabinow (Ed.), *Ethics: Subjectivity and truth (essential works of Michel Foucault, 1954–1984)* (pp. 281–301). New York: New York Press.

Hallberg, L. R. (2006). The "core category" of grounded theory: Making constant comparisons. *International Journal of Qualitative Studies on Health and Well-Being, 1*(3), 141–148. doi:10.1080/17482620600858399

Jacobs, F., Claringbould, I., & Knoppers, A. (2016). Becoming a 'good coach'. *Sport, Education and Society, 21*(3), 411–430. doi:10.1080/13573322.2014.927756

Jones, L., & Denison, J. (2017). Challenges and relief: A Foucauldian disciplinary analysis of retirement from professional association football in the United Kingdom. *International Review for the Sociology of Sport, 52*(8), 924–939. doi:10.1177/1012690215625348

Kelly, S. (2008). Understanding the role of the football manager in Britain and Ireland: A Weberian approach. *European Sport Management Quarterly, 8*(4), 399–419. doi:10.1080 /16184740802461652

McMahon, J., Zehntner, C., McGannon, K., & Lang, M. (2020). The fast-tracking of one elite athlete swimmer into a swimming coaching role: A practice contributing to the perpetuation and recycling of abuse in sport? *European Journal for Sport and Society* (Advance online publication). doi:10.1080/16138171.2020.17 92076

Mielke, D. (2007). Coaching experience, playing experience and coaching tenure. *International Journal of Sports Science & Coaching, 2*(2), 105–108. doi:10.1260/174795407781394293

Piggott, D. (2012). Coaches' experiences of formal coach education: A critical sociological investigation. *Sport, Education and Society, 17*(4), 535–554. doi:10.1080/1 3573322.2011.608949

Potrac, P., Jones, R., & Armour, K. (2002). 'It's all about getting respect': The coaching behaviors of an expert English soccer coach. *Sport, Education and Society, 7*(2), 183–202. doi:10.1080/1357332022000018869

Rynne, S. (2014). 'Fast track' and 'traditional path' coaches: Affordances, agency and social capital. *Sport, Education and Society, 19*(3), 299–313. doi:10.1080/1357 3322.2012.670113

Watts, D. W., & Cushion, C. J. (2017). Coaching journeys: Longitudinal experiences from professional football in Great Britain. *Sports Coaching Review, 6*(1), 76–93. doi:10.1080/21640629.2016.1238135

11 Time's Up! Indigenous Australian Sportsmen and Athlete Transitions

Megan Stronach

Cultural Issues in Athlete Transitions

As the various chapters in this book demonstrate, scholarship into the complex subject of athlete transitions has covered a range of sports and athletes and addressed both teams and individuals. However, both academic researchers and sport managers have generally adopted a rather generic and, therefore, largely undifferentiated perspective on the transition needs of elite athletes (Stambulova & Alfermann, 2009). This seems problematic because, as Stambulova and Alfermann put it, 'the universal knowledge about "athletes in general" seems insufficient to explain the behavior of athletes from different cultures' (Stambulova & Alfermann, 2009, p. 292). According to these scholars, both researchers and policymakers have treated athletes who leave sport as socio-culturally similar subjects with common issues of adjustment (Stambulova & Alfermann, 2009). This is a problem as the underlying distinctive social, demographic, and ethno-cultural factors brought to sport by athletes from diverse backgrounds and locations suggests that they will also have a diverse range of needs as they transition to the post-sport career.

Research by Ryba and Stambulova (2013), Stambulova and Alfermann (2009) and others (see chapter 1) indicates that athletes' perceptions of their transitions are infused by their cultures. Therefore, when studying athlete transitions, we should consider cultures in more depth and treat them as discrete contexts with particular sets of characteristics. Stambulova and Alfermann (2009) argued that because people internalise meanings from their cultural contexts, it is impossible to separate their development and behaviour from these frameworks. It is also important, they claimed, to appreciate that cultural context is fairly rigid; it cannot be readily changed by an individual. Thus, to further deepen contemporary understanding of athlete transition, it is important to consider athletes in their group contexts, using approaches that deal specifically with culture-specific differences. In recent years, a handful of researchers have carried out studies with these aims in mind. Many of these are reported in *Athletes' careers across*

146　*Megan Stronach*

cultures (Stambulova & Ryba, 2013), resulting in a deeper understanding of the specific ethno-cultural situations and needs of these athlete groups.

In an Australian context, there has been limited scholarship about adjustment to life after sport of Indigenous athletes—with some literature emanating from medicine, sociology, and sport psychology (Chambers, Gordon, & Morris, 2013; Martin, Fogarty, & Albion, 2014), but little from within sport management (some exceptions being Stronach, 2012; Stronach, Adair, & Taylor, 2014). It comes as something of a surprise that in a country that prides itself on its cultural diversity, the experiences of such an important minority group—Indigenous Australians—are still to be explored.

Conversely, there is considerable interest in the recruitment of Indigenous athletes *into* elite sport as well as support mechanisms to assist them with adjusting to life as full-time professional performers (see, for examples, Light, Evans, & Lavallee, 2019; Nicholson, Hoye, & Gallant, 2011). Consequently, it is now less likely that an Indigenous person will be 'mainstreamed' by sport organisations and treated as 'just another player' without ethno-cultural needs of their own (Light et al., 2019; Nicholson et al., 2011). This reflects the realisation by several sports in Australia that Indigenous athletes have particular ethno-cultural needs upon their recruitment into elite sport. These needs are sometimes met by mentoring from experienced Indigenous sportspeople, based on expectations that Indigenous athletes will have ethno-culturally specific adjustment needs in making the transition from 'rookie' to seasoned performer. In short, the nature and extent of pressures and disciplines associated with professional sport and media attention are typically unfamiliar to Indigenous people, regardless of whether they come from remote, rural, or urban communities. There is, therefore, a clear need for investigations in the Australian context into adjustment to life after sport of Indigenous athletes.

Background

Aborigines and Torres Strait Islanders, the Indigenous peoples of Australia, have societies and cultures that extend over 60,000 years. From the late eighteenth century, however, their traditional way of life was slowly eroded by the impact of European settlement and accelerated during the nineteenth century by the imposition of colonial laws and practices that subjugated and ostracised the original inhabitants. By the turn of the twentieth century, it was widely presumed, at least amongst whites, that Aborigines were a 'dying race'. Indigenous Australians nonetheless survived against great odds, such as their lack of immunity to European diseases, loss of traditional hunting territories, and state-sanctioned policies, allowing the removal of Aboriginal children from their parents and permanent relocation with white families (Reynolds, 2008). In the twenty-first century, Aborigines and Torres Strait Islanders, once the sole custodians of the Australian continent, comprise about 3.3% of the national population. The pernicious legacy of colonialism remains with Indigenous disadvantage evident across virtually every socio-economic indicator. Aboriginal people have, for example, significantly lower life expectancy than other Australians (AIHW, 2019), much higher levels of unemployment (ABS, 2018), considerably lower levels of education and income (ABS, 2018), and are vastly over-represented in the nation's prisons (Korff, 2018). In summary, Indigenous people have a multitude of reasons for feeling disenchanted by and disengaged from Australian society, past, and present.

For a few talented Indigenous athletes, however, sport has provided career opportunities, and in recent decades, Indigenous Australian athletes have become high-profile performers in three major sports (Korff, 2008). As mentioned, Indigenous Australians currently make up about 3.3% of the national population (ABS, 2018), but Australian Rules Football (i.e. AFL), rugby league (i.e. NRL), and boxing feature significant proportions of Indigenous Australian males competing at the elite level. Indeed, they are now statistically over-represented, constituting up to 14% in the football codes alone (Light et al., 2019). These three sports, both in professional and amateur ranks, offer glamour, status, financial reward, and a means of overcoming racism. Boxers have won silver and bronze medals at Olympic Games and produced numerous professional world champions, while footballers have achieved success and recognition at the highest echelons of their codes. Despite this proud history, little is known about the adjustment to life after sport of these athletes.

Identified Issues

Research by Stronach (2012) examined the transition experiences of 30 Indigenous Australian athletes. The focus was the athlete transition process for professional and amateur Indigenous athletes in the AFL, NRL, and boxing and the impact of sport beyond the playing field for these athletes, at a time when they could no longer rely on their physicality to sustain a career. The research has enabled some understanding of the situations and decision-making of these athletes around their transition to the post-sport career. How they move to this next phase of life proved to be a major challenge. Four areas of relevance, unique to this group of athletes, were identified.

The Primacy of Athletic Identity

Over many decades, Indigenous athletes have demonstrated abundant sporting prowess, becoming high-profile performers in Australian sporting culture (Hume & May, 2019; Korff, 2019a). As mentioned earlier, Indigenous Australians represent 3.3% of the national population (ABS, 2018), but are statistically over-represented in each of the three sports in focus here. Whilst these figures were recognised prior to the research, the impact

148 *Megan Stronach*

of this involvement was poorly understood. One outcome was the concept of athletic identity (AI).

AI as a concept is said to be the degree to which an individual identifies with the athlete role and can be defined as 'the degree of importance, strength, and exclusivity attached to the athlete role that is maintained by the athletes and influenced by environment' (Li, 2006, p. 22). The athletic role is an important social dimension of self-concept influencing experiences, relationships with others, and pursuit of sport activity. AI that is strong, but not exclusive, may have lasting psychological benefits for the athlete (Chang, Wu, Kuo, & Chen, 2018). However, athletes who place too much emphasis on sport may experience psychological and physical drawbacks both throughout their career and upon retirement. AI is considered a major factor influencing adjustment to termination from a sport career, and athletes found to be most likely to have career and adjustment difficulties were young males in high-profile and high-income sports, notably the football codes, because of their high levels of AI (Martin et al., 2014).

AI is measured by the Athletic Identity Measurement Scale (AIMS) (Brewer, Van Raalte, & Linder, 1993), and overall, athletes in the study recorded relatively high measures on this scale. Comments from some of the athletes who scored particularly high on the AIMS demonstrated difficulties after sport career termination as well as emotional and social adjustment to post-sport life. For example, David (retired 1997 from AFL) said, 'I lost a lot of confidence, I went into a state of depression—you're going to go from hero to zero'. Similarly, Billy (retired 1989 from professional boxing) lamented, 'it wasn't easy to say goodbye because boxin' . . . was everything'. Brian (retired 1993 from AFL) mourned, 'the loss of that whole environment, your mates, your footy club, the culture . . . the enthusiasm of the fans—you crave the relationship'.

Sport is, from an early age, the only life that many professional and elite Indigenous athletes know. Whilst conventional wisdom indicates that education is the door to economic opportunity, many of the male Indigenous athletes had embraced the idea that sport, not education, was the most viable means of attaining financial security. Generally, as the Indigenous athletes scored high on the AIMS, their educational or vocational interests, which were in conflict with the athletic role, were often sacrificed, or put on hold, until athletic pursuits were settled. Several had left school early or quit education programmes. They felt justified in choosing sport over education, albeit with some regret at having no real academic qualifications at the end of their playing career. In addition, many of the athletes described serious ongoing physical health problems related to their sport careers that were likely to restrict their capacity to work in a physically demanding position for any length of time. With the intense focus on the demands of sport, the athletes also sacrificed other sources of identity and self-fulfilment. Indeed, many athletes' sense of who they were—that is, their self-identity—was closely linked with their sport careers.

The Natural 'Black' Athlete

Sporting acumen has long been a source of pride for many Indigenous Australian people. However, there is a widespread and long-standing stereotypical belief about 'natural' sporting talent and that Indigenous people are 'naturally' suited to competitive sport and 'naturally' talented as performers (Adair & Stronach, 2011; Evans, Wilson, Dalton, & Georgakis, 2015). A typical example of such strong self-belief in 'innate' Indigenous physical abilities was provided by Jerry (retired 1989 from boxing):

> You know yourself, you can go anywhere in Australia, any school in Australia, the best athlete is what? The best sportsman is what? Indigenous people. They're gifted, high fighters, running, speed, more balance, rhythm, timing—they're gifted.

Thirty-three-year-old Alex (retired 2007 from NRL) expressed his conviction about Indigenous people as 'natural' athletes. However, he also hinted at the importance of cultural practice and the strength of familial examples:

> I think it's been passed on. And I mean when you look at a lot of the top athletes, they do have that look and physique of a natural-born warrior. And it's something I think when you look at a lot of the sports that we do are hand-eye, speed, co-ordination, and that comes down I think to our ancestors and our fore-fathers.

Alex was acknowledging the importance of skills handed down from parents and the challenges of growing up in a remote environment, which in its own way necessitated athleticism if food was going to reach the campfire. 'Well', he said, 'the kangaroos didn't jump in our laps!' However, this ongoing belief in the 'innate' abilities of Indigenous athletes fails to acknowledge other motivations at work, such as the incredible will and desire of Indigenous athletes to excel. Nathan (retired 2003 from AFL) expressed his exasperation:

> So you'll get people, you'll get commentators using language like, "Oh, this is magic". So, almost in a mythical sense. Which really irritates us [Indigenous] players, because what it does is saying to everyone else that somehow this is done a lot easier, and so we don't work as hard.

Again, this belief was acknowledged prior to the research, but its impact and relevance were poorly understood. Whilst there is no scientific evidence to support a belief in the so-called innate sporting abilities of Indigenous people, it nevertheless characteristically had the unintended effect of de-emphasising career pathways for Indigenous athletes where intellectual rather than physical capital was a prime requirement. Many of the

150 *Megan Stronach*

Indigenous athletes considered they were not 'naturally' suited to positions of responsibility or decision-making outside sport performance. They resented the lack of Indigenous personnel in administration, coaching, and management, yet few indicated a desire to assume a senior role in their sport.

Economic and Social Capital After Sport

Linked to both points, Indigenous athletes have an intriguing challenge: in sport, they are widely admired for their skills and talent, yet when retired from the playing field or boxing ring, they may struggle to preserve economic or social capital (Stronach, 2012; Stronach et al., 2014). This suggests that their time in sport, and indeed planning for life beyond it, is likely to be particularly challenging.

Over one-third of the participants in the study had not completed secondary education; others lacked vocational qualifications, and several of them had few social contacts outside sport. What was seen was a small range of career choices, invariably underpinned by their desires to give back to their own communities and other Indigenous people. Generally speaking, the post-sport career aspirations of the group were limited to occupations that complemented either their physicality or particular Indigenous cultural values. The most common choices were as follows:

- Indigenous sport programmes/mentoring
- Community coach/personal trainer
- Youth/community work

Critically, the figures indicated that 18 (or 58.1%) of the men did not see a career outside sport at all, with 7 choosing to work in Indigenous sport programmes, and 11 selecting a career in community coaching or personal training. A further seven (or 25.8%) of the athletes saw their futures fully engaged with Indigenous community, youth, and welfare programmes. This situation is suggestive of what has been called identity foreclosure (Brewer & Petitpas, 2017), where individuals make commitments to roles without considering alternatives.

The athletes' belief that a normal career progression was linked to community development was described by Johnny (retired 2009 from AFL). He described a profound belief in his role as an Indigenous man:

> I believe I'm put here to help more Indigenous people. In what role and capacity, that's where it comes in the next five or ten years, and that's what I'm working on at the moment. There's another side of me that wants to do some other stuff in communities, and basically use my profile to get things done, I suppose. But in the end—put it down—I'm here to help.

Time's Up! Indigenous Australian Sportsmen   151

Working in remote and dysfunctional Indigenous communities has noble intentions, but the practicality of turning such activity into a career is fraught with difficulties, and such a commitment may be detrimental to the economic well-being of ex-athletes themselves. Few community support roles generate much (or indeed any) income, and there is little prospect, from within that environment, for further opportunities for professional development. Indeed, there have been very few opportunities for Aboriginal people, within sport, for post-athletic employment. The coaches, administrators, marketers, media commentators, and so on are overwhelmingly from non-Indigenous backgrounds. Life after sport can also be difficult for Indigenous athletes who come from rural or remote communities and wish to return, for there is often limited employment in such regions. Many retired footballers and boxers want to give 'something back' to their communities and thus act as mentors, but often lack the skills to know how to make a difference.

Racism and Racialisation in Australian Sport

Indigenous Australian athletes face the persistent prospect of racism and racialisation in Australian society. Racism used to be an endemic part of on-field sport, but since racial vilification rules were introduced into Australian sports in the mid-1990s, athletes are probably more likely to face bigotry and discrimination outside the playing field or boxing ring (Korff, 2019b; NASCA, 2019). The implication, therefore, is that Indigenous athletes, during their time in the spotlight, may be somewhat shielded from excesses of racism as a consequence of their celebrity status, yet their time in that bubble is finite.

In 2000, Aboriginal researcher Darren Godwell (2000) argued that Indigenous males are at risk of being typecast in life as being good at sport, with social myths and racial stereotyping limiting the range of life and career possibilities that could be available to them. Jerry (retired 1989 from boxing) and Nathan (retired 2003 from AFL) referred to what they perceived to be the 'invisibility' of Indigenous people in team, club, and organisation management positions, arguably a consequence of racialisation and stereotyping. They pointed out that few former players made the career transition to administrative and leadership roles within the multi-million dollar businesses of the AFL or the NRL, or even boxing organisations:

> Every sport in Australia you got a committee, and I'll tell you what, there's hardly no Aborigines on them. No Aborigines, all white people.
>
> (Jerry)

> And how you know that occurs is when you see no AFL Aboriginal coaches, managers, board members and all that, so that the perception

152 *Megan Stronach*

is that they're not accountable. You won't see any . . . well, we've had a few captains, so that helps.

(Nathan)

A deeper issue relating to Indigenous invisibility was discussed by Alex (retired 2007 from NRL). He claimed that Indigenous people are frequently and deliberately overlooked by media and marketing companies and, therefore, denied opportunities that are more likely to be offered to non-Indigenous athletes:

> There's only a small window of opportunity for elite athletes to be able to use their image, and you've got a good manager or company behind you that feel as if they can use your image. I mean you look at a lot of our Olympians that are branded with the multi-vitamins, your sports telecasts—they do have long careers along those paths. A little bit harder for, I think, for Indigenous people. It's always sort of crossed my mind, "why isn't it our people up there?"

A picture emerged of chronic under-representation of Indigenous people in coaching, management, and media that was more significant in the football codes. A normal progression is often from player to coach or manager, but this pathway seems not to be pursued by Indigenous football players, or the younger boxers. In terms of careers after sport, this Indigenous invisibility has the effect of reducing the post-sport career opportunities available to Indigenous athletes. Whilst the underlying reasons for this are complex and not easily fully understood, there were suggestions of a belief (and even an ingrained self-belief) that whilst Indigenous players may perform well on the ground, they are not suitable to lead or manage. This situation highlights the complex way in which racialisation manifests. A double standard emerges, one that asserts that Indigenous players are acceptable but Indigenous managers are not, and one that an absence of Indigenous personalities in the media or in the conference rooms of the football leagues is acceptable.

Athlete Career Programmes

The study of athlete transition amongst Indigenous Australian athletes also examined policies and programmes (where they existed) established by sport organisations. As previously mentioned, key sport organisations now invest heavily in programmes to recruit Indigenous athletes (especially those from rural or remote settings) into elite-level sport, and there are culturally appropriate support mechanisms to assist them with adjusting to life as full-time professionals in urban settings.

The AFL Players' Association (AFLPA), as well as the NRL and Rugby League Players' Association (RLPA), deliver comprehensive programmes

Time's Up! Indigenous Australian Sportsmen   153

to support retiring athletes. These player welfare programmes provide athletes with a range of education and job skill training programmes, as well as access to professional services such as dieticians, sports psychologists, counsellors, and social workers. However, although these programmes are welcome, they have a weakness in that they demonstrate little understanding of ethno-cultural diversity for participants, and, therefore, the potentially varied needs of individuals from diverse backgrounds. This includes, of course, Indigenous athletes. As Ryan and Thorp (2013, p. 158) succinctly put it, 'individually tailored approaches would be far more beneficial than blanket service provision which fails to address athletes' personal sport histories (and futures)'.

Boxers who had been part of the Australian Institute of Sport (AIS) elite boxing squad had received support and career counselling from the Athlete Career and Education (ACE) (Chambers et al., 2013) programme personnel. This is regarded as the industry standard for the management of athlete career and education matters and a framework within which to develop welfare and training services for athletes. Many boxers had encountered Vocational Education and Training (VET) programmes, and indeed, several had commenced the training for their chosen vocation (most often the Certificate III in Fitness or Youth support work) whilst on scholarship at the AIS. Yet, only two had actually completed the training requirements.

Although there are transition programmes in some sports (i.e. the AFL and NRL), others (like professional boxing) have no support mechanism in place (Stronach & Adair, 2010; Stronach et al., 2014). Furthermore, many of the respondents argued that existing career transition programmes, although well intended, do not comprise people with any experience of, or understanding about, the complexities of retirement for Indigenous people. Their connections to wider kinship networks, their wish to engage with often distant communities, and thus their sense of responsibility for a group, rather than just themselves, are not easily communicated to career advisers who work within an individualistic paradigm. Indigenous Australian athletes hold a special set of personal values: pride in their Indigenous heritage, unique kinship and community obligations, and a commitment to support disadvantaged Indigenous people, in a formal or informal capacity. The obligation to give back to family and community was regarded as the natural order of Indigenous men. Several athletes described their own difficult, even dysfunctional family backgrounds, assuming that these experiences imbued them with the skills to provide expert assistance to others in similar situations.

National Sporting Organisations (NSO) such as the Australian Institute of Sport (AIS), the AFL, and the NRL have conventional programmes, but to date there have been no custom-designed programmes to accommodate the needs of cohorts from diverse backgrounds. At the other end of this career sequence, there are athlete transition programmes for athletes, but few involve culturally nuanced support initiatives. This is vitally needed for

154 *Megan Stronach*

marginalised groups like Indigenous people as well as women, differently abled sportspeople, and other CALD groups (Stambulova & Ryba, 2014).

This brief overview suggests that Indigenous Australian athletes are likely to face a complex experience in sport: lauded during their time on the ground or in the ring, but outside that space—particularly once their playing careers are over—they have even bigger challenges.

Implications for Practice

The research (Stronach, 2012; Stronach et al., 2014) provided an opportunity for the voices of 30 Indigenous athletes to be heard and as well garnered information from programme and athlete managers, coaches, and officials. What became clear is that Indigenous athletes have complex needs in terms of preparing for life beyond sport and then transitioning upon the point of retirement.

Elite Indigenous Australian athletes are highly competent and focused individuals who have the opportunity to be seen as exemplars for Indigenous people to enter sport with a wider sense of self and move into other occupational spheres once their sport career is past. But to do this, they need appropriate support and career counselling throughout their athletic careers. Support services available to the athletes during their sport careers had generally been provided by non-Indigenous people. However, Indigenous athletes require culturally appropriate support, and the athletes themselves believed that this support should ideally come from other Indigenous people. Indeed, the athletes themselves expressed a need for Indigenous mentors to help them with their transition experiences. Whilst it may not be feasible, logistically, for all Indigenous athletes around Australia to have access to a counsellor with Indigenous heritage, a base-line position ought to be that personnel involved in Indigenous development and transition programmes undergo education in culturally appropriate ways to engage with athletes of varying cultural backgrounds. This might be usefully supplemented by non-Indigenous sports administrators educated about the nuances of Aboriginal culture, needs, and aspirations in workplace settings.

Areas of need are as follows:

- Encouragement and support from coaches and managers to actually complete VET and other academic programmes
- Support to access a broader range of career pathways, which also complement Indigenous values of 'giving back' to community, such as teaching, health and police work
- For many of the former athletes, community support work will likely remain philanthropic and purely voluntary. However, if Indigenous athletes are provided with appropriate leadership and mentoring skills, such as those provided by the National Aboriginal Sporting Chance Academy

(NASCA), the NRL's 'One Community', or the AFL's 'Flying Boomerang' programmes, it can also be socio-culturally virtuous and 'life-changing'. Leadership training provided in these programmes is valuable and worthy preparation with many potential transferable applications, and similar programmes could be developed by boxing organisations.

- As elite athletes, these athletes have much to contribute to their sports organisations. A normal progression is often from athlete to coach or manager, but this pathway seems not to be pursued by Indigenous athletes. It appears that the cause is nothing to do with potential or ability, but simply to the belief that whilst Indigenous athletes may perform well on the ground or in the ring, they are not suitable to lead, manage, or coach. Therefore, a concerted effort is needed from those in positions of authority to invalidate this stereotypical belief and bring about a shift in attitudes, policies, and practices.

Conclusion

All of these factors mean that Indigenous Australian sportsmen face complex post-sport challenges due to (a) the primacy of their AI, (b) assumptions about their natural acumen as athletes, (c) profound commitments to extended families and communities, and (d) the impact of racialised stereotypes. Athletic retirement is, therefore, likely to be particularly challenging for Indigenous sportspeople in Australia. Consequently, providers of athlete career and education programmes need to develop policies and provide resources that cater for the complex transition needs of Indigenous athletes.

References

Adair, D., & Stronach, M. (2011). Natural born athletes? Australian Aboriginal people and the double-edged lure of professional sport. In J. Long & K. Spracklen (Eds.), *Sport and challenges to racism* London: Palgrave Macmillan.

Australian Bureau of Statistics. (2018). *2076.0 — Census of population and housing: Characteristics of aboriginal and Torres strait Islander Australians, 2016.* Retrieved from www.abs.gov.au/AUSSTATS/Abs@.Nsf/7d12b0f6763c78caca257061001cc5 88/5f17e6c26744e1d1ca25823800728282!OpenDocument

Australian Institute of Health and Welfare. (2019). *Deaths in Australia.* Retrieved from www.aihw.gov.au/reports/life-expectancy-death/deaths/contents/life-expectancy

Brewer, B., & Petitpas, A. (2017). Athletic identity foreclosure. *Current Opinion in Psychology, 16,* 118–122.

Brewer, B., Van Raalte, J., & Linder, D. (1993). Athletic identity: Hercules' muscles or Achilles' heel? *International Journal of Sport Psychology, 24,* 237–254.

Chambers, T., Gordon, S., & Morris, T. (2013). Athletes' careers in Australia. In N. Stambulova & T. Ryba (Eds.), *Athletes' careers across cultures* (pp. 17–30). London and New York: Routledge.

156 *Megan Stronach*

Chang, W. H., Wu, C.-H., Kuo, C.-C., & Chen, L. H. (2018). The role of athletic identity in the development of athlete burnout: The moderating role of psychological flexibility. *Psychology of Sport and Exercise, 39*, 45–51. https://doi.org/10.1016/j.psychsport.2018.07.014

Evans, J., Wilson, R., Dalton, B., & Georgakis, S. (2015). Indigenous participation in Australian Sport: The perils of the 'panacea' proposition. *Cosmopolitan Civil Societies, 7*(1), 53–79.

Godwell, D. (2000). Playing the game: Is sport as good for race relations as we'd like to think? *Australian Aboriginal Studies, 1&2*, 12–19.

Hume, C., & May, C. (2019). Indigenous Australians and sport. *Clearinghouse for Sport and Physical Activity*. Retrieved from www.clearinghouseforsport.gov.au/knowledge_base/organised_sport/sport_and_government_policy_objectives/indigenous_australians_and_sport

Korff, J. U. (2008). Aboriginal indigenous sport. *Creative Spirits*. Retrieved from www.creativespirits.info/aboriginalculture/sport/

Korff, J. U. (2018). Aboriginal prison rates. *Creative Spirits*. Retrieved from www.creativespirits.info/aboriginalculture/law/aboriginal-prison-rates

Korff, J. U. (2019a). Famous aboriginal sportspeople. *Creative Spirits*. Retrieved from www.creativespirits.info/aboriginalculture/sport/famous-aboriginal-athletes

Korff, J. U. (2019b). Racism in aboriginal Australia. *Creative Spirits*. Retrieved from www.creativespirits.info/aboriginalculture/people/racism-in-aboriginal-australia

Li, H. Y. (2006). *Validation of the athletic identity measurement scale with a Hong Kong sample.* (Doctor of Applied Psychology (Sport Psychology)). Victoria University, Melbourne. Retrieved from http://wallaby.vu.edu.au/adt-VVUT/public/adt-VVUT20060918.101003

Light, R., Evans, J., & Lavallee, D. (2019). The cultural transition of Indigenous Australian athletes into professional sport. *Sport, Education and Society, 24*(4), 415–426.

Martin, L., Fogarty, G., & Albion, M. (2014). Changes in athletic identity and life satisfaction of elite athletes as a function of retirement status *Journal of Applied Sport Psychology, 26*(1), 96–110.

NASCA. (2019). Counteracting racism. *The Challenge*. Retrieved from https://nasca.org.au/the-challenge/counteracting-racism/

Nicholson, M., Hoye, R., & Gallant, D. (2011). The provision of social support for elite indigenous athletes in Australian football. *Journal of Sport Management, 25*, 131–142.

Reynolds, H. (2008). *Nowhere People*. Camberwell, VIC: Penguin Books.

Ryan, C., & Thorpe, H. (2013). Athletes' careers in New Zealand (Aotearoa): The impact of the graham report and the carding system. In N. Stambulova & T. Ryba (Eds.), *Athletes' careers across cultures* (pp. 148–159). London and New York: Routledge.

Ryba, T., & Stambulova, N. (2013). Turn to a culturally informed career research and assistance in sport psychology. In N. Stambulova & T. Ryba (Eds.), *Athletes' careers across cultures* (pp. 1–16). London and New York: Routledge.

Stambulova, N., & Alfermann, D. (2009). Putting culture into context: Cultural and cross-cultural perspectives in career development and transition research and practice. *USEP, 7*, 292–308.

Stambulova, N., & Ryba, T. (Eds.). (2013). *Athletes' careers across cultures*. London and New York: Routledge.

Stambulova, N., & Ryba, T. (2014). A critical review of career research and assistance through the cultural lens: Towards a cultural praxis of athletes' career. *International Review of Sport and Exercise Psychology, 7*(1), 1–17.

Stronach, M. (2012). Retirement experiences: The case of elite Indigenous Australian boxers. In P. Sotiaradou & V. De Bosscher (Eds.), *Managing high performance sport.* London: Routledge.

Stronach, M., & Adair, D. (2010). Lords of the square ring: Future capital and career transition issues for elite Indigenous Australian boxers. *Cosmopolitan Civil Societies: An Interdisciplinary Journal, 2*(2), 46–70.

Stronach, M., Adair, D., & Taylor, T. (2014). Game over: Indigenous Australian sportsmen and athletic retirement. *Australian Aboriginal Studies, 2,* 40–59.

12 Transitions in Disability Sport

Jeffrey J. Martin and Eva Prokesova

Introduction

> All the different opportunities that have come my way—that I know never would have happened—and so, overall, it probably has been the best thing that has ever happened to me, just because so much of my life right now, so much of how I see myself, somehow links back to that.
>
> (Hammer et al., 2019, p. 369)

Sport can be an incredibly meaningful element of athletes' lives leading to a strong sense of self-regard and an excellent quality of life (Martin, 2017). This chapter opening quote exemplifies how meaningful being a Paralympian can be. At the elite-level sporting careers are typically short lived (e.g. 5–6 years; Witnauer, Rogers, & Saint Onge, 2007) relative to most non-elite sport careers such as university professors or farmers. Despite the brevity of a professional career athletes have typically trained and competed for many years (e.g. 10–20), often starting in early childhood (e.g. 8 years old). The commitment devoted to sport over such a long time often leads to a strong athletic identity (AI), which can make leaving sport difficult. The adjustment to leaving sport may be particularly challenging for athletes with disabilities and especially elite athletes such as Paralympians. Relative to able-bodied athletes, Paralympians may be forced out of sport for unique reasons such as the classification system or having to deal with injuries that exacerbate their impairments (Bundon, Ashfield, Smith, & Goosey-Tolfrey, 2018; Martin, 2017).

Paralympic sport has become increasingly competitive over the past 10–20 years necessitating increased dedication by potential Paralympians relative to only 5–10 years ago (Martin, 2011). For instance, world records and Paralympic winning times have dropped significantly over the past 20 years (Grobler, Ferreira, & Terblanche, 2015; Lepers, Stapley, & Knechtle, 2014). Whilst a strong AI may make leaving sport difficult, a strong and exclusive AI is particularly problematic. The following quote illustrates how one elite disabled athlete viewed sport retirement:

> I honestly believe it is very closely related . . . as if you were to lose a baby. Just like a miscarriage. It is just the sorrow inside and it is something

Transitions in Disability Sport 159

that you have looked forward to and planned for and boom it is taken away . . . all of a sudden you get back and that focus is gone and guess what . . . so are you basically. If you are not involved in sports anymore you are really nobody—that is exactly how you are treated when you get back.

(Wheeler, Malone, VanVlack, Nelson, & Steadward, 1996, p. 389)

The purpose of this chapter is to update and expand upon earlier work on disability sport and retirement (Guerrero & Martin, 2018; Martin, 1996, 1999, 2000, 2011, 2017; Martin & Wheeler, 2011). We first briefly review able-bodied work that also applies to athletes with disabilities. Second, we provide a fuller discussion of sport-specific retirement research. We pay particular attention to the unique elements of having impairments and the structure (i.e. the classification system) of Paralympic sport that may make leaving sport for athletes with disabilities different from able-bodied sport athlete retirement.

Third, we examine research showing how athletes cope with leaving sport and briefly review institutional support services provided by national organisations. Fourth, we address a recent line of research on social activism by Paralympians and present that work as a vehicle for transitioning out of sport and into a meaningful career or avocation (Braye, 2016; Choi, Haslett, & Smith, 2019; Haslett, Choi, & Smith, 2020; Smith, Bundon, & Best, 2016). Finally, we propose a few future research ideas and note the practical ramifications resulting from our review.

Leaving Sport

Athletes with and without disabilities have much in common and those similarities extend to the challenges of leaving sport (Martin, 2017). Athletes leaving sport have described it as an identity crisis (Hill & Lowe, 1974), a traumatic event (Blinde & Stratta, 1992; Oglivie & Howe, 1982), a role loss (Hill & Lowe, 1974), and career (Blinde & Stratta, 1992) and social death (Lerch, 1982). Factors contributing to emotional problems after leaving sport include a strong commitment to sport, an exclusive AI (Baillie, 1993; Hill & Lowe, 1974; Ogilvie & Howe, 1982; Thomas & Ermler, 1988), and a loss of autonomy and control of personal development during the athletic career (Thomas & Ermler, 1988; McGown & Rail, 1996).

It is important to note that many writers report that most athletes make the transition out of sport successfully (Martin, 2017; Sinclair & Orlick, 1993) and some perceive the transition to post-sport life positively to pursue other life goals (Coakley, 1983). It is not uncommon for some athletes to express relief at not having to cope with the stress of training and competing (Blinde & Greendorfer, 1985; Greendorfer & Blinde, 1985). Nonetheless, leaving sport for some athletes can be emotionally difficult.

Martin (1996, 1999, 2000) and others have suggested that leaving sport may present unique challenges to athletes with disabilities (Makoff, Vanden

Auweele, & VanLandewijck, 1999; Patatas, De Bosscher, Derom, & De Rycke, 2020; Schaeffer & Bergman, 1994; Wheeler, 2003; Wheeler et al., 1996, 1999). Upon retirement, disability sport athletes might have unsolved disability-related emotional issues that they face when they exit sport, resulting in significant emotional distress (e.g. depression). Athletes may also end up with a secondary disability such as an overuse injury (e.g. shoulder tendonitis) from overtraining (e.g. Burnham, May, Nelson, Steadward, & Reid, 1993). Secondary disabilities make coping with the post-sport world difficult. For instance, the functional aspects (e.g. wheeling) associated with activities of daily living (ADLs) may be compromised (Wheeler et al., 1996, 1999). Other authors have suggested that athletes with disabilities may find it particularly challenging to cope with their impairment when they leave sport.

Such challenges may be the result of a rapid transition to Paralympic sport shortly after an acquired disability (Asken, 1989; Wheeler et al., 1996, 1999). For example, sport may help athletes both cope and avoid dealing with disability (Asken, 1989). As a result, upon leaving sport, they may have to cope more overtly with their disability without the support that sport provides (e.g. teammate social support). Research with athletes with disabilities has shown that many athletes view sport as the most important activity in their lives (Wheeler et al., 1996, 1999), a way to demonstrate personal mastery (Mackoff et al., 1999) and an essential part of their personal identity (Wheeler et al., 1996). One athlete reported,

> When we are on the track, I think we don't look at ourselves as disabled. When we're in our racing chair it is like putting on a uniform; it's like you are out of it now; you are out of the disability. It gives you that. It's like putting a Superman vest on.
>
> (Wheeler et al., 1996, p. 388)

However, athletes often neglect other aspects of their lives, such as important relationships, preparing for post-sport life in general and career development (Wheeler et al., 1996, 1999). An athlete in the Wheeler et al.'s (1996) investigation noted,

> I didn't have a balance in my life. That's where all the injuries were' that's where all the emotional and mental turmoil was as well. Because I never allowed myself to do other things, because I had my whole identity wrapped up in athletics.
>
> (Wheeler et al., 1996, p. 388)

Martin (1999) conceptualised the transition experiences of athletes with disabilities in a loss framework. He suggested that athletes with disabilities experience a range of losses including psychological, social, and physiological losses. Psychological losses (e.g. reduced mastery experiences) are

Transitions in Disability Sport   161

associated with a strong AI and self-esteem resulting in the potential for negative (e.g. anger) reactions upon leaving sport. Social losses include loss of teammates and the inability to remain engaged in disability sport (e.g. acting as a coach or administrator). Physiological losses also occur as athletes lose the health and fitness benefits associated with sport and endurance training.

Transition theorists indicate that neglecting important social relationships (e.g. spouse, friend) predicts difficulties with transitioning out of sport (Schlossberg, 1981; Martin, 1996). Wheeler and colleagues found that athletes with disabilities perceived a lack of support from their peer group as well as administrators in their sport organisations after they retired (Wheeler et al., 1996, 1999). Athletes with disabilities who fully commit themselves to sport to the exclusion of important relationships, career interests, and hobbies may be at risk for post-career difficulties such as heightened feelings of loneliness due to reduced team social support.

Researchers in disability sport have identified negative emotional experiences upon leaving sport such as feelings of anger, depression, grief, hollowness/emptiness, sadness, and mourning (Wheeler et al., 1996, 1999; Makoff et al., 1999; Schaefer & Bergman, 1994). Symptoms of depression meeting the criteria for a major depressive episode have been reported retrospectively (Wheeler et al., 1996, 1999). Athletes also report symptoms consistent with unresolved grieving and clinical depression long after they have retired. One athlete reported,

> it's like somebody in your family died. It's like a death in your family and that thing that was this person or whatever that was so important to you just disappeared. I think you go through all the grieving things you do when somebody dies.
>
> (Wheeler et al., 1999, p. 228)

However, consistent with able-bodied research in the area (e.g. Blinde & Greendorfer, 1985), disability sport transition research has also shown that athletes may be excited and happy to leave sport. Athletes often look forward to leaving the stresses and strains of the competitive sport environment behind as well as chronic pain from overuse injuries. Athletes have also reported that the time to enjoy other important aspects of a well-rounded life is also embraced (Wheeler et al., 1996, 1999). For example, one athlete noted,

> It was just knowing, that there were other things out there for me to explore. I was 'into' (getting) a career and I wanted to pursue things differently in my career. . . . I just wanted to explore ordinary life. I wanted to finish school and establish a career. I was ready to move on.
>
> (Wheeler et al., 1996, p. 391)

162 *Jeffrey J. Martin and Eva Prokesova*

The majority of athletes interviewed in the Wheeler et al. (1996, 1999) studies coped well with their daily lives and recalled many poignant and pleasant memories as they left sport. However, others were angry at administrators in sports organisations who they perceived as simply allowing them to slip away from sports. Retirement issues may also have performance ramifications. Martin and Ridler (2014) sought to determine whether retirement status was related to swimmers' performance at the World Championships. Seventeen percent of the athletes considering retiring were within one second of their time goal. In contrast, 45% of the athletes not considering retirement came within one second of their goal. Although the sample was small ($N = 17$), the results point towards a potential conundrum. Athletes may have disinvested in their AI as they contemplated retirement to prepare for leaving sport. However, that same disinvestment in AI may have played a role (e.g. reduced training time) in their poorer performance (Martin & Ridler, 2014). Worries about life after retirement may also have hurt athlete's performance preparation. These speculative explanations await further research.

Unique to Parasport is the phenomena of classification, which also has implications for retirement. In one study of Parasport athletes, a small number of them cited the following reasons for retiring (Bundon et al., 2018): "My classification changed and I was no longer eligible to compete", "My sport or event was eliminated from the Paralympic program", and "My class was eliminated from the Paralympic program". Because such reasons are out of an athletes control, they may be particularly difficult to cope with. In addition, if athlete's perceive that cheating in the classification process, which then leads to retirement, is rampant they may become particularly angry and disillusioned (Sanchez, 2020).

In brief, it is important for coaches, teammates, friends, spouses, sport psychologists, and sport administrators to understand the valuable experiences that sport provides, the importance of sport in athletes' lives, and the challenges they face in leaving sport. As noted earlier, the Paralympics is growing in competitiveness, sophistication, and complexity and the sport demands of athletes are increasing (e.g. increased media attention). It is not clear how this might exacerbate or attenuate any difficulties athletes face in transitioning out of sport. Clearly, helping athletes leave sport is just as important as helping athletes attain excellence whilst in sport (Martin, 2017).

Coping Effectively

A number of factors help athletes cope with leaving sport. Researchers have indicated that athletes need effective coping strategies and strong social support and should engage in retirement planning (Martin, 2011; Martin & Wheeler, 2011). In retirement, maintaining regular physical activity is an important coping strategy as it helps athletes remain fit and healthy.

Social support can also be found in many exercise settings in addition to maintaining contact with former teammates. Maintaining or re-establishing prior non-sport social support mechanisms is also of value. Social support from teammates is an important predictor of life satisfaction (Atkinson & Martin, 2020).

Recent research with high-level wheelchair basketball players and rugby players indicates that the traits such as personality qualities of grit, hardiness, and resilience all predict life satisfaction, suggesting they may be adaptive in helping athletes achieve a good quality of life upon leaving sport (Atkinson & Martin, 2020; Martin, Byrd, Watts, & Dent, 2015). Recent research efforts have suggested that the personality factor of conscientiousness is also related to retirement planning via effective goal-setting practices (Demulier, Le Scanff, & Stephan, 2013).

The following quote indicates that taking on non-athlete sport roles helps athletes cope.

> I began coaching once I had stopped training and cannot recall actually retiring. The coaching filled the void and I didn't miss not competing. This has allowed me to stay involved and still mix with the elite group of players. A lot of these players were young developing players when I was still playing, and I often make comparisons with them and reflect that back to my own career.
>
> (Lavallee, Gordon, & Grove, 1997, p. 137)

Coaches, athletic trainers, physical therapists, and sport psychologists should also be aware of and monitor athlete training workloads closely, and minor injuries should be addressed quickly with appropriate rest in order to avoid chronic overuse injuries. Peer athlete mentors report being optimistic in response to hypothetical scenarios about being helpful to peer mentees in managing their disability and sport. Although indirect, this evidence suggests that retired peer athlete mentors may also help newly retired athletes leave sport (Perrier, Smith, & Latimer-Cheung, 2015). However, peer athlete mentors have also reported struggling with potential mentees who appeared to need mentors with greater counselling skills. This suggests that adequate training is critical for any peer mentor who is thrust into a helping type of relationship. An example of a retirement planning strategy would be career consulting prior to leaving sport. This strategy is particularly important for elite Paralympians who are professional athletes. Leaders of pre-retirement interventions should concentrate on ensuring athletes maintain a diverse social network and engage in activities outside sport. Coaches can also help by speaking with their athletes early in their careers about post-career life.

Because some athletes may struggle when they leave sport, it seems reasonable that retirement programmes are available to Paralympians when they leave sport (Patatas et al., 2020). Psychological services (e.g. preparation for leaving sport) and ongoing support for athletes (Wheeler, 2003) are important elements of effective programmes. The International Paralympic Committee (IPC) career transition programme for athletes started in 2007. By 2009, athletes had access to the Adecco Athlete Career Program, which the International Olympic Committee (IOC) had developed for able-bodied athletes (see http://athlete.adecco.com/ and www.paralympic.org/athletes/career-programme/how). Able-bodied career assistance programmes are fairly common (Stambulova & Ryba, 2013), but research on their effectiveness is sparse. Bobridge and colleagues reported beneficial psychosocial outcomes from a 14-week-long programme that included increased confidence and awareness of the value of planning for the future whilst still actively competing (Bobridge, Gordon, Walker, & Thompson, 2003).

Coaches and sports organisations should consider developing and supporting such programmes so that athletes who are experiencing anxiety prior to or during their transition can be helped. Another important strategy is the provision of opportunities to remain engaged in sport (e.g. coaching). In disability sport, there has been a growing interest in activism in disability sport (Braye, 2016; Bundon & Hurd Clarke, 2015; Smith et al., 2016) and we present that next given that it may have retirement implications.

An activist identity is an individual orientation to be involved in social missions. An activist orientation includes social-political and problem-solving behaviour. Personal involvement in activism can range from passive, low-risk, institutionalised actions to more active, high-risk, unconventional behaviour to bring societal change (Corning & Myers, 2002). People with an activist identity are frequently involved in activities to change society for the better (Bundon & Hurd Clarke, 2015). Athlete activism is also seen when athletes use their visibility as a platform to express their opinions publicly, to raise awareness about social topics (e.g. disability rights, mental health issues, various forms of discrimination), and/or to advocate for social change (Tibbetts et al., 2017).

The Paralympic Games are recognised as the third largest sporting event in the world (Kropielnicki, Rollason, & Man, 2017). Because of the visibility of elite Paralympians, and cultural idolisation, Paralympians have the potential to make important contributions to promote social missions and point out inequities within and outside sport (Braye, 2016; Brittain & Beacom, 2016; Haslett & Smith, 2019; Smith et al., 2016). This enables Parasport athletes to present themselves as not only successful athletes or inspirational speakers but also people with wider social interests and concerns for social justice (Pate, Hardin, & Ruihley, 2014). The IPC also promotes the Paralympic Games as an instrument for disability activism and social change (Brittain & Beacom, 2016) so such efforts by athletes are consistent with the Paralympic institutional goals of activism.

However, it should be noted that some researchers do not perceive Paralympic sport as an optimal platform for disability activism. Braye, Dixon,

Transitions in Disability Sport   165

and Gibbons (2013) indicated that many of their participants (disabled non-athletes) viewed the characteristics and experiences of most people with disabilities as vastly different from a Paralympian, thereby limiting their ability to be effective advocates for all people with disabilities. At the same, however, Paralympians seemed to be criticised for not engaging in more activism. Despite Braye's (2016) concerns, many researchers perceive adapted sport as having potential to promote activism (Goodley, 2016; Martin, 2017; Shakespeare, 2016). Unfortunately, the number of studies in disability sport promoting activism is rather small (Braye, 2016; Bundon & Hurd Clarke, 2015; Haslett & Smith, 2019; Smith et al., 2016).

Nonetheless, researchers have suggested that retired Paralympians find activism meaningful. To promote activism within athletes who are not yet active and engaged, this may be done by narratives of athletes who are already involved in activism. Increasing athlete's social consciousness may prepare them to participate in social change and open up discussions about challenges that activism may present (Smith et al., 2016). Showing current athletes how to be involved in activism in safe ways, how to minimise potential risks, and providing recommendations about how to transfer from an active athletic career to activist retirement would help them make the transition out of sport (Smith et al., 2016).

Future Research

In regard to research directions, we have limited theory-based quantitative work of a longitudinal nature that would make a substantial contribution to the knowledge base. Examining psychological (e.g. coping skills), social (e.g. social support), technological (e.g. the use of Zoom or Skype to facilitate social support), and environmental (e.g. access to exercise facilities) predictors of the transitions to life after sport would be elucidating. Most commentaries on sport retirement are based on the premise that most athletes do not want to leave sport. However, the following quote indicates there are situations where athletes may remain in sport despite wanting to retire:

> I don't think I would have retired unless I had a job 'cause we had a baby so I wouldn't have been able to. I would've carried on doing [my sport] until I had a job or an income so that I could retire. When I was competing I was quite well paid . . . if you're in that position its quite difficult to retire.
>
> (Bundon et al., 2018)

This quote suggests another research question on athletes who wish to retire but feel pressured to continue for monetary considerations. Sanchez (2020) suggests that some athletes may leave Paralympic sport because they perceive that some Paralympians are cheating. Finally, with the 2020

Paralympics unexpectedly postponed due to the worldwide Coronavirus, many Paralympians may be forced to retire for a plethora of, as of yet unknown, potential direct (e.g. injury) and indirect (e.g. geographical relocation due to job loss) reasons. Understanding the unique emotional experiences of leaving sport under these two sets of unique challenges are two final avenues for future research.

Implications for Practice

There are a number of important practical applications resulting from the research we have reviewed. Firstly, athletes should be thinking about and planning for leaving sport long before retirement is eminent. Secondly, coaches, administrators, and sport psychologists should be discussing and helping athletes think about and plan for retirement. Finally, national organisations that lack institutional programmes should put them into place in order to provide guidance and a framework that supports athletes and support staff efforts. Programmes such as the "Heroes of disability sports" provide retired Brazilian athletes a year-long financial stipend to be advocates and publicise the Paralympic Movement. Such programmes may provide models for other national Olympic and Paralympic associations to emulate (Mauerberg-deCastro, Campbell, & Tavares, 2016).

References

Asken, M. J. (1989). Sport psychology and the physically disabled athlete: Interview with Michael D. Gooding, OTR/L. *The Sport Psychologist, 3*, 167–176.

Atkinson, F., & Martin, J. (2020). Gritty, hardy, resilient, and socially supported: A replication study. *Disability and Health Journal, 13*, 100839.

Baillie, P. (1993). Understanding retirement from sports: Therapeutic ideas for helping athletes in transition. *The Counseling Psychologist, 21*, 399–410. doi:10.1177/0011000093213004

Blinde, E. M., & Greendorfer, S. L. (1985). A reconceptualization of the process of leaving the role of competitive athlete. *International Review for the Sociology of Sport, 20*, 87–94.

Blinde, E. M., & Stratta, T. M. (1992). The sport career death of college athletes: Involuntary and unanticipated sports exits. *The Journal of Sport Behavior, 15*, 3–20.

Bobridge, K., Gordon, S., Walker, A., & Thompson, R. (2003). Evaluation of a career transition program for youth-aged cricketers. *Australian Journal of Career Development, 12*, 19–27. doi:10.1177/103841620301200204

Braye, S. (2016). 'I'm not an activist': An exploratory investigation into retired British Paralympic athletes' views on the relationship between the Paralympic games and disability equality in the United Kingdom. *Disability & Society, 31*, 1288–1300.

Braye, S., Dixon, K., & Gibbons, T. (2013). 'A mockery of equality': An exploratory investigation into disabled activists views of the Paralympic games. *Disability & Society, 28*, 984–996.

Transitions in Disability Sport 167

Brittain, I., & Beacom, A. (2016). Leveraging the London 2012 Paralympic games: What legacy for disabled people? *Journal of Sport and Social Issues, 40*, 499–521.

Bundon, A., Ashfield, A., Smith, B., & Goosey-Tolfrey, V. L. (2018). Struggling to stay and struggling to leave: The experiences of elite para-athletes at the end of their sport careers. *Psychology of Sport and Exercise, 37*, 296–305.

Bundon, A., & Hurd Clarke, L. (2015). Honey or vinegar? Athletes with disabilities discuss strategies for advocacy within the Paralympic movement. *Journal of Sport and Social Issues, 39*, 351–370.

Burnham, R. S., May, L., Nelson, E., Steadward, R. D., & Reid, D. (1993). Shoulder pain in wheelchair athletes: The role of muscle imbalance. *The American Journal of Sports Medicine, 21*, 238–242.

Choi, I., Haslett, D., & Smith, B. (2019). Disabled athlete activism in South Korea: A mixed-method study. *International Journal of Sport and Exercise Psychology*, 1–15.

Coakley, J. J. (1983). Leaving competitive sport: Retirement or Rebirth. *Quest, 35*, 1–11. doi:10.1080/00336297.1983.10483777

Corning, A. F., & Myers, D. J. (2002). Individual orientation toward engagement in social action. *Political Psychology, 23*, 703–729.

Demulier, V., Le Scanff, C., & Stephan, Y. (2013). Psychological predictors of career planning among active elite athletes: An application of the social cognitive career theory. *Journal of Applied Sport Psychology, 25*, 341–353.

Goodley, D. (2016). *Disability studies: An interdisciplinary introduction.* London: Sage.

Greendorfer, S. L., & Blinde, E. M. (1985). Retirement from intercollegiate sport: Theoretical and empirical considerations. *Sociology of Sport Journal, 2*, 101–110.

Grobler, L., Ferreira, S., & Terblanche, E. (2015). Paralympic sprint performance between 1992 and 2012. *International Journal of Sports Physiology and Performance, 10*, 1052–1054.

Guerrero, M., & Martin, J. (2018). Para sport athletic identity from competition to retirement: A brief review and future research directions. *Physical Medicine and Rehabilitation Clinics, 29*, 387–396.

Hammer, C., Podlog, L., Wadey, R., Galli, N., Forber-Pratt, A. J., Newton, M., . . . Greviskes, L. (2019). Understanding posttraumatic growth of paratriathletes with acquired disability. *Disability and Rehabilitation, 41*, 674–682.

Haslett, D., Choi, I., & Smith, B. (2020). Para athlete activism: A qualitative examination of disability activism through Paralympic sport in Ireland. *Psychology of Sport and Exercise, 47*, 101639.

Haslett, D., & Smith, B. (2019). Disability sport and social activism. Routledge handbook of disability activism. In M. Berghs, T. Chataika, Y. El-lahib, & A. K. Dube (Eds.), *Routledge handbook of disability activism* (pp. 197–208). London: Routledge.

Hill, P., & Lowe, B. (1974). The inevitable metathesis of the retiring athlete. *The International Review of Sport Sociology, 9*, 5–29.

Kropielnicki, K., Rollason, T., & Man, C. (2017). *Global sports impact report 2017.* Retrieved February 10, 2020, from www.sportcal.com/PDF/GSI/Report/GSI_Report_2017_Sample_Pack_v1.pdf

Lavallee, D., Gordon, S., & Grove, J. R. (1997). Retirement from sport and the loss of athletic identity. *Journal of Personal and Interpersonal Loss, 2*, 129–147.

Lepers, R., Stapley, P. J., & Knechtle, B. (2014). Analysis of marathon performances of disabled athletes. *Movement & Sport Sciences-Science & Motricité, 84*, 43–50.

168 Jeffrey J. Martin and Eva Prokesova

Lerch, S. H. (1982). *Athlete retirement as social death: An overview.* Paper presented at the 3rd annual meeting of the North American Society for the Sociology of Sport, Toronto, Canada.

Makoff, D., Vanden Auweele, Y., & VanLandewijck, Y. (1999). *Transition out from elite disability sports: The social support aspect. Abstract.* 10th The International Symposium of Adapted Physical Activity, Barcelona/Lleida, Spain. May 1999.

Martin, J. J. (1996). Transitions out of competitive sport for athletes with disabilities. *Therapeutic Recreation Journal, 30,* 128–136.

Martin, J. J. (1999). Loss experiences in disability in sport. *Journal of Loss and Interpersonal Loss, 4,* 225–230.

Martin, J. J. (2000). Sport transitions among athletes with disabilities. In D. Lavallee & P. Wylleman (Eds.), *Career transitions in sport: International perspectives* (pp. 161–168). Morgantown, WV: Fitness Information Technology, Pub.

Martin, J. J. (2011). Athletes with disabilities. In T. Morris & P. Terry (Eds.), *The new sport and exercise psychology companion* (pp. 609–623). Morgantown, WV: Fitness Information Technology, Pub.

Martin, J. J. (2017). *Handbook of disability sport and exercise psychology.* New York: Oxford University Press.

Martin, J. J., Byrd, B., Watts, M. L., & Dent, M. (2015). Gritty, hardy, and resilient: Predictors of sport engagement and life satisfaction in wheelchair basketball players. *Journal of Clinical Sport Psychology, 9,* 345–359.

Martin, L., & Ridler, G. (2014). *The impact of retirement status on athletic identity and performance expectations: A study of Paralympic swimmers at a major international competition.* Abstracts of the 28th International Congress of Applied Psychology. Paris: International Association of Applied Psychology (IAAP).

Martin, J. J., & Wheeler, G. (2011). Psychology. In Y. Vanlandewijck & W. Thompson (Eds.), *The Paralympic athlete* (pp. 116–136). London, England: International Olympic Committee.

Mauerberg-deCastro, E., Campbell, D. F., & Tavares, C. P. (2016). The global reality of the Paralympic Movement: Challenges and opportunities in disability sports. *Motriz: Revista de Educação Física, 22,* 111–123.

McGown, E., & Rail, G. (1996). Up the creek without a paddle: Canadian women sprint racing canoeists retirement from international sport. *Avante, 2*(3), 118–136.

Ogilvie, B. C., & Howe, M. A. (1982). Career crisis in sport. In T. Orlick, J. T. Partington, & J. H. Salmela (Eds.), *Mental training for coaches and athletes* (pp. 176–183). Ottawa: Sport in Perspective and Coaching Association of Canada.

Patatas, J. M., De Bosscher, V., Derom, I., & De Rycke, J. (2020). Managing parasport: An investigation of sport policy factors and stakeholders influencing paraathletes' career pathways. *Sport Management Review, 23*(5), 937–951.

Pate, J. R., Hardin, B., & Ruihley, B. (2014). Speak for yourself: Analysing how US athletes used self-presentation on twitter during the 2012 London Paralympic Games. *International Journal Sport Management and Marketing, 15,* 142–162.

Perrier, M. J., Smith, B. M., & Latimer-Cheung, A. E. (2015). Stories that move? Peer athlete mentors' responses to mentee disability and sport narratives. *Psychology of Sport and Exercise, 18,* 60–67.

Sanchez, R. (2020, March). Dirty pool at the Paralympics: Will cheating ruin the games? *Sports Illustrated.* Retrieved from www.si.com/olympics/2020/03/03/paralympiccheating

Schaeffer, Y., & Bergman, Y. (1994). *Unpublished research observations presented by Hutzler, Y.* at The International Symposium of Adapted Physical Activity, Oslo, Norway, May 22–26, 1995.

Schlossberg, N. K. (1981). A model of analyzing human adaptation to transition. *The Counseling Psychologist, 9,* 2–18.

Shakespeare, T. (2016). The Paralympics-superhumans and mere mortals. *The Lancet, 38,* 1137–1139.

Sinclair, D., & Orlick, T. (1993). Positive transitions from high performance sport. *The Sport Psychologist, 7,* 138–150.

Smith, B., Bundon, A., & Best, M. (2016). Disability sport and activist identities: A qualitative study of narratives of activism among elite athletes' with impairment. *Psychology of Sport and Exercise, 26,* 139–148.

Stambulova, N. B., & Ryba, T. V. (2013). Setting the bar: Towards cultural praxis of athletes' careers. In N. B. Stambulova & T. V. Ryba (Eds.), *Athletes' careers across cultures* (pp. 235–254). London and New York: Routledge.

Thomas, C. E., & Ermler, K. L. (1988). Institutional obligations in the athletic retirement process. *Quest, 40,* 137–150. doi:10.1080/00336297.1988.10483895

Tibbetts, E., Longshore, K., Cropper, R., Lipsky, S., Brutus, A., Bonura, K. B., & Galli, N. (2017). Supporting the athlete in society: Athlete-activism. *Sport Psychologists Works, 5,* 1–2.

Wheeler, G. D. (2003). *Adapted physical activity. Athletes in transition.* Edmonton, Alberta: University of Alberta Press.

Wheeler, G. D., Malone, L. A, VanVlack, S., Nelson, E. R., & Steadward, R. (1996). Retirement from disability sport: A pilot study. *Adapted Physical Activity Quarterly, 13,* 382–399.

Wheeler, G. D., Steadward, R. D., Legg, D., Hutzler, Y., Campbell, E., & Johnson, A. (1999). Personal investment in disability sport careers: An international study. *Adapted Physical Activity Quarterly, 16,* 219–237.

Witnauer, W. D., Rogers, R. G., & Saint Onge, J. M. (2007). Major league baseball career length in the 20th century. *Population Research and Policy Review, 26,* 371–386.

13 A Holistic Perspective to Elite Athletes' Career Development and Post-Sport Career Transition in an African Context

Tshepang Tshube, Leapetswe Malete and Deborah L. Feltz

Elite Athletes' Career Development

Athletic Talent Identification and Development

Talent identification, recruitment, and development across different fields including business, art, sport, music, and education have attracted significant interest in research (Abbott & Collins, 2002; Bruner, Erickson, Wilson, & Côté, 2010; Oreck, Baum, & Owen, 2004). Recruitment and talent identification agencies around the globe spend a significant amount of money to identify talented individuals and match them with the right corporations and the right career path development. Researchers in sport studies have been challenged to develop the most effective talent identification and development strategies (Coutinho, Mesquita, & Fonseca, 2016; Grissom, Redding, & Bleiberg, 2019; Henriksen, Stambulova, & Roessler, 2010). For example, a number of journals including the *Journal of Talent Development and Excellence*, the *Journal of Sport Sciences*, and the *Consulting Psychology Journal: Practice and Research* have devoted special issue publications to athletic talent identification and development and coaching elite performances (Baker & Schorer, 2010; Cooper, 2019; Durand-Bush & Salmela, 2002). The surge in research further intensified the ongoing debate on the nature versus nurture's contribution to athletic talent identification and excellence. The long-term athletic development (LTAD) model is another example of the efforts to develop effective talent identification and development strategies (Balyi, Way, & Higgs, 2013). Although the LTAD is beyond the scope of this chapter, its stage-based approach to children and youth sport focusing on the psychosocial, environmental, and human development trajectories is compelling (Bruner et al., 2010; Côté & Vierimaa, 2014). The model has been piloted in many countries including Botswana.

East Africans, particularly Kenyan middle- and long-distance runners, have dominated elite sport for over 40 years (Pitsiladis, Onywera, Geogiades, O'Connell, & Boit, 2004). Eldoret is the most popular town in the Kenyan

Holistic Perspective to Elite Athletes' Career 171

Rift Valley and lies at an altitude around 2,100 m (7,000 ft). This is arguably the most popular recruitment centre for middle- and long-distance runners in the world. Elite distance coaches, agents, and recruiters frequent Eldoret in search for distance runners. The Kenyan success in middle and long distance has further extended the debate on genetic and environmental contributions to athletic success. Some scholars (Burke, 2016; Pitsiladis et al., 2004; Rosen, 2019) have argued that the most successful Kenyan runners originate from a numerically small tribe, which is about 3% of the total population, hence a possible genetic factor to Kenyan athletic success. Even though there is a genetic contribution, lifestyle and environmental factors have been cited as major contributors to Kenyan long- and middle-distance dominance (Onywera, 2009; Pitsiladis et al., 2004).

Early talent identification and development scholars (Green, 2005; Henriksen, Stambulova, & Roessler, 2010b) assessed innate prerequisites for athletic excellence. Cross-sectional designs were used to extrapolate key characteristics on adolescents with the hope to predict athletic excellence (Morris, 2000). In addition to assessment and extrapolation, early researchers placed significant emphasis on the quality and quantity of training required for athletic excellence (Durand-Bush & Salmela, 2002; Ford et al., 2011). These two approaches informed research and practice for athletic excellence. Recent studies, however, have challenged this unidimensional approach to athletic talent identification and development (Levy & Ruggieri, 2019).

Contextualised Athlete Development

Pre-adolescent qualities do not automatically predict athletic excellence in adulthood. The unidimensional approach to athletic talent identification and development prompted an increasing number of researchers to consider a multidimensional approach (Abbott & Collins, 2004; Huijgen, Elferink-Gemser, Lemmink, & Visscher, 2014; Simonton, 2001) to athletic talent identification and development. Therefore, recent research has considered and called for a cross-cultural (Bjørndal & Ronglan, 2018; Kuettel, Christensen, Zysko, & Hansen, 2018; Nam, Shin, Jung, Kim, & Nam, 2019) and a holistic approach to athlete development (Debois, Ledon, & Wylleman, 2015; Henriksen et al., 2010b; Lindgren & Barker-Ruchti, 2017; Wylleman & Reints, 2010). Henriksen et al. (2010a) conceptualised a holistic and lifespan approach as an approach that places significant emphasis on athletic context. For example, a consideration of athletic and non-athletic factors at micro (e.g. family, school, and peers) and macro (e.g. educational systems, national culture, and sport federations) levels play a pivotal role in athletes' career path and development (Chambers, Harangozo, & Mallett, 2019; Henriksen et al., 2010b; Tamminen et al., 2019).

The contextual environment surrounding athletes has a significant bearing on their career path and athletic success. The Environmental Success

172 *Tshepang Tshube et al.*

Factors (ESF) model (Henriksen et al., 2010b) outlines three key necessities for athletic success in a holistic environment. The first necessity is termed preconditions, which includes human (e.g. coaches, teachers, and team management), materials (e.g. training, competition, and studying materials), and financial factors (e.g. scholarship). The second necessity is the process, which refers to diverse and daily activities athletes engage in. Examples include training and class routines, camps, and competition. The third and last necessity is individual development and achievements. This necessity constitutes athletes acquiring psycho-social and athletic skills necessary for life and athletic excellence. An interplay between these factors leads to athletic success. The ESF model has been applied to a number of sports including soccer (Gledhill & Harwood, 2015; Zuber, Zibung, & Conzelmann, 2016) and track and field (Henriksen et al., 2010a). For example, Henriksen et al. (2010b) noted that a strong organisational culture, composed of open cooperation and a whole-person approach in track and field athletes, provided important basis for environment's success.

Africa, Latin America, and East Asia are amongst the least studied regions of the world when it comes to sport (Manuel Luiz & Fadal, 2011; Riot, O'Brien, & Minahan, 2019). In Africa, this dearth of research in athlete development and their transition out of sport has affected policy formulation and programmes for athlete career development. To promote research, build academic network, and mentorship in emerging countries, the *International Journal of Sport & Exercise Psychology* launched two special issue publications in 2016 and 2019 on sport psychology in emerging countries (Papaioannou, Schinke, & Schack, 2019). The journal paired an experienced author with a mentee from an emerging country to publish a sport psychology–related research. The first issue led to publications from countries such as Botswana, Tanzania, and South Africa. The second issue published six studies from countries such as Argentina, Brazil, and Ghana. Contributions to the first special issue included articles regarding the role of sport psychology in sport development in Botswana (Tshube & Hanrahan, 2016), the use of sport on HIV intervention (Sørensen, Maro, & Roberts, 2016), and mental toughness in South African tennis sport (Cowden & Meyer-Weitz, 2016). Tshube and Hanrahan (2016) noted that even though physical education is a new programme offered in Botswana, the programme plays a pivotal role in sport development. The government of Botswana in 2018 and 2019 gave six and 23 sport psychology graduate scholarships at the University of Botswana. The scholarships are an indication of the government's role and commitment to sport development.

The role of governments and the Africa Union in sport has a historical significance. For instance, governments of many newly independent countries in Africa are known to have used sport for nation building and African solidarity (Baker, 1987; Chipande & Banda, 2018). African governments still fund almost all sport-related activities in Africa. However, the funding is also relatively small compared to other social programmes. Several

Holistic Perspective to Elite Athletes' Career   173

attempts have been made to support elite athlete development, construction of sport facilities, and training of coaches through public private partnerships. However, this has failed to work due to the fact that private-sector engagement is very minimal and mostly confined to areas where marketing opportunities through public media are optimal, such as football leagues and tournaments. Therefore, athletes in Africa still experience a number of challenges including limited financial resources and inadequate sport facilities (Manuel Luiz & Fadal, 2011; Riot et al., 2019; Tshube & Feltz, 2015). These challenges have led to some elite athletes migrating to industrialised nations for lucrative contracts (Darby, 2007).

Providing elite athletes with high-performance training, high-tech sport facilities, and specialised services, such as sport medicine, is not a key priority (Riot et al., 2019). In a study that examined talent development environment in Nigeria (Elumaro, Georgios, Russell, & Tony, 2016), barriers such as lack of support at family level, limited resources to support school and community sport programmes, sports injuries, and lack of competitions hindered athlete development. Government, schools, and parents were identified as key stakeholders in facilitating athletic excellence. However, government funding for sport in many African countries is extremely limited. This is understandable considering many competing national priorities such as healthcare, education, and other socioeconomic challenges that could undermine the economic stability of many countries. Unfortunately, the underfunding of sport has been detrimental to holistic athlete development. For instance, athlete development programmes in many African countries lack deliberate athlete-centric structures that address lifespan athlete development, including attention to dual-career development, high-performance training, and retirement transition. This generates much interest on the process of holistic athlete development in this context.

Holistic Athlete Development

Decades of research on career development in elite sport has put the spotlight on important but highly complex processes that underlie athlete development and career transitions. This research has achieved significant milestones that include the broadening of our current understanding of athlete career development. Specific achievements include theory building (Stambulova, 2003; Stambulova, Alfermann, Statler, & Côté, 2009; Wylleman & Lavalle, 2004), which has improved explanations of the complex interrelated factors that underlie athlete development and career transitions (e.g. Henriksen et al., 2010b); increased diversity of athlete populations and contexts studied (e.g. Condello, Capranica, Doupona, Varga, & Burk, 2019; Tshube & Feltz, 2015); and, more importantly, convergence in the framing of the holistic and lifespan approach to athlete development (Wylleman & Reints, 2010). Much credit to this line of work goes to some of the early research on topics such as talent development, crisis transitions,

174 *Tshepang Tshube et al.*

and career termination (Alfermann, Stambulona, & Zemaityte, 2004; Côté, 1999; Durand-Bush & Salmela, 2002). More recent investigations focusing on the social and environmental factors have led to an emerging line of work on international and cross-cultural dimensions, which also include less studied contexts and athlete populations (Codelloo et al., 2019; Ryba & Stambulova, 2013; Tshube, Feltz, & Malete, 2018).

Multiple country studies on career transitions and dual-careers of elite African athletes and international student athletes are excellent examples of a developing trend in this line of work and advances in cross-cultural sport psychology. Although much still needs to be done, the current evidence points to the convergence of conceptual frameworks and athlete development pathways across contexts and cultures. For instance, emerging evidence suggests relevance of Wylleman and Lavalle's (2004) holistic athlete development model to African contexts. This model proposes a lifespan approach to understanding athlete career development and transition. It was conceptualised to cover various domains of an athlete's development, namely athletic, psychological, psychosociological, academic/vocational, and financial. Guided by ecological, reciprocal, and self-deterministic approaches, the holistic athlete development model considers the role of age and varying factors at each stage of an athlete's development. The factors include biological and chronological age, stage of athlete development, education, and the roles of significant others such as family, siblings, peers, coaches, and sport governing bodies, sponsors, and employers. Elements of this model have been confirmed in research on career development, dual-career, and post-sport career transition amongst Southern African Olympic athletes (Tshube & Feltz, 2015; Tshube et al., 2018). However, much remains unknown about barriers faced by athletes in the development process, which calls for more investigations of these factors.

Holistic Athlete Development in Africa

Research on Southern African Olympians (Tshube et al., 2018) confirms the four stages of the athlete career path proposed in the holistic career model and reported in other studies (Debois, Ledon, & Wylleman, 2015; Henriksen et al., 2010b). Although this research cannot claim to represent elite athlete development across Africa, a case can be made that it offers a cursory look at a typical career trajectory of an elite African athlete. Crosscutting themes that emerge from the research that are also supported by anecdotal evidence are the persistent historical and cultural influences in the organisation of sport and games that underlie the amateur model of elite sport in the African region. Even with that, key elements of the lifespan development model are evident. The age breakdown and influence of various actors across the four stages mirror what has been reported in the literature (e.g. Tekavc, Wylleman, & Cecić Erpič, 2015; Wylleman & Lavalle, 2004). These are some important overlaps between what is reported in the

Holistic Perspective to Elite Athletes' Career   175

Table 13.1 Athletes' entourage profiles by stage (adapted from Tshube et al., 2018)

Age 10.5	15	20	31
Start	*Junior*	*Senior*	*Retirement*
Teacher	Coach	Coach	Family
Parents	Teacher	Federation	Coach
Siblings	Parents	Parents	Federation
Ext family	Federation	Friends	Friends

literature and findings from the Southern African study (see Table 13.1, Tshube et al., 2018): the mean initiation and retirement ages, the role of coaches, and dual-career trajectories on athlete development. In the African context, the school (teachers and coaches) plays a prominent role in early stages of sport development. Parental role is negligible, whilst school and community sports are almost non-existent at the junior level. National and international sport federations feature prominently from the senior years (around 20 years old) through retirement. Whilst variations exist between countries and regions, strong similarities exist, most likely because of shared cultures and histories. Sport development across Africa is a predominantly a by-product of education systems that have strong ties to countries' colonial histories. Most of the evidence shared in this chapter is derived from studies on countries that share sport cultures and colonial histories.

Although these stages are in line with the holistic, lifespan development model, the structure of most African sport systems seems to have understated effects on athlete career trajectories. These include athletes' challenges to maintain a delicate balance between good academic performance and excellence in sport because access to sport in the junior and early senior years is mainly through education systems. Maintaining this balance can be very stressful and, in many cases, leads to early termination of sport careers, especially for athletes who perceive a thriving academic and professional career. On a positive note, it also reinforces the development of a dual-career approach from very early on. Limited professional sport and limited out of school elite junior sport opportunities have a role to play in these difficult choices. Most elite junior athletes from these contexts who do not transition past junior high school or do not get noticed by national sport associations and are also likely to drop out or terminate sport early because of lost support from school sports or financial burdens on themselves or their families if they were to continue. Available data from Southern Africa suggests athletes struggle to balance school and sport during the early years of their athletic careers and that this persists through senior years. This has an influence on post-sport career transition and adaptation, because elite athletes are compelled to think and prepare themselves for dual careers from very early on. Limited professional sport opportunities, low incentives from athletic careers, and persistent cultural perceptions of sport as something to be pursued for leisure and not as a profession are most likely behind early dual-career investments amongst elite Southern Africa. This may vary by country, race, socioeconomic circumstances, educational background, and history of sport participation. Athlete development in the senior and pre-retirement stages takes significant personal investment and support from coaches and national sport associations/federations.

Psychological and Psychosocial Development

Psychological, psychosocial, and financial factors feature prominently in the holistic athlete development framework and have become some of the key topics of investigation (Condello et a., 2019; Tekavc et al., 2015; Trussel, 2014). This is not surprising considering their power to serve as both facilitators and constraints to holistic athlete development. Typical psychological topics in the literature include athletic identity, motivation, sport enjoyment, depression, and burnout. The psychosocial domain comprises a myriad of factors that are at the intersection of psychological and social factors within an athlete's environment. Investigations have largely focused on how these factors affect athlete transitions across various stages. Examples include the facilitative and constraining roles of coaches, friends, parents, siblings, and intimate relationships on athlete transitions across stages. For instance, in the youth sport area, early sport specialisation and parental roles have been widely studied. Financial factors, including scholarships, sponsorships, and grants from national federations and endorsements, are also known to facilitate or constrain athlete transitions.

Research on many of these issues amongst Southern African elite athletes is relatively sparse. However, emerging evidence offers some interesting contextual perspectives. For instance, whilst there may be concerns about the high rate of early sport specialisation and its associated negative outcomes such as overuse injuries and burnout in other parts of the world, evidence from the Africa context suggests this is not yet a major concern. In this region, early specialisation is very minimal because junior school sports programmes are structured to enable multiple sport participation (Malete, 2006; Tshube et al., 2018). Limited parent and family involvement in youth sport and low perceived incentives from athletic careers may be contributing factors. The amateur orientation of the sport systems in low- and middle-income countries like Botswana, Namibia, and Zimbabwe may also lead to lower levels of social and psychological challenges typical of a more commercial orientation. This is likely to be an outcome of the low perceived value of an investment in elite competition and its associated challenges in these countries. Nonetheless, challenges exist. Many athletes lament poor parental and family support, difficulty balancing the workload from school and sport, poor academic emotional support services, and

Holistic Perspective to Elite Athletes' Career 177

financial struggles to remain competitive at the highest level (Tshube & Feltz, 2015). Even though the depth and specific impact of these challenges are largely unknown, there is no doubt that they exert a huge toll on the athletes' emotional wellbeing and overall development. The potential but general underperformance of African elite athletes at global sport events like the Olympics, Commonwealth Games, and World Student Games may be an indicator of the impact of these challenges on athlete development. The overall paucity of research on mental health and wellbeing of elite athletes observed (Rice et al., 2016) extends to the African context.

Academic Development and Life-Skills Education

As indicated previously, the recurring theme of the amateur orientation of elite sport in the African context reinforces a dual-career orientation that also explains junior school dropout for some athletes and shorter athletic careers overall. Narratives from retired Olympians who had dropped out of school at about 16 years included stories of difficulty managing the demands of school and sport, lack of academic mentors and tutoring services, education systems that could not accommodate unique needs of student athletes, and high failure rates (Tshube & Feltz, 2015). Whilst most elite athletes who go into college complete their collegiate education, there are many who drop out of college and also fail to continue with their athlete careers after college. A good example is the case of a field hockey national team player from South Africa who dropped out of college but still could not attain his dream to play the sport professionally because he could not qualify for any team. In line with evidence from the extant literature (e.g. Alfermann et al., 2004; Ryan, 2015; Wylleman & Reints, 2010), when African athletes struggle with schoolwork, do not get enough academic support, and are forced to make a choice between school and sport, academic careers suffer even when prospects of an athletic career are highly uncertain. Overall, a dual-career focus enabled by the structure of sports in Africa mostly leads to relatively easier post-career retirement transitions and adaptation.

An area that is also largely neglected in the literature is life-skills education especially during the mastery and discontinuation phases of athlete development (approximately from 25 years of age). This is despite the opportunities such education offers to building resiliency and enhancing athletes' capabilities to manage numerous challenges they face in sport and life. Gould and Carson (2008) define life-skills as internal personal assets that can be facilitated or developed through sport and transferred to non-sport settings. The assets may include tangible and intangible skills and competencies like leadership, personal finance, problem-solving, goal setting, emotional control, hard work, and self-esteem. A review of the life-skills literature shows a significant focus on youth sport because of its youth development orientation and paucity of evidence with elite athletes who are in the senior, mastery, or pre-retirement stages. There is also limited appreciation of the role life-skills straining could play in enhancing the health and wellbeing of elite athletes (e.g. Holt, Tamminen, Tink, & Black, 2009; Pierce, Gould, & Camiré, 2017).

Despite its facilitative potential, life-skills education of elite African athletes and its potential impact on coping, career transitions, and adaptation are largely under-researched and unknown. Life-skill learning is also believed to happen vicariously because there are no known programmes that directly target elite athletes. Programmes for youth athletes in this region are largely in their infancy, and most of the emerging evidence is based on broad-based cross-cultural surveys of youth in sport-for-development programmes. Based on the concerns and needs of Southern African elite athletes across the various stages of development, such as managing competing dual-career interests, financial strain, dropping out of school or sport, and early retirement from sport (Tshube et al., 2018), it seems the model for life-skills transfer proposed by Pierce et al. (2017) is worth exploring in this context. This model follows a life-long development approach and is guided by an ecological framework. It considers the individual, learning contexts (school, sport, family, and extra-curricular), the socio-cultural environment, and their roles in the transfer process.

Retirement Transition and Post-Sport Career Adaption

Research on elite athletes' retirement transition and post-sport career adaption has historically been conceptualised and studied through thanatology and gerontology models (Blinde & Greendorfer, 1985; Crook & Robertson, 1991). These models studied athletes' retirement as an event. Recent research transitioned to examine elite athletes' retirement as a process (Wylleman & Lavalle, 2004). These studies mostly explored causes of retirement and transition (Fernandez, Stephan, & Fouquereau, 2006; Lavallee, Grove, & Gordon, 1997), post-sport career adaptation and challenges (Ekengren & Stambulova, 2017; Fedotova, Statsenko, Skvortsov, & Zaitsev, 2017), effective interventions for elite athletes' retirement transition (Silva et al., 2020), and the role of cultural context in supporting elite athletes' retirement transition (Stambulova, 2017; Stambulova et al., 2020). Retirement from elite sport has been associated with feelings of disorientation, void, frustration, depression, and identity loss (Kerr & Dacyshyn, 2000; Knights, Sherry, & Ruddock-Hudson, 2016). Some studies on elite athletes' retirement linked athletic retirement with social rebirth and positive retirement experiences (Coakley, 1983). Other commonly stated reasons are deselection, injury, age, and free choice. Overall, the most ideal and successful transitioning is associated social rebirth and positive retirement experiences, or when an athlete feels fulfilled. Literature specific to Africa (Rintaugu, Mwisukha, & Monyeki, 2016; Tshube & Feltz, 2015; Tshube et al., 2018) indicates that lack of financial and social support are some of the major challenges elite athletes in Africa have to navigate during post-sport retirement. The noted challenges are not unique to athletes' retirement. Even though African athletes are some of the most successful in their respective sport fields, studies and anecdotal evidence indicates that they are some of the most disadvantaged athletes in the world. Athletes often decry of lack of compensation, unfair treatment, corruption, and poor training facilities (Agbo, 2019; Mokganedi, 2011). For example, Ghana flew three million US dollars in cash to the 2014 FIFA World Cup to avert players' boycott of the cup (Sport, 2014). Athletes do not always trust that sport administrators in their respective countries will pay allowances and cash bonuses. Kenya's Chef de Mission to the 2016 Olympic games was one of the five Kenyan officials arrested for stealing over $250,000 meant for athletes' support in preparation for the Rio 2016 Olympic games (Gurdian, 2016). These issues certainly have an effect on elite athletes' career paths and retirement transition. In addition to corruption in sport, lack of compensation, and help with transition out of sport, most African countries do not have policies that guide athletes on dual career. Hence, most of them opt out of school to pursue sport. Even though there is limited literature on dual career and athletes' retirement in Africa, studies carried out in Africa (Rintaugu et al., 2016; Tshube & Feltz, 2015; Tshube et al., 2018) indicate that lack of dual-career support services has implications for elite athletes' retirement transition challenges. In one of the *New York Times* investigative journalism reports on Kenyan Runners, the investigation revealed that most Kenyan runners have not finished high school, use their sport earnings to support extended family members, and, consequently, 75% of former top-level athletes do not have sustainable income (Rosen, 2019). The challenges are not unique to Kenya; newspaper and academic reports from other African countries (Maseko & Surujlal, 2011; Okpara & Akpodonor, 2019; Tiro, 2018; Tshube & Feltz, 2015) make a case for African governments to provide dual-career support services to avert post-sport career challenges.

Future Research Directions

The literature on career development and retirement transition of talented athletes in Africa is so limited that there is much to explore. Overall, regardless of the phase of athlete development or retirement transition, further research is needed to expand the knowledge of elite athlete development from more countries in Africa. Thus far, research has explored career development of elite athletes from Botswana, Ghana, Kenya, Namibia, Nigeria, South Africa, Tanzania, and Zimbabwe. Except for Namibia, these countries share a British colonial past that tied sport to education. Apart from selected sports like ruby, cricket, and, most recently, soccer in South Africa, elite commercial sport has been slow to develop in most of these countries. However, there is much diversity in culture, education, and sport within the African continent, and elite athletes in Northern African countries, such as Algeria, Egypt, Morocco, and Tunisia, may have different challenges, support systems, and sport governing bodies that should be identified and studied. In addition, little research has focused on women in elite sport in African countries and the special circumstances that they may have to navigate in order to be successful (e.g. sexism, childcare, religious beliefs) (Sikes & Bale, 2014). In all of these contexts, more longitudinal research is needed that follows athletes over the course of their careers and into retirement, and as we suggested previously, the model for life-skills transfer proposed by Pierce et al. (2017) is worth exploring in this context.

In terms of life-skill learning, little is known regarding the extent of life-skill knowledge amongst elite African athletes. What life-skill knowledge do African athletes have, and how do they compare by country? Where did they learn these skills given that there are no known formal instructional programmes that target elite athletes? Answers to these questions will help coaches and sport federations develop life-skill programmes that build the competencies athletes need to manage numerous challenges they face in their path to success.

In addition, in helping athletes in their pursuit of athletic success in a holistic environment, coaches and teachers in African countries should be surveyed and interviewed regarding how they view their role on the holistic development of athletes. What do coaches and teachers think is their responsibility for an athlete's development and transitions across stages? Is there an antagonistic relationship between academic and athletic goals for the athlete? Lastly, how do coaches develop their own knowledge for holistic development of athletes? In examining how coaches learn researchers are starting to use social network analysis to identify the structures of coaches' networks and how they influence each other in informal learning situations (Walker, 2020). Answers to these questions may help uncover the facilitative and constraining roles of coaches and teachers on athlete development and transitions across stages.

In terms of mental wellbeing, more comparative studies of elite athletes in African countries with their counterparts from European and North American countries would be helpful to gain a better understanding of these athletes' mental health and wellbeing and how that may differ in the African context. Factors such as athletic identity, motivation, sport enjoyment, depression, and burnout could be compared at various stages of athletes' development and post-career adaptation. As we noted previously, a lack of early sport specialisation and an earlier dual-career focus enabled by the structure of sports in Africa may have a more positive effect on the emotional health of African athletes than with athletes in countries where there is greater pressure to specialise early in one's sport development and avoid other identity development. On the other hand, athletes in more developed countries may have more sports in which to sample, better coaching, more parental and academic support, and better sports medicine

Holistic Perspective to Elite Athletes' Career 181

access that could negatively affect the emotional health of African athletes. Research is needed to explore these potential differences.

Implications for Practice

At the programmatic level, research that compares the types of career assistance programmes for athletes in European and American countries to those in African countries could help in finding best practices to assist retiring. African athletes can make better post-career transitions into life as productive members of their society. For instance, Canada, the United States, Australia, and most industrialised countries have had career assistance programmes to help athletes during their athletic career transitions for two decades (Chambers et al., 2019; Lenton, Bradbury, & Sayers, 2020; Pearson & Petitpas, 1990; Stambulova et al., 2020), but it is unknown whether National Olympic Committees and federations in Africa have similar programmes for their athletes. Canada has recently developed a total athlete wellness programme, called Game plan (2020) that strives to support national team athletes to live better and more holistic lives. Similar programmes can be developed by African sport federations to help athletes focus on health, education, and career opportunities both during their high-performance career and beyond. Mentorship and life-skills programmes that specifically enhance financial literacy, entrepreneurship, and psychosocial health are likely to help with post-career adaptation. Developing sport systems that intentionally reinforce a dual-career orientation and adaptive athletic identities is key.

Historically, much of the past research on athlete development has emphasised the competitive process and the individual athlete with limited attention to context and other factors. In this chapter, we have tried to address cross-cultural issues and a holistic and lifespan approach to athlete development and career transition within an African context. Future research suggestions also emphasise this holistic and lifespan perspective to ultimately be able to provide better programmes to help African athletes in their holistic athlete and life development and career transitions.

References

Abbott, A., & Collins, D. (2002). A theoretical and empirical analysis of a "state of the art" talent identification model. *High Ability Studies, 13*(2), 157–178. doi:10.1080/1359813022000048798

Abbott, A., & Collins, D. (2004). Eliminating the dichotomy between theory and practice in talent identification and development: Considering the role of psychology. *Journal of Sports Sciences, 22*(5), 395–408. https://doi.org/10.1080/0264 0410410001675324

Alfermann, D., Stambulona, N., & Zemaityte, A. (2004). Reactions to sports career termination: A cross-national comparison of German, Lithuanian, and Russian athletes. *Psychology of Sport and Exercise, 5*, 61–75.

182 *Tshepang Tshube et al.*

Agbo, A. (2019, August 23). Africa games: Fear in rabat as Nigeria athletes threaten to boycott events. *Best Choice Sports.* Retrieved from https://bestchoicesports.com. ng/africa-games-fear-in-rabat-as-nigeria-athletes-threaten-to-boycott-events/

Baker, J., & Schorer, J. (2010). Identification and development of talent in sport: Introduction to the special issue. *Talent Development & Excellence, 2*(2), 119–121.

Baker, W. J. (1987). *Sport in Africa: Essays in social history* (J. A. Mangan, Ed.; 1st ed.). New York: Holmes & Meier Pub.

Balyi, I., Way, R., & Higgs, C. (2013). *Long-term athlete development.* Champaign, IL: Human Kinetics.

Bjørndal, C. T., & Ronglan, L. T. (2018). Orchestrating talent development: Youth players' developmental experiences in Scandinavian team sports. *Sports Coaching Review, 7*(1), 1–22. https://doi.org/10.1080/21640629.2017.1317172

Blinde, E. M., & Greendorfer, S. L. (1985). A reconceptualization of the process of leaving the role of competitive athlete. *International Review for the Sociology of Sport, 20*(1–2), 87–94. https://doi.org/10.1177/101269028502000108

Bruner, M. W., Erickson, K., Wilson, B., & Côté, J. (2010). An appraisal of athlete development models through citation network analysis. *Psychology of Sport and Exercise, 11*(2), 133–139. doi:10.1016/j.psychsport.2009.05.008

Burke, J. (2016, August 1). Eldoret: The Kenyan town trying to "run away from poverty." *The Guardian.* Retrieved from http://www.theguardian.com/world/2016/ aug/01/eldoret-the-kenyan-town-trying-to-run-away-from-poverty

Chambers, T. P., Harangozo, G., & Mallett, C. J. (2019). Supporting elite athletes in a new age: Experiences of personal excellence advisers within Australia's high-performance sporting environment. *Qualitative Research in Sport, Exercise and Health, 11*(5), 650–670. https://doi.org/10.1080/2159676X.2019.1605404

Chipande, H. D., & Banda, D. (2018). Sports and politics in postcolonial Africa. In M. S. Shanguhyia & T. Falola (Eds.), *The Palgrave handbook of African Colonial and postcolonial history* (pp. 1263–1283). Palgrave Macmillan. https://doi. org/10.1057/978-1-137-59426-6_50

Coakley, J. (1983). Leaving competitive sport: Retirement or rebirth? *Quest, 35*, 1–11.

Cooper, S. (2019). Introduction to the special issue on coaching elite performers. *Consulting Psychology Journal: Practice and Research, 71*(2), 62–71. http://dx.doi. org/10.1037/cpb0000140

Condello, G., Capranica, L., Doupona, M., Varga, K., & Burk, V. (2019). Dual-career through the elite university student-athletes' lenses: The international FISU-EAS survey. *PLoS One, 14*(10). https://doi.org/10.1371/journal.pone.0223278

Côté, J. (1999). The influence of the family in the development of talent in sport. *The Sport Psychologist, 13*, 395–417.

Côté, J., & Vierimaa, M. (2014). The developmental model of sport participation: 15 years after its first conceptualization. *Science & Sports, 29*, S63–S69. https:// doi.org/10.1016/j.scispo.2014.08.133

Coutinho, P., Mesquita, I., & Fonseca, A. (2016). Talent development in sport: A critical review of pathways to expert performance—Patrícia Coutinho, Isabel Mesquita, António M Fonseca, 2016. *SAGE, 11*(2), 276–293.

Cowden, R. G., & Meyer-Weitz, A. (2016). Mental toughness in South African competitive tennis: Biographical and sport participation differences. *International Journal of Sport and Exercise Psychology, 14*(2), 152–167. https://doi.org/10.1080/ 1612197X.2015.1121509

Crook, J. M., & Robertson, S. E. (1991). Transitions out of elite sport. *International Journal of Sport Psychology, 22*(2), 115–127.

Darby, P. (2007). Out of Africa: The exodus of elite African football talent to Europe. *WorkingUSA, 10*(4), 443–456. https://doi.org/10.1111/j.1743-4580.2007.00175.x

Debois, N., Ledon, A., & Wylleman, P. (2015). A lifespan perspective on the dual career of elite male athletes. *Psychology of Sport & Exercise, 21*, 15–26.

Durand-Bush, N., & Salmela, J. H. (2002). The development and maintenance of expert athletic performance: Perceptions of world and Olympic champions. *Journal of Applied Sport Psychology, 14*(3), 154–171. https://doi.org/10.1080/10413200290103473

Ekengren, J., & Stambulova, N. (2017). *Returning home after playing abroad: Re-adaptation challenges of elite Swedish handball players* (pp. 531–531). Retrieved from http://urn.kb.se/resolve?urn=urn:nbn:se:hh:diva-34653

Elumaro, A. I., Georgios, A., Russell, M., & Tony, W. (2016). *Talent development environment in Nigeria: Athletes' perceptions of barriers, opportunities and facilitators.* https://doi.org/10.11648/j.ajss.20160406.11

Fedotova, I. V., Statsenko, M. E., Skvortsov, V. V., & Zaitsev, V. G. (2017). Age-specific profiles of retired athletes" heart rate variability and psychoemotional status in post-retirement adaptation period. *Theory and Practice of Physical Culture, 9*, 20.

Fernandez, A., Stephan, Y., & Fouquereau, E. (2006). Assessing reasons for sports career termination: Development of the athletes' retirement decision inventory (ARDI). *Psychology of Sport and Exercise, 7*(4), 407–421. https://doi.org/10.1016/j.psychsport.2005.11.001

Ford, P., Croix, M. D. S., Lloyd, R., Meyers, R., Moosavi, M., Oliver, J., . . . Williams, C. (2011). The long-term athlete development model: Physiological evidence and application. *Journal of Sports Sciences, 29*(4), 389–402. https://doi.org/10.1080/02640414.2010.536849

Game Plan. (2020). Retrieved from www.mygameplan.ca/

Gledhill, A., & Harwood, C. (2015). A holistic perspective on career development in UK female soccer players: A negative case analysis. *Psychology of Sport and Exercise, 21*, 65–77. https://doi.org/10.1016/j.psychsport.2015.04.003

Gould, D., & Carson, S. (2008). Life skills development through sport: Current status and future directions. *International Review of Sport and Exercise Psychology, 1*, 58–78. doi:10.1080/ 17509840701834573.

Green, B. C. (2005). Building sport programs to optimize athlete recruitment, retention, and transition: Toward a normative theory of sport development. *Journal of Sport Management, 19*(3), 233–253. https://doi.org/10.1123/jsm.19.3.233

Grissom, J. A., Redding, C., & Bleiberg, J. F. (2019). Money over merit? Socioeconomic gaps in receipt of gifted services. *Harvard Educational Review, 89*(3), 337–369. https://doi.org/10.17763/1943-5045-89.3.337

Gurdian, S. (2016, November 22). Kenya official found 'hiding under bed' before Rio 2016 corruption arrest. *The Guardian.* Retrieved from www.theguardian.com/sport/2016/nov/22/kenya-official-hiding-under-bed-rio-2016-arrest

Henriksen, K., Stambulova, N., & Roessler, K. K. (2010a). Successful talent development in track and field: Considering the role of environment. *Scandinavian Journal of Medicine & Science in Sports, 20*(s2), 122–132. https://doi.org/10.1111/j.1600-0838.2010.01187.x

Henriksen, K., Stambulova, N., & Roessler, K. K. (2010b). Holistic approach to athletic talent development environments: A successful sailing milieu. *Psychology of Sport and Exercise, 11*(3), 212–222. https://doi.org/10.1016/j.psychsport.2009.10.005

Holt, N. L., Tamminen, K. A., Tink, L. N., & Black, D. E. (2009). An interpretive analysis of life skills associated with sport participation. *Qualitative Research in Sport and Exercise, 1*, 160–175. doi:10.1080/ 19398440902909017

Huijgen, B. C. H., Elferink-Gemser, M. T., Lemmink, K. A. P. M., & Visscher, C. (2014). Multidimensional performance characteristics in selected and deselected talented soccer players. *European Journal of Sport Science, 14*(1), 2–10. https://doi.org/10.1080/17461391.2012.725102

Kerr, G., & Dacyshyn, A. (2000). The retirement experiences of elite, female gymnasts. *Journal of Applied Sport Psychology, 12*(2), 115–133. https://doi.org/10.1080/10413200008404218

Knights, S., Sherry, E., & Ruddock-Hudson, M. (2016). Investigating elite end-of-athletic-career transition: A systematic review. *Journal of Applied Sport Psychology, 28*(3), 291–308. https://doi.org/10.1080/10413200.2015.1128992

Kuettel, A., Christensen, M. K., Zysko, J., & Hansen, J. (2018). A cross-cultural comparison of dual career environments for elite athletes in Switzerland, Denmark, and Poland. *International Journal of Sport and Exercise Psychology*, 1–18. https://doi.org/10.1080/1612197X.2018.1553889

Lavallee, D., Grove, J. R., & Gordon, S. (1997). The causes of career termination from sport and their relationship to post-retirement adjustment among elite-amateur athletes in Australia. *Australian Psychologist, 32*(2), 131–135. https://doi.org/10.1080/00050069708257366

Lenton, A., Bradbury, T., & Sayers, J. (2020). Elite sport retirement: Elite New Zealand athletes' perceptions of retirement interventions. *Journal of Sport Behavior, 42*(1), 50.

Levy, J. J., & Ruggieri, J. (2019). Personality, styles, and orientations in sport: Pros, cons, and guidelines for predicting sport performance. In *APA handbook of sport and exercise psychology, volume 1: Sport psychology* (Vol. 1, pp. 79–98). American Psychological Association. https://doi.org/10.1037/0000123-005

Lindgren, E.-C., & Barker-Ruchti, N. (2017). Balancing performance-based expectations with a holistic perspective on coaching: A qualitative study of Swedish women's national football team coaches' practice experiences. *International Journal of Qualitative Studies on Health and Well-Being, 12*(Suppl 2). https://doi.org/10.1080/17482631.2017.1358580

Malete, L. (2006). Goal orientations, sport ability, perceived parental influences and youth's enjoyment of sport and physical activity in Botswana. *International Journal of Applied Sports Sciences, 18*, 89–107.

Manuel Luiz, J., & Fadal, R. (2011). An economic analysis of sports performance in Africa. *International Journal of Social Economics, 38*(10), 869–883. https://doi.org/10.1108/03068291111170415

Maseko, J., & Surujlal, J. (2011). Retirement planning among South African professional soccer players: A qualitative study of players' perceptions. *African Journal for Physical Activity and Health Sciences*, 157–171. https://doi.org/10.4314/ajpherd.v17i4.

Mokganedi, M. (2011, May). Mmegi online: BAA accused of neglecting athletics team. *Mmegi Online*. Retrieved from www.mmegi.bw/index.php?sid=8&aid=875&dir=2011/May/Tuesday17/

Morris, T. (2000). Psychological characteristics and talent identification in soccer. *Journal of Sports Sciences, 18*(9), 715–726. https://doi.org/10.1080/02640410050120096

Nam, B. H., Shin, Y. H., Jung, K. S., Kim, J., & Nam, S. (2019). Promoting knowledge economy, human capital, and dual careers of athletes: A critical approach to the global sports talent development project in South Korea. *International Journal of Sport Policy and Politics, 11*(4), 607–624. https://doi.org/10.1080/19406940.2019.1615974

Okpara, C., & Akpodonor, G. (2019, May 13). Nigeria's sports heroes: Tales of the dimming stars. *The Guardian Nigeria News—Nigeria and World News.* Retrieved from https://guardian.ng/sport/nigerias-sports-heroes-tales-of-the-dimming-stars/

Onywera, V. O. (2009). East African runners: Their genetics, lifestyle and athletic prowess. *Genetics and Sports, 54,* 102–109. https://doi.org/10.1159/000235699

Oreck, B., Baum, S., & Owen, S. (2004). Assessment of potential theater arts talent in young people: The development of a new research-based assessment process. *Youth Theatre Journal, 18*(1), 146–163. https://doi.org/10.1080/08929092.2004.10012570

Papaioannou, A. G., Schinke, R. J., & Schack, T. (2019). Special issue: Sport and exercise psychology in emerging countries—Part II. *International Journal of Sport and Exercise Psychology, 17*(1), 1–84.

Pearson, R. E., & Petitpas, A. J. (1990). Transitions of athletes: Developmental and preventive perspectives. *Journal of Counseling & Development, 69*(1), 7–10. https://doi.org/10.1002/j.1556-6676.1990.tb01445.x

Pierce, S., Gould, D., & Camiré, M. (2017). Definition and model of life skills transfer. *International Review of Sport and Exercise Psychology, 10*(1), 186–211. doi:10.1080/1750984X.2016.1199727

Pitsiladis, Y. P., Onywera, V. O., Geogiades, E., O'Connell, W., & Boit, M. K. (2004). The dominance of Kenyans in distance running. *Equine and Comparative Exercise Physiology, 1*(4), 285–291. https://doi.org/10.1079/ECP200433

Rice, S. M., Purcell, R., De Silva, S., Mawren, D., McGorry, P. D., & Parker, A. G. (2016). The mental health of elite athletes: A narrative systematic review. *Sports Medicine, 46,* 1333–1353. doi:10.1007/s40279-016-0492-2

Rintaugu, E. G., Mwisukha, A., & Monyeki, M. A. (2016). From grace to grass: Kenyan soccer players' career transition and experiences in retirement. *African Journal for Physical Activity and Health Sciences, 22*(1:1), 163–175. https://doi.org/10.4314/ajpherd.v22i1:1

Riot, C., O'Brien, W., & Minahan, C. (2019). High performance sport programs and emplaced performance capital in elite athletes from developing nations. *Sport Management Review.* https://doi.org/10.1016/j.smr.2019.11.001

Rosen, J. W. (2019, April 22). For Kenyan runners, winning can be a road to ruin. *The New York Times.* Retrieved from www.nytimes.com/2019/04/22/sports/kenyan-runners.html

Ryan, C. (2015). Factors impacting carded athlete's readiness for dual careers. *Psychology of Sport and Exercise, 21,* 91–97.

Ryba, T. V., & Stambulova, N. (2013). The turn towards a cultural informed approach to career research and assistance in sport psychology. In N. Stambulova & T. V. Ryba (Eds.), *Athletes Careers Across cultures* (pp. 1–16). New York: Routledge.

Sikes, M., & Bale, J. (2014). *Women's sport in Africa.* New York: Routledge.

Silva, A. M., Nunes, C. L., Matias, C. N., Jesus, F., Francisco, R., Cardoso, M., . . . Minderico, C. S. (2020). Champ4life study protocol: A one-year randomized controlled trial of a lifestyle intervention for inactive former elite athletes with overweight/obesity. *Nutrients, 12*(2), 286. https://doi.org/10.3390/nu12020286

Simonton, D. K. (2001). Talent development as a multidimensional, multiplicative, and dynamic process. *Current Directions in Psychological Science, 10*(2), 39–43. https://doi.org/10.1111/1467-8721.00110

Sørensen, M., Maro, C. N., & Roberts, G. C. (2016). Gender differences in HIV related psychological variables in a Tanzanian intervention using sport. *International Journal of Sport and Exercise Psychology, 14*(2), 135–151. https://doi.org/10.1 080/1612197X.2015.1121511

Stambulova, N. B. (2003). Symptoms of a crisis-transition: A grounded theory study. In N. Hassmen (Ed.), *SIPF yearbook* (pp. 97–109). Örebro, Sweden: Örebro University Press.

Stambulova, N. B. (2017). Crisis-transitions in athletes: Current emphases on cognitive and contextual factors. *Current Opinion in Psychology, 16*, 62–66. https://doi.org/10.1016/j.copsyc.2017.04.013

Stambulova, N. B., Alfermann, D., Statler, T., & Côté, J. (2009). ISSP position stand: Career development and transitions of athletes. *International Journal of Sport and Exercise Psychology, 7*, 395–412.

Stambulova, N. B., Ryba, T. V., & Henriksen, K. (2020). Career development and transitions of athletes: The international society of sport psychology position stand revisited. *International Journal of Sport and Exercise Psychology*, 1–27. https://doi.org/10.1080/1612197X.2020.1737836

Tamminen, K. A., Page-Gould, E., Schellenberg, B., Palmateer, T., Thai, S., Sabiston, C. M., & Crocker, P. R. E. (2019). A daily diary study of interpersonal emotion regulation, the social environment, and team performance among university athletes. *Psychology of Sport and Exercise, 45*, 101566. https://doi.org/10.1016/j.psychsport.2019.101566

Tekavc, J., Wylleman, P., & Cecić Erpič, S. (2015). Perceptions of dual career development among elite level swimmers and basketball players. *Psychology of Sport and Exercise, 21*, 27–41. doi:10.1016/j.psychsport.2015.03.002

Telegraph Sport (2014, June 26). *Ghana flies $3 million in cash to players in Brazil to avert potential boycott over world cup appearance fees.* Retrieved from www.telegraph. co.uk/sport/football/teams/ghana/10927168/Ghana-flies-3-million-in-cash-to-players-in-Brazil-to-avert-potential-boycott-over-World-Cup-appearance-fees.html

Tiro, B. (2018, August 31). *BNSC, BNOC discuss life after sport—the patriot on Sunday.* Retrieved from www.thepatriot.co.bw/sport/item/6055-bnsc,-bnoc-discuss-life-after-sport.html

Trussel, D. E. (2014). Contradictory aspects of organized youth sport: Challenging and fostering sibling relationships and participation experiences. *Youth & Society, 46*(6), 801–818.

Tshube, T., & Feltz, D. L. (2015). The relationship between dual-career and post-sport career transition among elite athletes in South Africa, Botswana, Namibia and Zimbabwe. *Psychology of Sport and Exercise, 21*, 109–114. https://doi.org/10.1016/j.psychsport.2015.05.005

Tshube, T., Feltz, D. L., & Malete, L. (2018). *International Journal of Coaching Science, 12*(2). Retrieved from www.riss.kr/search/Search.do?detailSearch=true&search Gubun=true&queryText=znCreator,Tshepang&colName=re_a_kor

Tshube, T., & Hanrahan, S. J. (2016). Sport psychology in Botswana: A prime breeding ground. *International Journal of Sport and Exercise Psychology, 14*(2), 126–134. https://doi.org/10.1080/1612197X.2016.1142462

Walker, L. (2020). Understanding how central nodes establish positions of influence in coach social networks. *Journal of Sport and Exercise Psychology, 42S.*

Wylleman, P., & Lavalle, D. (2004). A developmental perspective on transitions faced by athletes. In M. Weiss (Ed.), *Developmental sport and exercise psychology: A lifespan perspective* (pp. 507–527). Morgantown, WV: Fitness Information Technology.

Wylleman, P., & Reints, A. (2010). A lifespan perspective on the career of talented and elite athletes: Perspectives on high-intensity sports. *Scandinavian Journal of Medicine & Science in Sports, 20*, 88–94.

Zuber, C., Zibung, M., & Conzelmann, A. (2016). Holistic patterns as an instrument for predicting the performance of promising young soccer players—A 3-years longitudinal study. *Frontiers in Psychology, 7.* https://doi.org/10.3389/fpsyg.2016.01088

14 Autobiographical Insights Into Athlete Transitions From Sport

Kitrina Douglas

Passing the Ball

'Why didn't you sign for Arsenal or Everton then?' she asked after he paused. He'd been telling her a story about a football game he used to play on the way home from school each day. He'd first pick teams, Liverpool v Ipswich, Man United v Arsenal, and Chelsea v Leeds, for example. Then, he'd kick the ball at the first gatepost, and if it hit, it meant it was 1–0 to Chelsea. The next gatepost provided an opportunity for Leeds to equalise. If he hit the post, the game ended 1–1, and on to the next two teams he went, through the entire first division, every day, all the way home from school and all recorded in his notebook. It sounded such fun, so creative and all his own idea. A few years later, scouts invited him to Highbury, home of Arsenal and Goodison park, home of Everton, for trials, after which he was offered a contract to play professionally.

'My father didn't believe in professional sport', he replied matter of factly, 'so he wouldn't let me sign, he wanted me to have a 'safe' (he raised his eyebrows) job, but I played semi-pro for Hearts on release from the Navy when I was in Edinburgh'.

At 6, she was too young perhaps to form an opinion. She just absorbed the story about a little boy making up games and playing football, having fun and being asked to play professionally by two of the country's top teams.

Practice 1

The sun had not long been up and its orange light made the practice ground appear magical. She loved these mornings, cool air on her skin, hidden pockets of warm air, a musky aroma rising from the grass.

As she squeezed each shot, it fizzed through the stillness but hardly made a sound as it settled near the white post she was aiming at 70 yards away. And it was always exactly 70 yards to start with. Her grouping of hit balls around the white post suggested she was no normal golfer; in fact, if you did not know better, you would be excused for thinking the balls had been placed by the post as opposed to being hit from the length of a football pitch away.

Autobiographical Insights on Transition   189

Her next shot was so accurate that it pitched fully onto the 3-inch-wide post and ricocheted off making a loud *crack*, it was the only sound. Further up the field movement that stopped with the noise drew her attention. Three deer had been passing, now, they stood motionless and became statuettes in the sun's spotlight, as they watched her. She stared back, not moving, aware of slender legs, long bodies and a dignified presence. The lead deer turned its head from her to draw the morning air through its nostrils, then it bent its neck and swept the dewy grass with its nose. Raising its head again something beckoned it back on its journey. The other deer looked from her to the larger deer, and followed on.

Her body went back to hitting, but her mind was filled with words. They arrived as silently and unexpected as the deer, they filled her head with joy, as had the deer. Like the deer, they would not move, so she emptied them out on a piece of paper. The only paper she could find was a page from her yardage book, but the lines came flooding out.

As she wandered up the range to collect the balls, she hummed a new tune and allowed the words to drop into her melody and out popped a ditty. She would not be so grandiose to call it a song, but she sang it just the same, maybe to herself, maybe to the deer or maybe to remind her of that moment with the deer. (adapted from Douglas, 2016)

Practice 2

After an afternoon exploring the mountains and taking ice creams by the lake, they returned to grassy field. The sun had not lost its heat but was turning red and creating shapes and shadows across the tightly cropped grass. Nathan pulled out the big tournament bag and balls and, with the remains of the baguette, wandered over to the empty range. Carefully placing the bag down so that its flat surface formed 'the stumps', he took a club from the bag in readiness to defend his wicket. She wandered 20 yards away.

Adopting a sideways stance, Nathan took a step forward making an imaginary swipe at a ball with a cricket swing, left elbow up, front foot forward, then, in front of the bag, he patted down a few uneven patches of grass and awaited delivery. It arrived like a guided missile chipped on target, but he anticipated its flight, and before the ball connected with the waiting bag, he swung forward and took the rising ball flush on face of the club, THWACK into the distance.

'Nice hit!' she shouted, watching the ball fly overhead.

There was a harmony between them, a symphony being played without a conductor.

Later, Nathan took a putter and walked to the green whilst she took a pitching wedge and went off to await him throwing the ball over. When he did, it came to rest in a divot so she acted out for the imaginary cameras, 'What sort of a lie is that?' looking to the heavens. Putting the ball way back in her stance, she closed the face of the club, put her hands forward

190 *Kitrina Douglas*

and began to commentate, 'Douglas facing an impossible shot'. Then she focused, became silent, allowed her body to remember the move and hit the ball. Moments later, after the ball came to rest 4 feet from the pin, she returned to her commentary, 'Ooooh, what a shot! Leaving her foursomes partner a little tester'.

'The pressure's on her partner now', Nathan said, taking up the commentary and lining up the putt from several angles. Then he stood to the ball, and smoothly struck it into the hole.

*

In 1996, as a high-performance professional athlete and undergraduate student, I was shocked by the singular way athletes' lives were being represented in the scientific literature presented to me in lectures and seminars. Within golf, the sport that I played for 20 years, the available literature suggested that women were consumed by their profession, physically isolated by travel and insulated from everyday reality of mainstream society (Crosset, 1995). This type of narrative script was not restricted to research amongst female golfers. Across sport research, these types of findings were mirrored by scholars who, at times, went as far as to suggest that the professional athlete 'has, and *must* have', such a narrow focus on winning 'it is *impossible* for him (or her) to be much else' (Werthner & Orlick, 1986, p. 337, my italics). Put bluntly, I was being informed that it was impossible (not difficult or challenging even) for me to 'be' anything else! *Not daughter, sister, aunty, friend, counsellor, coach, journalist, storyteller* or any of the other identities important to me. Sitting amongst the '96 cohort of Sport and Exercise Science students at the University of Exeter, I looked at the lecturer in disbelief and silence, as he talked with authority about a population I was a member of—high-performance athletes.

In social science research, we now have a much better idea about how individuals lose their voice and agency, of which the above is an example. I may have been a successful business woman, earning a living in professional sport, yet in this context I was silenced. My life and experience did not seem to count. At the time, as an undergraduate, I did not possess the narrative resources to question the literature and ask, '*isn't the very fact I am in the lecture testimony that not all athletes are this way?*' Wasn't I, in Carl Popper's terms, at least one 'Black Swan' that proved their theory wrong? Another explanation was that I was deluded. That winning *really* was everything to me and I was in denial? I mention this now, at the start of this chapter as a reminder to myself, of a need to really listen to participants, to hear and to identify my own biases and assumption when analysing and making statements about others' lives. What other explanations were there?

Learning how my life can be subsumed in a story that does not represent me was an important lesson. I learned that the claims these authors made

Autobiographical Insights on Transition   191

about their data were less generalisable than they were claiming. The irony of this is not lost on me now, some 20 years later. One of the challenges I am often faced with given my valuing of life history, single case, biographical and autoethnographic research is that some researchers criticise this research on the basis that it is impossible to learn from these methodologies as they are not generalisable, and—being based on one person's experience and subjectivity, they are not credible. Yet, here was I not fitting the mould of research that was supposed to be generalisable and objective.

There are, of course, a huge number of researchers who also value the learning, insights and theoretical generalisations that can be made from a single case, and it is on such a basis in this chapter that I use my own sport experience as a vehicle for exploring professional sport and the types of identity work that might make transitions less problematic.

A Call to Stories

The opening quote to this chapter 'if you want to know me . . . you must know my story' provided an opening to share three stories about practice—the art of transforming a novice into an expert and a way we maintain improvements in performance once we attain that level. If we, within the scientific community, want to understand an individual's life, and why he or she might experience difficulty during their transition from sport, then there is much to be learned by exploring 'back' stories. And not just of the individual athlete, but also the stories available in the construction of an identity and sense of what is valued and how values are created and transmitted. In *The Renewal of Generosity*, Arthur Frank (2004) reminds us that

> Stories do not merely narrate events. They convey on action and actor—either one or both—the socially accredited status of being worth notice. To render narratable is to claim relevance for action, and for the life of which that action is part. . . [and to] render present what would otherwise be absent.
>
> (Frank, 2004, p. 62)

My aim here is to 'render narratable' stories that have been silenced and/or lost from my experiences in sport and place these alongside stories that others believe are 'worth' noticing. I have a number of reasons for doing this. One is to provide examples of complex identity developments and how the values and stories we are born into (that form our ideological apparatus) play a role in shaping who we become. We cannot take the individual athlete out of their context if we want to understand them and create interventions that reduce distress and trauma leaving sport.

Louis Althusser (1971) coined the term *interpellation* to describe how an individual, because they have been shaped to act in certain ways by the ideology they are embedded within, responds when he or she is called or

192 *Kitrina Douglas*

'hailed'. In sport terms, we can see this with the dominant scripts available in professional sport culture. Here, athletes are interpellated to understand that winning brings honour and glory and losing will bring humiliation, embarrassment and shame. If someone questions the amount of hard work, dedication and sacrifice expected, we are thus called to respond, 'no pain no gain'. However, this narrative script aligns with only one available narrative and is a hallmark of the performance narrative (Carless & Douglas, 2012, 2013a, 2013b: Douglas & Carless, 2006), which dominates in sport and allows little deviation and exploration.

Mark Freeman and Alistair MacIntyre extended the concept of an individual's actions being shaped by forces outside the individual, suggesting that personal history begins even before birth, 'The story of my life', MacIntyre wrote (1984, p. 205), 'is always embedded in those communities from which I derive my identity. I am born with a past; and to try to cut myself off from that past, in the individualist mode, is to deform my present relationship'. Sharing stories from my past and the past of my parents, therefore, has the capacity to illuminate the process of interpellation. That is, they enable me to see the ways in which I respond according to others' expectations of me and that these that relate to the 'rituals' and 'practices' I learned through my family, community and culture and provide the means to resist the dominant storylines by providing counterstories.

The opening stories about 'practice' provide three counter stories—that is, they do not follow the expected performance narrative template (Douglas & Carless, 2006), which includes training, hard work and/or dedication. Rather, the narrative plot deviates to reveal a different route to into professional sport and excellence.

For those familiar with my work, it will come as no surprise that here, as I often do, I draw on arts-based and storytelling methodologies. Given I have written extensively about my motives and rationale for doing so, I will not devote space to these methodologies here.[1] Rather, in what follows I draw from a collage of published autoethnographic research (written by me) along with news reports (written by journalists) to explore specific moments from my entry, life-in and departure from the professional golf tour with the hope that it expands the narrative possibilities open to athletes and researchers regarding career transition from sport.

Sharing stories told about me has the added lens of showing how myths are created about sport heroes, which in turn influence both the general public's understanding about what it takes to excel in sport and the expectations of athletes, coaches and others in the performance environment regarding what is valued *in sport* and what it takes to excel. It is the messiness of these issues that I would like to address in this chapter.

I commenced my academic journey a few weeks after walking off the golf course in what was to be my last professional tournament, though I did not know this at the time. The following extract, from my PhD thesis, tells the tale.

Walking Down the Mountain

On 4 September 1996, I went to the ladies' toilet. On the way there, I turned my head awkwardly and experienced a sharp pain in my neck, which restricted my head from turning. Not a huge problem, you might think. I was, however, on the tenth hole of the Oxfordshire Golf Course, playing in the English Open—a professional golf tournament with a £200,000 prize fund—and I was one of the top players in Europe. In a very humorous 30 minutes, one of my playing partners demonstrated on the other, in the middle of the fairway, how her mother, a physio, would 'unlock' a patient's neck. She then offered to do the same for me. The spectators lining the fairway had no idea why one golfer in our group (Debbie Dowling another top pro) suddenly sat on the grass in compliance to instructions from the other player (a young woman I did not know that well) who proceeded to place an arm lock round Debbie's head, an act intended to give me confidence to let her do the same to me. *Not on your life* I thought, enjoying the show. By this stage, two groups were waiting to tee off behind us; thus, my indecision about what to do (play on or withdrawal) was holding up play. Officials were called in. An ambulance was dispatched. In the midst of the comedy of errors, I realised that, although just a minor injury, the St John's Ambulance medics would not be able to fix a muscle or tendon problem with a bandage, and so I declined a lift back in the ambulance and walked off the golf course (and out of professional tournament golf) and went and enjoyed a traditional afternoon cream tea at a luxury hotel on the river Thames in Marlow with a friend (Douglas, 2004, p. 1).

If the theories about professional sports people were to be trusted, I should have experienced some type of fracturing of my athletic identity in what could be termed a 'career-ending injury'—an identity, which according to the science literature, is 'supposed' to define me and my sense of self. Surely, after investing so much in my sport career and not being 'much else', what else of my 'self' was there?

At this point in the chapter, it might be useful to state that from my own research I recognise many athletes can and do experience a fracture of their sense of self from such departures (see, for example, Carless & Douglas, 2012, 2013a, 2013b; Douglas & Carless, 2006, 2009, 2015). The previous chapters also attest to this. Furthermore, I have witnessed participants, colleagues and friends exhibit and/or share stories about self-harming, attempted suicide, substance misuse, or loss of self-worth (Douglas & Carless, 2009, 2012a, 2012b, 2014, 2015) following deselection, career-ending injury, pregnancy and/or transition out of sport. At the same time, I have witnessed and evidenced, through the actions, behaviour and stories of other participants, colleagues and friends—along with my own subjective experiences and documented behaviours—that there are alternative types of journey (Douglas & Carless, 2015; Douglas, in press) that show an individual athlete's sense of self-worth is not always dependent on their rank

194   *Kitrina Douglas*

and performance—despite there being literature that says it must. There are, if you are able to notice them, alternative types of narrative plots that challenge the hegemony of the performance narrative.

Whilst the previous descriptions regarding a focus on winning certainly reflect the experiences and values of some athletes, they failed to recognise diversity—we are not all the same. Subsuming us all sends out a dangerous message and makes it more difficult to support athletes who do not want their athletic identity to dominate. Sport and winning does not mean the same thing to us all, we each have different journeys into sport, *different biographies* and so it follows that leaving sport through natural or forced transitions will also bring confer different meanings.

My first experience of dissatisfaction with traditional research came through reading Carole Gilligan's book *In a Different Voice* (Gilligan, 1993). In this hallmark text, Carole Gilligan reveals how women's voices and stories had been systematically silenced by traditional psychological approaches to identity and development. For Gilligan, 'The failure to hear the differences in (women's) voices stems in part from the assumption that there is a single mode of social experience and interpretation' (Gilligan, 1993, p. 173).

Gilligan was not alone. Narrative theorists also question the 'single monolithic culture', to suggest that 'many people experience themselves as caught between different cultural systems' (McLeod, 1997, p. 100). When these differing cultural systems are recognised, singular expectations of behaviour and responses become untenable as an individual's life is understood to be complex, contingent and multidimensional.

In the research that David Carless and I have been involved with over the past 20 years, we seem to have a pre-occupation with not cementing and finalising the lives of people we conduct research with, because we know from our own experiences what doing so feels like. Such experiences (of being misrepresented) have, I hope, led us to be more cautious of the claims we make for our 'data' and to look for those dimensions of life that are hidden or taboo. Being misrepresented has also provoked concerns with those things that are omitted from research because they are difficult or impossible to put into words. By this I mean, if asked by a researcher *how did you get to the top*, it may be easier (due to the narrative templates or scripts that are available to an athlete) for him or her to respond by saying he or she took a singular focus, was dedicated, and made sacrifices to invest in hours of training. There are many dangers with drawing on this type of dominant narrative, and the most problematic is that it cements and strengthens the 'myth' that there is only being *one way* to succeed in sport. It means actions and activities like singing, writing songs, or having spiritual experiences while hitting golf balls are omitted; thus, the actions and values of individuals for whom alternative explanations are important are in danger of having important dimensions of their self-concept ridiculed, undermined, trivialised and narrowed—all factors that contribute to problematic transition. If we hope to support healthier transitions, then perhaps, recognising (and listen and recognising) those dimensions of an athlete's life that fail to gain recognition may be more important than researchers and practitioners have realised.

In the remainder of this chapter, I share a small selection of counter stories with the aim of broadening the canvas regarding athletic transitions.

*

I hit my first ever golf ball all at the age of 17 while on holiday in Scotland with my family. The following extract from "Negotiating a relational identity" (Douglas, 2009) focuses on this event and the consequence.

Do You Fancy an Ice Cream?

The lure was the ice cream. He had offered them ice creams on the way back from the golf range. She and her little sister eagerly accepted the invitation to ice cream and even hit a few shots. This offer, 2 days later, was a little different.

'Do you fancy leaving school and playing golf for a year?' her dad asked, as if he was asking about ice creams again. She thought golf was boring, but school was pretty boring too . . . and she had no burning desire to do anything in particular. 'If you don't like it you can do your A levels,' he reasoned. It all sounded so simple driving along in the car, it wasn't an intense conversation, it didn't even seem particularly important, it was just like he was asking *do you fancy chocolate or vanilla?*

'If you like it', he continued, eyes not diverting from the road, 'but aren't very good, you do your A levels, but you will have a game you can play for the rest of your life. Golf's played everywhere. If you like it', he glanced over towards her shrugging his shoulders in the process, 'and you are good at it, no-one can stop you. You see, you can always finish your education, at any age, but with sport', there was a moment's pause, 'time is an issue, it's a little different'.

He left his proposal hanging. The ball, so to speak, was in her court. Of course, she did not know anything about golf, other than it was boring. She liked the smell of the lamb's wool sweaters in the golf shop though—she quite fancied having one of those. Three different options, no drawbacks, no pressure, only opportunities. She shrugged her shoulders: why not?

While she and her father had been rather under-whelmed regarding the gravity of her decision to leave school at 17, without qualifications and without skills in the activity she was pursuing, her teachers were not quite so at ease with the decision and announcement at the beginning of term:

'You're doing WHAT?' enquired her form teacher. 'I'm leaving school at Christmas to become a professional golfer', she said. 'Do you think you have reached the standard then? It's very difficult to make it in professional sport you know! Do you think you are good enough?'

196 *Kitrina Douglas*

'I don't know', she replied in all honesty, but enjoying the drama, 'I haven't even played yet'.

*

A few months later, while completing my final term at school, I played in my first competition on another family holiday, this time in Portugal. I owned no golf clubs and did not have an official handicap.

Par Golf Magazine: Net Nothing!

> Ever heard of a two net nothing? It's a new one of us but Katrina Douglas, 36 handicap member of Long Ashton Golf Club scored one in the Algarve during the recent TAP amateur week. Playing in a four-ball with her partner, father Jim Douglas, she scored a two at the short 13th, one of the many holes on which she received two strokes start. So it counted as a hole in nought. Needless to say, she and Dad won the competition . . . with a net 60! Now 17 year old (Kit for short), who started playing golf only in August, plans to take up golf full-time, playing and practising every day, in the hope of becoming a proette. 'I'm not much good yet,' she says, 'but I've been told I've got some potential and as I'm a great sports lover I'd hate not to give myself the chance of becoming really good at golf'.
>
> (Par Golf, 1978)

After dropping out of school at Christmas, I joined a local golf course and took weekly lessons from Richard Bradbear at Burnham and Berrow golf club. How, when, where and what I practised was left to me. I watched the better players at the club for inspiration, I read a lot, made up games like my father had and played in the women's events each week. Two years later, I entered my first national competition, the 1980 Scottish Girls Championship. Again, recorded very helpfully by the British media.

The Scotsman

> It took Jane Connachan just six holes to increase her overnight lead of three to double figures, with her playing partner, Kitrina Douglas collapsing under the pressure of poor putting. After four putting the third any lingering chance of a contest vanished when the English girl followed that immediately with a brace of sevens.
>
> (Scotsman, 1980)

The following year Gordon Cosh, the friend of my father's from the driving range story, invited me to go on holiday to Florida with his family over Christmas.

Autobiographical Insights on Transition   197

Trust

He didn't look up from the paper, he just asked the question: 'Are you taking a bible with you?' In the excitement of what to pack on her first trip to America, a bible hadn't figured on her list. So she took a moment to consider her options. A simple 'no' might look as if she didn't care, saying yes would be a lie, so she came up with: 'They're all too big, too heavy', hoping it would be an end to the matter. It wasn't.

'I'll buy you a travel one', he said, from behind the broadsheet. Which he did, with the instructions to read a chapter every day, which she did.

In the dark bedroom, she fumbled to find the bathroom door knob, uneasy, ashamed, slightly tense and, at 5 am, still half asleep. Pausing to make sure she had not disturbed the sleep of her roommates Annie and Tanya she turned the handle in slow motion while holding her breath. Her skin acknowledged the coolness of the sterile room, but it was only once the door was softly closed and locked tight, that she put the light on, the toilet seat down, and commenced reading.

She wondered why reading this book was such a problem in front of her two friends. She wondered why she was driven to read even though her father did not check up on her or ever ask her about it. She began where he suggested, the search for wisdom and understanding, the proverbs of renowned philosopher, Solomon: *He who refreshes others will be refreshed. A kind hearted woman gains respect, but ruthless men gain only wealth.* Her bum went numb on the hard seat, but the reading captured her thoughts. What should her behaviour be towards others? What sort of heart did she have? *A kind answer turns away wrath.* How *should* she respond?

Six months later her father died. She continued reading.

Wouldn't He Be Proud Now?

The press corps did not want to disrupt the polite hand-shakes following the 1982 British Amateur Championship final, but, if *their* stories were to take centre stage in the Sunday papers copy needed to be filed before the football results and it was already 3:50 pm and they were in the middle of the 16th hole. This being golf, however, the rush to circle the winner was dignified.

The usual cliché questions surfaced first, about the game and how she came from behind. *Daily* Telegraph reporter Marie Clark then slipped in her question. This one, however, came as a shock to the young champion:

'Wouldn't your father have been proud of you now?' Clarke asked, as much as statement or assumption as a question. The journalist's story had, of course, already been written, about the *21 year old* who *only started golf four years ago*, and had taken *a year off school, beaten every member of the British team* and that *her father had died a few months earlier.* Clarke simply needed a *yes* from the player to show she actually interviewed the girl.

198   *Kitrina Douglas*

The reply was as much a shock to the journalists as the question had been to the player:

'No'.

Faces looked up from note books, pens stopped, earnest expressions and eyes pinned attention on the relative unknown. The words were out, however, before the young player realised she was disagreeing with the world's top journalists. The words were out before she had thought through the ramifications of annoying this group of men and women. The pause in the furious scribbling provoked a further response, but, in those few moments, she could not find words to bridge the divide, so she once again stepped on thin ice searching for the words.

'No', she said firmly shaking her head, 'my father was proud of *me*, not what I did today, not hitting a ball round the golf course'.

Daily Express

How a 50–1 Shot Turned Into a Champion

> Last weekend the long legged 5ft 9 Miss Douglas 21 turned the form book of women's golf into a comic strip. The 50–1 long shot became British Champion after mowing down five internationals in a sensational march to the title. . . . When we met one question was: stroke play or match play? Revealingly she answers "As long as I'm winning, I don't mind which. I hate losing." Competitiveness came from her father, Jim, head of a construction firm and a footballer for Edinburgh's Hearts. Sadly, he did not see his daughter's triumph. He died last month at 51 with a heart illness.
>
> (Heager, 1982)

One of my motives behind me wanting to win that particular British Amateur Championship was because the Curtis Cup (an important bi-annual team event between the United States & United Kingdom) was taking place in the United States and I wanted be part of a British team on a US trip, I did not want to play for Great Britain in the United Kingdom. In addition, I did not have the finances (since my father's death) to continue playing amateur golf indefinitely, I needed either to find work or to turn professional. Winning this event led to selection for the British team and the chance to travel to Europe and the United States.

Two years later, I was dropped from the British team, and in April the following year (1984) 2 weeks after signing professional forms, I played in my very first professional tournament. The Ford Classic at Woburn Golf Club.

Sunday Telegraph

Douglas in Fairy-Tale Beginning

> KITRINA DOUGLAS'S victory in the Ford Classic was . . . the stuff of fairy tales. To win your first tournament, only a fortnight after turning professional

Autobiographical Insights on Transition 199

is enough in itself, but to win it only six years after taking up the game is almost certainly without precedent. Miss Douglas she said she did not try to think about winning, only playing "steady golf" and her stomach turned a summersault when she found, much to her surprise, that she was two shots clear. It left a certain amount of egg on the faces of the selectors but she refused to gloat, "I did this to prove to myself, not to show them."

(Williams, 1984)

Scotsmail

Kitrina Has the Superstar Image

[A]nd the talent and personality to transform British golf's garden party image. . . . She is a tough competitor and that quality comes from hours of competitive practice at her home club where she plays the men off their own tees for money and rarely loses.

(McDonnel, 1984)

The Guardian

Captivating Kitrina

Kitrina Douglas's four-shot victory in her first tournament as a professional was a heart warming sight even for two women from the LGU, which has excluded her from the Curtis Cup match next month. There is no animosity on either side. Penny Taylor, Chairman of the LGU said, "After playing the Vagliano and being rejected, she was the most marvellous entertainer. It was quite admirable". The other LGU representative said Miss Douglas had written a wonderful letter of appreciation on turning professional. "We get plenty of criticism and we don't get many letters like that. It was a marvellous gesture from a lovely girl".

(Khan, 1984)

The media capture what they need to sell newspapers, but alongside 'performance', there was plenty going on 'off' the course. The following, from a story called 'Confession' (Douglas, 2018) provides just one example of some the important things that are left out, unreported and not news 'worthy'.

The sweltering summer afternoon heat and huge galleries meant it would take ages to leave the course so I settled with a private 'players only' lounge where a television in the corner of the room was showing the Pope's visit. Slumping down, off came my shoes and socks and I ordered a cold drink. A few minutes later, as the waitress placed the food down, Leanne, another player, came and sat down.

I knew Leanne was a catholic, attended mass regularly and believed very different things about access to God, sin and absolution to me. The *troubles*

200   *Kitrina Douglas*

in my father's country, Ireland, bombs, deaths and blood shed only highlighted the fissure between protestants and Catholics. So, as we sat side by side, there was an invisible chasm existing between us.

I noticed how visibly enthused and moved Leanne was watching the pope.

'Its so wonderful', she said little knowing that the player next to her had no time for this religious leader, little respect for what he stood for, and saw him as a bloke dressed in his fancy gear, waving to the crowd. Yet, despite all those misconceptions and biases, as we began talk about aspects of our individual faiths, we found similarities in fundamental truths. While watching events unfolding on the television, I can only describe the moment as something spiritually bridging and joyous, and well, I felt a goodness I cannot describe. It brought access to a different perception about those who professed a catholic faith and I was changed.

'I can't believe I've really enjoyed talking to you about this', I said, 'me too' she returned. 'We should do it again', she said. I found myself agreeing.

Soon meetings were regularly taking place and other players of similar, different or no faith joined us. In time I became the Sheppard of this little flock, responsible for organising a time, a place to meet after play in all the different countries we visited. Through our gatherings, we supported each other's spiritual growth, communion and friendship, and anyone was welcome. Yet, I hated the time organising this meeting stole from doing other things, like my practice, site seeing and exploring, getting myself ready for the event, or just having *not* to bother being the organiser. At the same time, I thought it was the right thing to do, so I always did it. But, I would complain to God, '*look*', I'd say slightly annoyed, '*I need to practice*', or '*I'm tired, I need to rest, it's been a long day*' or '*I've an important game tomorrow*', and then the next day I would confound the record books and win another big event. Then I'd say, '*ok God; guess I didn't need the practice*'. And we'd organise barbeques, gigs and Leanne went with me to buy my first guitar, taught me new chords and to play *Donald Where's Your Trousers*, which made me laugh, and we would sing. I used our contacts in the United Kingdom to find homes for tour players who weren't from Europe, who needed a place to stay, showing care, and practical support and because it's the right thing to do.

The Sunday Times

Leading Lady Kitrina's Winning Act

> It has taken the phenomenal Kitrina Douglas only three months of her professional career to become Europe's leading money winner. The fact is that this leggy West Country girl seemed destined for greater stardom on the stage, and when she carried off the gold medal for acting at the Bath festival Kitrina's tutor was convinced she had a spectacular future in the theatre. She is one of the most ebullient and irrepressible characters on the European tour and always ready for a giggle. Yet there is a more solemn side

Autobiographical Insights on Transition 201

to her. She is genial enough, seldom stays in the same places as her fellow professionals. As soon as she finishes her round she leaves the course, eats and returns to the practice ground to work for a couple of hours. It is this relentless drill that has taken her to the top in her first season.

(The Sunday Times, 1984)

June 2004, Psychology Workshop

I had not seen Leanne in quite a few years but any space between us evaporated as we exchanged stories round her kitchen table. Still, there was a lot to catch up with. She was now a head pro, the national golf coach, ran a golf shop and had a same sex partner. Quite a change. I had dropped out of the tour, completed a sport science degree then a PhD, was doing commissioned research as an independent researcher, still doing commentary for the BBC, and, my reason for visiting her area of the country was delivering workshops to women golfers.

'You know', she said, mid-sentence,

> I tell my students about you, that you would be on the practice ground before everyone else and still there at the end of the day, you had such a dedicated work ethic, I tell my students, *that's how you have to practise, that's what you have to do to get to the top.*

Implications for Practice

The media (like the researchers mentioned earlier) write about what is of concern to them. Their horizon of interest (Althusser, 1971; Bakhtin, 1984) centred on how golf tournaments are won. To do so, they 'cherry pick' from the action and events and then draw on war metaphors to create an image and identity of a young woman who is like a soldier, 'mowing down' the opposition, 'marching' to the title, and being a 'tough' competitor who invests herself in 'relentless drill'. This last metaphor provides a useful example to consider how athletes' lives are used to promote one way of becoming successful in sport. An event (hitting balls on a practice ground) is used to create a cultural understanding of what actions are necessary to train a soldier for war. From these narrative building blocks, they then link 'the drill' with 'how to get to the top of sport' and write:

> [A]s soon as Kitrina finishes her round she leaves the course, eats and returns to the practice ground to work for a couple of hours. It is this relentless drill that has taken her to the top in her first season.
>
> (The Sunday Times, 1984)

Yet, this story omits other important events and explanations, which equally contribute to optimal performance and, I believe, to mental health and

202 *Kitrina Douglas*

sustaining a multidimensional identity. Namely, that I left the golf course to have fun, go sight-seeing and explore, to arrange meetings with peers where spiritual growth was central, to learn about a new town, new language, new food, to learn to play the guitar and sing and so on (see Douglas, in press, 2009, 2014). In contrast, the news media, their descriptions and how they define my practice as 'relentless drill' shape how my identity is seen by others, and when I win, the 'relentless drill' becomes a map for others. Over time, as this identity becomes cemented and narrowed by others, it becomes a vehicle to shape and police other athletes' lives. It also informs what the public know and expect from young sport people. While undoubtedly I spent hours on the practice range, it was not experienced as relentless drill. Ironically, it is equally possible that not valuing winning (to the extent that it was everything), learning to play a musical instrument, taking on responsibilities for the well-being of others, and doing 'non-performance' related activities, played a part in me winning. More importantly, their story could not be more different to how I describe hitting balls or how I self-identify.

Over time, it can be difficult to sustain and value dimensions of our 'self' and identity if the only thing people are presented with, and ask is about, and the only thing valued in our culture, is related to how you win/won (see Carless & Douglas, 2013a). The power of the performance narrative is difficult to usurp, and whether an individual athlete self-identifies with the stories created about them or not, we can become entrapped in a story not our own. For Alec Grant, narrative entrapment means 'you get this narrative biography superimposed on you and then people react towards you as if you are this label' (Grant, 2017, 2020). Like many of the soldiers I have carried out research with (Carless & Douglas, 2016a, 2016b; Douglas & Carless, 2015, 2016), high-performance athletes are often not as tough as their public image portrays, many are vulnerable and insecure and have difficulty living up to what others expect of them. The problem we face (the research community) is not so much with the individual as it is with challenging dominant narratives that portray soldiers only as tough, powerful and strong and athletes as healthy, mentally strong and empowered.

Without my father showing me a different way to harness sporting potential, without him suggesting I read a particular book and value wisdom, humility and caring for others, without being trusted to feel like I could take my own route, without playful events created with both my parents and friends—and their valuing and showing an interest in what went on off-course—I may not have written songs, had sustaining relationships, been creative on and off the golf course, and I may have experienced that time as relentless drill and sacrifice.

Life is too rich and complex to reveal it all, so researchers, news media, coaches as well as professional athletes all, to some degree, filter, sift and sort information. Consequently, it is the systematic amplification of some

Autobiographical Insights on Transition 203

stories over others that can, over time, begin to narrow how athletes narrate their lives and experiences. An individual's ability to sustain an alternative story—an integral part of a multidimensional identity which we know is life and mental health sustaining—is largely due to alternatives types of stories and actions being available and valued (McLeod, 1997). Counterstories, like those shared here, about life in sport, that are not about winning, keep the past alive for the storyteller, yet I am not the sole beneficiary. Sharing alternative representations about life in sport and the journey to the top also keep future possibilities alive for others by challenging the monologue the performance narrative and adding to the pool of alternative narrative resources.

Note

1. In the following publications, David Carless and I provide methodological insights to the use of stories, storytelling:

> Carless, D., & Douglas, K. (2016) My eyes got a bit watery there: Using stories to explore emotions in coaching research and practice at a golf programme for injured, sick and wounded military personnel. *Sports Coaching Review,* 197–215.
> Carless, D., & Douglas, K. (2016). Narrating Embodied Experience: Sharing Stories of Trauma and Recovery. *Sport, Education & Society.* 21(1), 47–61.
> Douglas, K., & Carless, C. (2015). Finding a counter story at an inclusive, adapted, sport and adventurous training course for injured, sick, and wounded soldiers: Drawn in—drawn out. *Qualitative Inquiry,* 454–456.
> Douglas, K., & Carless, D. (2010). Restoring connections in physical activity and mental health research and practice: A confessional tale. *Qualitative Research in Sport and Exercise, 2*(3), 336–353.
> Douglas, K., & Carless, D. (2009). Exploring taboo issues in high performance sport through a fictional approach. *Reflective Practice, 10*(3), 311–323.
> Douglas, K., & Carless, D. (2008). Using stories in coach education. *International Journal of Sports Science and Coaching, 3*(1), 33–49.

References

Althusser, L. (1971). *Ideology and ideological state apparatuses. Lenin and philosophy, and other essays* (B. Brewster, Trans). London: New Left Books.
Bakhtin, M. (1984). *Problems of Dostoevsky's poetics.* Minneapolis: University of Minnesota Press.
Carless, D., & Douglas, K. (2016a). When two worlds collide: A story about collaboration, witnessing and life story research with soldiers returning from war. *Qualitative Inquiry, 23*(5), 375–383.
Carless, D., & Douglas, K. (2016b). Narrating embodied experience: Sharing stories of trauma and recovery. *Sport, Education & Society, 21*(1), 47–61.
Carless, D., & Douglas, K. (2013a). Living, resisting, and playing the part of athlete: Narrative tensions in elite sport. *Psychology of Sport and Exercise, 14*(5), 701–708.

Carless, D., & Douglas, K. (2013b). "In the boat" but "selling myself short": Stories, narratives, and identity development in elite sport. *The Sport Psychologist, 27,* 27–39.

Carless, D., & Douglas, K. (2012). Stories of success: Cultural narratives and personal stories of elite and professional athletes. *Reflective Practice, 13*(3), 387–398.

Crosset, T. W. (1995). *Outsiders in the clubhouse: The world of women's professional golf.* New York: Suny.

Douglas, K. (2004). What's the drive in golf: Motivation and persistence in women professional tournament golfers (Doctoral Thesis). University of Bristol.

Douglas, K. (2009). Storying my self: Negotiating a relational identity in professional sport. *Qualitative Research in Sport, Exercise & Health, 1*(2), 176–190.

Douglas, K. (in press). "And I dedicate this win to . . .": Performing grief in high performance sport. *Autoethnography.*

Douglas, K. (2018). Confession. In L. Turner, N. P. Short, A. Grant, & T. E. Adams (Eds.), *International perspectives on autoethnographic research and practice* (pp. 96–104) Oxen, UK: Routledge.

Douglas, K., & Carless, D. (2012a). Membership, golf and a story about Anna and me: Reflections on research in elite sport. *Qualitative Methods in Psychology Bulletin, 13*(1), 27–33.

Douglas, K., & Carless, D. (2012b). Taboo tales in elite sport: Relationships, ethics, and witnessing. *Psychology of Women Section Review, 14*(2), 50–56.

Douglas, K., & Carless, C. (2014). Sharing a different voice: Attending to stories in collaborative writing. *Cultural Studies-Critical Methodologies, 14*(6), 610–618.

Douglas, K., & Carless, D. (2016). My eyes got a bit watery there: Using stories to explore emotions in coaching research and practice at a golf programme for injured, sick and wounded military personnel. *Sports Coaching Review,* 197–215.

Douglas, K., & Carless, C. (2015). Finding a counter story at an inclusive, adapted, sport and adventurous training course for injured, sick, and wounded soldiers: Drawn in—drawn out. *Qualitative Inquiry,* 454–456.

Douglas, K., & Carless, D. (2006). Performance, discovery, and relational narratives among women professional tournament golfers. *Women in Sport and Physical Activity Journal, 15*(2), 14–27.

Douglas, K., & Carless, D. (2009). Abandoning the performance narrative: Two women's stories of transition from professional golf. *Journal of Applied Sport Psychology, 21*(2), 213–230.

Douglas, K., & Carless, D. (2015). *Life story research in sport: A narrative approach to understanding the experiences of elite and professional athletes.* London: Routledge.

Frank, A. (2004). *The renewal of generosity: Illness, medicine and how to live.* Chicago and London: University of Chicago Press.

Freeman, M. (2010). *Hindsight.* New York: Oxford University Press.

Gilligan, C. (1993). *In a different voice: Psychological theory and women's development.* Cambridge, MA: Harvard University Press.

Grant, A. (2020). Autoethnography. In K. Aranda (Ed.), *Critical qualitative health research* (pp. 159–177). New York and London: Routledge.

Grant, A (2017). Qualitative conversations. *YouTube, [video file].* Retrieved from www.youtube.com/watch?v=a38pB97glok

Heager, R. (1982, May). How a 50-1 shot turned into a golf champion. *Daily Telegraph.*

Khan, E. (1984, May). Why ignore Douglas? *The Guardian.*

Autobiographical Insights on Transition   205

MacIntyre, A. (1984). *After virtue: A study in moral theory* (2nd ed.). Notre Dame, IN: University of Notre Dame Press.

McLeod, J. (1997). *Narrative and psychotherapy.* London: Sage.

McDonnel, M. (1984). Kitrina has the superstar image *Scotsmail.*

Par Golf Magazine. (1978, January). Net nothing! *Par golf magazine.*

Scotsman Newspaper (April 1980).

Werthner, P., & Orlick, T. (1986). Retirement experiences of successful Olympic athletes. *International Journal of Sport Psychology, 17,* 337–363.

Williams, M. (1984, May). Douglas in fairy-tale beginning. *Sunday Telegraph.*

The stories included here are adapted from a number of previous published stories including:

Douglas, K. (2014a). Challenging interpretive privilege in elite and professional sport: One [athlete's] story, revised, reshaped, reclaimed. *Qualitative Research in Sport, Exercise and Health, 6*(2), 220–243.

Douglas, K. (2009). Storying my self: Negotiating a relational identity in professional sport. *Qualitative Research in Sport, Exercise & Health, 1*(2), 176–190.

Douglas, K. (2018). Confession. In L. Turner, N. P. Short, A. Grant, & T. E. Adams (Eds.), *International perspectives on autoethnographic research and practice* (pp. 96–104) Oxen, UK: Routledge.

Conclusion

Deborah Agnew

Of all the experiences in sport, the one commonality is retirement. It will happen at some point in an athlete's career, so, in this sense, it is expected. Yet, so many athletes are unprepared for life after sport. The perspectives from around the world presented in this book share this common thread that, while retirement from sport is expected, it can be difficult. It is hoped that the stories shared here will help athletes, practitioners, academics and those who care for athletes as they leave sport to better understand the retirement experiences of athletes, so that athletes in the future can enjoy the fulfilling retirement they deserve.

Going forward, it is clear that we need evidence-based practices for helping athletes transition into life after sport. Both athletic and non-athletic factors affect the retirement transition; therefore, it is not enough to take an individual approach to athlete retirement. As practitioners, we need to look beyond the individual alone. The developmental approach advocates for the link between past career experience, present situation and plans for the future to be prominent in retirement transition planning. We know that many athletes do not prepare for life after sport, particularly those who experience a less predictable end to the timing of their retirement, for instance with a career-ending injury or deselection from a team. Athletes often fail to make the connection between their sports-related skills and their life beyond sport. We know that up to one in five athletes will require professional assistance in the transition out of sport: it is not by chance that career assistance programmes have been initiated in the United Kingdom, the Netherlands, Australia, the United States and Canada (Stambulova, Alfermann, Statler, & Côté, 2009). However, we also know that a high percentage of athletes are not accessing these programmes (Flanagan, 2018).

In order to assist athletes who are retiring from sport, it is clear that a whole-person, whole-career approach is needed and that any care provided to athletes needs to be both culturally specific and appropriate. As discussed in chapter 1, pre-retirement planning facilitates the transition out of sport. Again, although there are many career assistance programmes now being offered to athletes, we know that there is limited engagement by athletes in

Conclusion 207

such intervention programmes. In particular, programmes that place the onus on the athlete to ask for assistance have limited effectiveness because the athlete is often unable or unwilling to ask for help. It is clear that assistance needs to be offered or even made a part of the exit from sport process, rather than requiring athletes to ask. Retirement programmes need to be accessible and relevant and target athletes at many stages of their career. Current athletes need to be involved in pre-retirement planning, but assistance needs to be available to 'in-between' athletes who are leaving professional sport. Given it can take up to 2 years for athletes to successfully transition out of sport, assistance also needs to be ongoing.

The timing of assistance programmes has been found to be an important factor for college athletes. Chapter 2 demonstrates that only a small percentage of college athletes make it to the professional level, meaning that many are retiring from sport before their professional career has even begun. This leaves college athletes at a higher risk of experiencing difficult transitions. Similarly, athletes with a disability can have unique reasons for retiring from sport, such as changes to the classification system (see chapter 12). Whilst sport may help athletes cope with their disability, retirement can often see athletes experience a secondary disability such as an overuse injury from their involvement in sport, which can complicate the retirement transition.

As emphasised by chapter 3, the current structures in sport that are designed to support athletes may actually hinder their ability to cope with life after sport. Athletes become used to those involved in the sport doing everything they can to assist them. However, the 'real world' expects athletes to be self-sufficient, thus in retirement athletes may be vulnerable to difficulties. Athletes can and should be encouraged to take responsibility for decisions and actions themselves. This is particularly relevant for para-athletes who are positioned as dependent when they may not be.

Chapter 4 identified retirement from sport as a critical period for doping vulnerability. Preparing for the end of their career may lead some athletes to doping in an effort to prolong their career. Injured athletes are particularly vulnerable to doping and, for those who have experienced a doping ban, this may be the catalyst for retirement. Piffaretti's (2011) three-phase model requires a systematic follow-up in the acute phase, the realisation phase and the acceptance phase because athletes who have experienced a doping ban may have heightened and prolonged distress and are at risk of serious mental health issues. Programmes that are designed to support the athlete during these phases should be focused on psychological, physical and occupational matters. It is arguable that all athletes and not just those who have experienced a doping ban would benefit from such a programme.

Frankl (1984) stated that being unable to change a situation challenges us to change ourselves. Once athletes have accepted the end of their careers, they can be open to new opportunities; thus, retirement can be a positive turning point that increases well-being. However, it is important to

208 *Deborah Agnew*

acknowledge that retirement is not the only transition athletes can make. Chapter 5 is unique in that it considers multiple transitions in sport that can significantly impact an athlete's life and can raise issues that precede retirement. Support for athletes, therefore, needs to be continual throughout careers and lasting into retirement and beyond. As Chapters 8 and 9 highlight, it is not only the athlete who can experience a difficult transition out of sport, but the families and those who care for athletes during this time as well. Their experiences must also be acknowledged, with appropriate resources by organisations and sport governing bodies directed towards caring for the athletes and those who support them.

Parents are central figures in their children's athletic careers who can bear witness to their child's helplessness and loss of identity upon retirement from sport. Chapter 9 provides support for the 'in-between' stage as athletes move beyond sport. During this stage, parents often provide psychological, and material support for athletes, along with educational and career guidance, which is an important role given the lack of formal transition programmes in many sports. However, parents often feel ill-prepared for this role and do not, or cannot, necessarily understand what the athlete is going through. Therefore, parents can feel anger at the lack of formal programming in sports from coaches, clubs, organisations and governing bodies. Much of the academic literature focuses on the experience of the athlete, yet it must be recognised that athletes do not go through the transition out of sport process alone. Support initiatives for parents and other significant others who care for athletes during the transition out of sport phase are needed.

Athletes who are deselected are particularly at risk of experiencing retirement transition difficulties. As explored in chapter 8, the methods for clubs within the same sport in deselecting athletes vary, with some procedures being more distressing than others. Being deselected in a single meeting heightens the distress for the athlete. Given retirement is a process, it is recommended that deselecting athletes is also a process rather than a single meeting, which would allow for the systematic follow-up in psychological, physical and occupational areas as recommended by Piffaretti (2011).

Chapter 10 provided an overview of coaching positions being regarded as the next logical step for athletes at the conclusion of their careers. Some athletes can be perceived as being fast-tracked through necessary qualifications into coaching positions. The trust and respect earned as an athlete is favoured by directors appointing coaches because it is believed an athlete, especially one who has been part of the club as a player, will uphold the culture of the club. Having athletes coach the club they have played for can be dangerous, however, as it can impact on the development of a coaching identity. Allowing athletes broader experiences by coaching at clubs with which they have not been affiliated may allow space for positive coach identity construction.

Conclusion 209

The fast-track coaching career also appears to only be available for some players. Chapter 11 identifies pathways in sport to administration, management and coaching are limited for Indigenous athletes are often only perceived as having natural athletic ability, not academic ability. Therefore, there is a lack of progression opportunities from athlete to coach even though many Indigenous athletes have expressed a desire to follow this pathway. Planning for retirement for Indigenous athletes is, therefore, likely to be particularly challenging because of the small range of career choices and the lack of vocational qualifications. Indigenous athletes require culturally appropriate support from other Indigenous people, but the under-representation beyond a playing role needs to be addressed. At the very least, non-academic support personnel need to be educated about the nuances of Australian Aboriginal culture in order to make a meaningful contribution to supporting the transition out of sport.

Similarly, chapter 13 recognises that African athletes are often perceived as having a natural ability for running. Athlete development programmes in Africa often lack athlete-centred approaches that address lifespan development, including dual-career development and retirement transition. Notably though in Southern Africa, the sport system encourages a balance between good academic performance and excellence in sport, which athletes can find challenging. In a holistic approach to athlete development, psychological, psychosocial and financial factors feature prominently. These areas, along with life-skills education that is lacking in Africa, are significant factors in assessing influence on post-career coping and adaptation. It is also important to note that different sports and different countries have different sport systems; therefore, further research is needed to understand the complexities of these systems in order to develop the most appropriate interventions for athletes.

Athletes are vulnerable to experiencing identity loss upon retiring from sport. Athletic identity is often formed from a young age, which can limit the opportunities to develop other identity components. Athletic identity can also be based on athletic performance, which is problematic. Chapter 6 emphasises the need to allow space for athletes to explore outside pursuits. Whilst this may be perceived as contrary to improving sports performance, to not allow opportunities may see the athlete fail to develop skills outside sport, which can then leave them unprepared for life after sport. It is important to focus on the whole person and not just performance to decrease the dominance of athletic identity.

Furthermore, it is limiting to box athletes into one component of identity. As Kitrina Douglas shows in chapter 14, it is possible for athletes to have multiple dimensions to their identity, and they are not necessarily all focused on winning. Kitrina's story serves as a reminder for practitioners caring for athletes who transition out of sport to listen to the athletes as well as recognise their own biases and assumptions around what the athlete is going through. We need to recognise the complex context in which

210 *Deborah Agnew*

athletes perform, develop identity and become who they are. Chapters 1, 11, 13 and 14 have shown that cultural context is important if we are to design appropriate and successful interventions to facilitate smoother transitions out of sport. If we want to understand athlete retirement transition experiences, we need to first listen to the athletes' stories.

There is not one-way athletes are 'supposed' to experience retirement transitions. Whilst there may be similar components, athlete transition experiences are unique and individuals, therefore, designing intervention programmes based on a one-size-fits-all approach are unlikely to be successful. This provides a challenge for sports administrators, organisations, medical staff and governing bodies. However, it is a challenge that must be met. A clear message through the chapters of this book is that pre-planning for retirement is a crucial element in the successful transition out of sport. Therefore, retirement cannot be an afterthought, not for athletes or for those who care for them both in and as they leave professional sport. We have a responsibility to allow space for outside sport discussions and interests, so the athletes are not continually focused on being an athlete while also being told by media and broader society that being an athlete is all they are.

Despite the need to focus on sports performance during their careers, it is not enough to perceive an athlete as only an athlete. Approaches to caring for athletes during their careers, through the transition process and in life after sport must be holistic and must recognise athletes have a life outside sport. The significant contribution of those who care for athletes such as parents, family, friends and medical staff needs to be acknowledged with appropriate support and resources funnelled into developing the required skills to assist athletes during this difficult time.

The body of literature on athlete retirement from sport is growing, with more becoming known on athlete experiences of retirement and what is needed for a successful transition out of sport. However, this book highlights that athlete experiences in retirement, although important, are not the only experiences we need to understand. Future research needs to be longitudinal in nature and follow athletes throughout their careers and into retirement from sport and beyond. It is when we take a lifespan approach that encourages the whole individual and the entirety of their experiences that we can be in the best position to support athletes as they leave professional sport.

References

Flanagan, L. (2018, February 11). Finding new meaning after an Olympic Career. *The Atlantic*. Retrieved from www.theatlantic.com/education/archive/2018/02/finding-new-meaning-after-an-olympic-career/553004/

Frankl, V. (1984). *Man's search for meaning: An introduction to logotherapy*. New York: Simon & Schuster.

Piffaretti, M. (2011). Psychological determinants of doping behaviour through the testimony of sanctioned athletes. *World Anti-Doping Agency*. Retrieved from www.wada-ama.org/sites/default/files/resources/files/learning_about_determinants_m.piffaretti_final_report_6.2011def.pdf

Stambulova, N., Alfermann, D., Statler, T., & Côté, J. (2009). ISSP position stand: Career development and transitions of athletes. *International Journal of Sport and Exercise Psychology*, 7(4), 395–412.

Index

academy 66, 68, 69, 131, 132, 136
academy coach 131, 133, 135
academy directors 131–33, 136
activism 4, 159, 164, 165
adaptation 9, 12, 13, 15–17, 40, 118,
119, 121, 175, 177, 178, 180, 181,
209; Conceptual Model 11, 117;
period 12, 17
adjustment 10, 12, 16, 22, 24, 26–28,
71, 111, 119, 120, 145–48, 158;
disorder 23
agency 23, 39, 40, 43, 74, 190
alcohol misuse 23, 24, 27, 61, 85, 87
American football 21
anger 51, 52, 61, 66, 102, 113–17, 161,
162, 208
anti-doping 46, 47, 50, 51, 53, 54
anxiety 22, 23, 24, 62, 65, 66, 69, 72, 86,
91, 164
athletic identity 1, 3, 12, 14, 15, 17, 25,
28, 50, 68, 72, 76, 79, 86, 87, 130,
139, 147, 148, 158, 176, 180, 181,
193, 194, 209
Athletic Identity Measurement Scale
(AIMS) 148
Australian (rules) football 74, 101,
103–05, 109–11, 147–53, 155

basketball 21, 36, 163
best practice 53, 181
boxing 147–55

career: assistance 11, 18, 36, 38, 41, 42,
53, 55, 76, 78, 79, 88, 109, 116, 136,
149, 153, 154, 163, 179, 181, 206;
development 10, 35, 36, 67, 72, 76,
101, 105, 113, 132, 136, 147, 459, 160,
170–73, 179, 208; disruption 25, 50,
84, 86, 91, 193; dual careers 4, 11–13,

17, 77, 173–81, 208; paradigm/
cultural praxis 12; planning 10, 14,
16, 18, 35, 43, 55, 60, 72, 75, 76, 102,
116, 122, 136, 140, 141, 150, 151,
152, 154, 161, 163, 165, 206, 209;
post-sport 41, 43, 52, 55, 76, 129,
133, 136; programs 12, 37, 53, 152,
153, 155, 164, 181, 206; reflection
28; termination 9, 10, 14, 17, 27, 50,
54, 59–61, 74, 86, 108, 114, 117, 119,
120, 148, 174; trajectory 1, 15, 42, 48,
49, 65, 103, 130, 137, 158, 171, 174,
175, 180; transitions xviii, 2, 4, 13, 17,
25, 26, 33–35, 53, 71, 87, 123, 141,
173, 181, 192
celebrity 74, 151
coach 3, 10, 11, 14, 15, 17, 25, 32,
35–38, 40–42, 48, 54, 58, 61, 62,
64–66, 115, 116, 118–20, 122, 129,
130–34, 137–42, 150–52, 154, 155,
131–64, 166, 171–76, 180, 190, 192,
201, 202, 208, 209
coaching 34, 37, 39, 42, 53, 60, 61,
86, 90, 103, 122, 123, 129, 130–42,
150, 152, 163, 164, 170, 180, 203,
208, 209
collegiate athletes 2, 21–26, 113, 177
concussion 26, 27
control 26, 46, 54, 55, 88, 102, 103, 105,
108–10, 115, 118–20, 122, 132, 133,
159, 162, 177
coping 1, 3, 4, 9, 22, 27, 35, 53, 54, 55,
74, 85–90, 92, 93, 102, 118, 122, 160,
162, 165, 178, 209
corruption 179
cross-cultural 4, 12, 171, 174, 178, 181
culture 4, 15, 17, 18, 39, 40, 47, 58, 59,
64, 66, 68, 74, 79, 92, 104, 118, 132,
133, 139–41, 145–47, 149, 154, 171,

Index   213

172, 174, 175, 189, 192, 194, 202, 208, 209
cycling 48, 49

Danish athletes 9, 12–16
delisting 101–03, 105–07, 109, 110
depression 21–27, 51, 59–61, 72, 74, 85, 86, 148, 160, 161, 163–66, 207
deselection 1, 3, 35, 69, 102–04, 106–08, 119, 178, 193, 206, 208
doping 2–4, 46–55, 207

ecological framework / approach 10, 12, 17, 174, 178
education 1, 12–16, 39, 41, 53, 54, 72, 88, 89, 118, 129, 132, 140–42, 147, 148, 150, 154, 155, 170, 172–75, 177–79, 181, 195, 209
emotional distress 105, 112, 114, 116–18, 148, 159, 161, 166, 176, 177, 180, 181
emotions 14, 16, 17, 21–23, 25, 27–29, 47, 50, 52, 54, 121, 122, 160
employment 16, 34, 38, 41, 42, 43, 51, 53, 55, 101, 103, 105, 107–09, 116, 118, 120, 134, 151
environmental factors 10–12, 14, 16, 17, 25, 47, 48, 53, 57, 58, 64, 66, 67, 77, 79, 87, 92–94, 108, 110, 120, 130–32, 138–40, 148, 149, 151, 161, 165, 170–74, 176, 178, 180, 192

faith 200
fatigue 23, 24
financial factors 11, 176
football (soccer) 3, 58–61, 63, 64, 66, 68, 69, 84, 85, 87–94, 114, 130, 131, 133, 135–38, 140, 141, 172, 173, 179, 189, 197, 198

gambling 61, 85, 87, 92
goals 28, 47, 54, 113, 115, 116, 159, 180
golf 4, 188, 190, 192–99, 201, 202

high-performance disability sport 32–34
holistic 4, 10, 11, 12, 17, 52, 77, 79, 170–76, 180, 181, 209, 210

ice hockey 21
identity 1, 3, 9, 12, 14, 15, 17, 21, 25, 27, 28, 33, 50, 55, 59–61, 64, 65, 67–69, 71–79, 85–90, 92, 102, 103, 114, 115, 119, 130, 133, 136, 139, 140,

142, 147, 148, 159, 160, 164, 176, 178, 180, 191–95, 201–03, 208–10; crisis xvii, 72, 73, 79, 85, 119, 159; foreclosure 15, 25, 72, 150
income 13, 14, 34, 49–51, 60, 147, 148, 151, 165, 176, 179
indigenous athletes 3, 145–55, 209
injury 1, 3, 14, 25, 26, 28, 35–37, 43, 48–50, 54, 59, 60, 62, 63, 65, 67, 69, 75, 84–87, 89–91, 93, 102, 106, 118, 119, 122, 158, 160, 163, 166, 173, 176, 178, 193, 206, 207
interventions 18, 23, 27, 51, 52, 77–79, 87, 94, 122, 123, 163, 172, 178, 191, 207, 209, 210
isolation 51, 73, 116, 190

lack of control 102, 109, 120
life after sport 1, 60, 76, 101, 104, 130, 146, 147, 151, 165, 206, 207, 209, 210
life satisfaction 1, 13, 15, 22, 163
life-skills 18. 55. 177. 178. 180. 181. 209
lifespan approach 4, 10, 11, 17, 42, 103, 119, 171, 173–75, 181, 209, 210
long-term athlete development 36, 170
loss 1, 14, 15, 23, 25, 39, 47, 50, 52, 60, 61, 67, 72, 73, 75, 84, 85–87, 90, 92, 102, 103, 114, 116, 119, 141, 146, 148, 159, 160, 161, 166, 178, 193, 208, 209

media 11, 34, 36, 50, 51, 53, 64, 66, 75, 79, 146, 151, 152, 162, 173, 196, 199, 201, 202, 210; social media 63, 64
mental health 3, 9, 21–26, 29, 47, 51, 59, 63, 66, 68, 79, 84–90, 92, 94, 106, 110, 164, 177, 180, 201, 203, 207; psychological distress 1, 21–25, 75, 121, 122; psychosocial difficulties 2, 10, 21, 23, 24, 26, 27, 29, 164, 170, 174, 176, 181, 209
mentors 15, 42, 43, 103, 131, 143, 150, 151, 154, 163, 172, 177, 181
Moving On! Program 27

narrative inquiry 73, 103
NCAA 21, 27
networks 9, 15, 16, 25, 28, 42, 43, 54, 87–89, 94, 107, 116, 120, 123, 137, 153, 163, 172, 180

pain 26, 61, 93, 114, 122, 161, 192, 193
para-athletes 32, 35, 40–43, 72
Paralympics 2, 32, 33, 35–42, 162, 166

214 *Index*

parents 3, 48, 113–23, 138, 146, 149, 173, 175, 176, 180, 192, 202, 208, 210
performance xvii, 3, 17, 32–34, 38, 40, 41, 47–50, 53, 54, 64, 67, 69, 72–77, 86, 101, 129–33, 136, 137, 140, 141, 150, 162, 170, 173, 175, 177, 181, 190–92, 194, 199, 201–03, 209, 210
Polish athletes 9, 12, 14–16
pre-retirement planning 9, 16, 27, 87, 92, 94, 115, 155, 163, 206, 207
professionalisation 2, 32–35, 37–39, 41, 43

quality of life 23, 26, 158, 163

racism 147, 151
rehabilitation 32, 35, 36, 44, 53, 54, 59, 90
relationships 9, 17, 21, 26, 52, 59, 60, 113, 116, 130, 121, 138, 142, 148, 160, 163, 176, 192, 202
role theory 71
rugby league (NRL) 147, 153, 149, 151, 152, 153, 155
rugby union 130, 131, 133, 136–38, 140, 141

sacrifice 122, 148, 192, 194, 202
sanctions 47–54
self-worth 86, 92, 93, 193
sleep disturbance 23, 24
social status 18, 102
social support 9, 25, 26, 28, 86–89, 94, 117, 121, 121, 123, 160–63, 165, 178
sport management 33, 34, 146
sport managers 37, 145
stakeholders 33, 130–33, 136, 138, 142, 173
stigma 51, 76, 77, 79, 93, 94
stress 10, 22, 25, 41, 43, 72, 117, 159, 191, 175; stressors 1, 22, 23, 26

student athletes 12, 21, 23–29, 174, 177
sub-elite sport 101, 103
substance use 24, 46, 51; substance misuse 22, 122, 193
Swiss athletes 11, 13–16
Sydney Olympics 33, 36, 37

talent 77, 131, 132, 136, 147, 149, 150, 170, 179, 199; development 4, 9, 36, 37, 170, 173; identification 4, 36, 37, 122, 138, 141, 170, 171
tennis 48–50, 172
transition: crisis 2, 10, 173; difficulty 18, 21, 22, 26, 60, 76, 79, 90, 91, 92, 102, 109, 110, 115, 116, 119, 123, 130, 136, 142, 151, 152, 176, 179, 191, 207, 208; non-normative 1, 18, 35, 78, 85, 89, 108, 193, 194; normative 1, 35, 85, 89, 193, 194; period 1, 4, 12, 107, 108, 110, 111, 120, 122; process 2, 9, 12, 17, 24, 27, 35, 102, 103, 104, 107, 108, 110, 115, 117, 138, 141, 147, 152–54, 164, 173, 206, 208, 210; programs 27, 53, 116, 153, 154; smooth 16, 72, 74, 77, 94, 129, 161, 177; successful 1, 2, 14, 16, 22, 25, 77, 78, 106, 108–10, 118, 121, 131, 133, 139, 159, 165, 175, 178, 179, 181, 191, 194, 207, 209, 210; unsuccessful 12, 14, 72, 121

WADA 46, 53
weakness 64, 68, 93
well-being 2, 17, 50, 63, 84, 88, 89, 94, 101–03, 105–10, 151, 202, 207
wheelchair basketball 36, 163
Wheelchair Rugby 36
winning 13, 39, 40, 47, 64, 74, 86, 88, 132, 190, 192, 194, 198–200, 202, 203, 209

Printed in the United States
by Baker & Taylor Publisher Services